Engaging Political Philosophy

Engaging Political Philosophy introduces readers to the central problems of political philosophy. Presuming no prior work in the area, the book explores the fundamental philosophical questions regarding freedom, authority, justice, and democracy. More than a survey of the central figures and texts, *Engaging Political Philosophy* takes readers on a philosophical exploration of the core of the field, directly examining the arguments and concepts that drive the contemporary debates. Thus the fundamental issues of political philosophy are encountered first-hand, rather than through intermediary summaries of the major texts and theories. As a result, readers are introduced to political philosophy by doing philosophy. Written in a conversational style, *Engaging Political Philosophy* is accessible to students and general readers. Instructors can use it in the classroom as a stand-alone textbook, a complement to a standard collection of historical readings, or as a primer to be studied in preparation for contemporary readings.

Robert B. Talisse is W. Alton Jones Professor of Philosophy, Professor of Political Science, and Chairperson of the Philosophy Department at Vanderbilt University. His research specialization is political philosophy, with special focus on democratic theory.

Engaging Political Philosophy

An Introduction

Robert B. Talisse

Routledge
Taylor & Francis Group

NEW YORK AND LONDON

First published 2016
by Routledge
711 Third Avenue, New York, NY 10017

and by Routledge
2 Park Square, Milton Park, Abingdon, Oxon, OX14 4RN

Routledge is an imprint of the Taylor & Francis Group, an informa business

© 2016 Taylor & Francis

Library of Congress Cataloging in Publication Data
Talisse, Robert B.
Engaging political philosophy : an introduction /
Robert B. Talisse. -- 1st ed.
pages cm
Includes bibliographical references and index.
1. Political science--Philosophy--History. I. Title.
JA71.T3547 2015
320.01--dc23
2015007295

ISBN: 978-0-415-80832-3 (hbk)
ISBN: 978-0-415-80833-0 (pbk)
ISBN: 978-0-203-14224-0 (ebk)

Typeset in Sabon
by Taylor & Francis Books

For my brother Mike and the political philosophers of our youth: Ray, Klaus, Jello, and D.H.

"They don't even know the question"

Contents

Preface

Academics do a lot of travelling to and from professional events, including conferences, lectures, and colloquia. These trips regularly require air travel, and so I often find myself making small talk on planes with fellow passengers. Nearly invariably, in the course of these conversations I will be asked my line of work. The typical reactions to the reply that I am a philosopher are disconcerting. Many people express surprise that philosophers (more likely, *professional* philosophers) still exist. I have recently taken to describing my line of work in a way that omits the word philosophy. Yet I was surprised to find that an alternate reply—that I work as a political theorist—also occasioned a strange reaction, albeit of a different kind. The prevailing assumption among my flight companions was that a political theorist was some kind of pundit, strategist, or lobbyist. Typically, I would be asked follow-up questions like, "So, who's going to win the next election?," "What do you say about immigration?," or, worst of all, "Are you a Conservative or a Liberal?" My subsequent explanation that political theorists are not in the first instance policy advocates or political commentators, but academics studying fundamental issues concerning justice, equality, freedom, authority, and the like, was often met with unabashed bewilderment. *The fact that* there is a profession in which people investigate such things seemed to lie at the heart of the puzzlement. The people I spoke with tended to take for granted that the political order (in the United States, at least) was well structured and that questions concerning justice, equality, freedom, authority, and the like were settled long ago. Some even projected the distinct impression that anyone who bothered in the present day to investigate such matters must be perverse, perhaps even politically dangerous. I can only imagine what the response would have been if I were to have mentioned that many political theorists are in the employ of public universities.

The fact that much of the standing political order is simply taken for granted in our everyday interactions is perhaps unsurprising. But that the political order should be seen as something that *ought to be* taken for granted is disturbing. After all, the complex world of governments, states, laws, courts, and other institutions is not simply *given*; we create these things, and fundamental philosophical questions concerning them are in fact far from settled. It still makes good sense to wonder why and whether political entities such as states should exist; and, alas, we are not yet clear about the natures of justice, equality, freedom, authority, and democracy. People still argue about what equality is, what justice demands, what makes a person free, who gets to give orders, and how we should be governed. Importantly, these matters are not disputed only among fringe radicals who oppose modern Western democracy. These questions are still hotly debated among mainstream academics seeking the best philosophical articulations of the ideals by which we live. Ongoing investigation into fundamental questions concerning the prevailing political order does not imply opposition to that order.

This occasions a related thought. The attitude that conceptual matters concerning politics are largely settled probably owes to the fact that the values and ideals associated with modern Western democracy are currently globally ascendant. Even the world's dictators pay significant lip service to the ideas of freedom, equality, and self-government; this is because nothing provides the veneer of legitimacy quite like the vocabulary of democracy. Indeed, throughout the world to characterize a policy or institution as democratic is often all it takes to justify that policy or institution. What is the value, then, of investigating the meaning and worth of ideas that everyone seems to agree upon?

At the risk of making philosophy seem all the more suspect, I note that philosophers have traditionally taken themselves to be social gadflies, querulous characters centrally concerned to disrupt consensus, unsettle agreement, and provoke disputation. It should be stressed that philosophers adopt this role not simply because they enjoy wrangling. The philosopher's thought, rather, is that widespread unanimity is often won by suppressing dissent, ignoring objections, and silencing doubts. The philosopher is hence made queasy by consensus, fearing that it may have been won by non-rational or oppressive means.

Although it often may seem that the philosopher is driven by a pathological attraction to troublemaking, the motivation, rather, is an abiding concern not only for the truth, but also for the cognitive health of those who believe what is true. We want not only to believe what is true; we also want to believe truths *for good reasons*. The philosopher's aim, then, is to protect against *false* or *merely apparent* agreement. And this is achieved through ongoing questioning and continually testing the considerations that undergird our central beliefs and deepest convictions.

This kind of activity might strike you as a perfectly appropriate way to gain the truth. Still, one might question its value once we already have the truth. Hence one might again wonder about the value of raising questions concerning the validity of democracy; if we *know* that democracy is the best form of government, what would be the point of questioning the belief that it is best? Philosophers propose that we should keep questioning that which is not only widely agreed upon, but also seems to be agreed upon for good reasons. What is the point of that?

Well, philosophers tend to draw a distinction between *coming to know* and *maintaining one's knowledge*. They tend to think that without proper maintenance, true beliefs can imperceptibly dissolve into false beliefs, and good reasons can crumble into mere platitudes. This is because in the absence of scrutiny of the kind upon which philosophers insist, we lose sight of the reasons and arguments that provide the basis for our beliefs. And this makes us less able to distinguish our beliefs from similar-sounding imposters. Without the maintenance that philosophical questioning provides, our living truths can easily devolve into dead dogmas, as one philosopher famously put it. Philosophy helps us to find out what is true; but it also helps us to maintain our grip on it. One might say, then, that it is especially important to subject our most fundamental, significant, and widespread ideals to philosophical scrutiny.

Such is the thumbnail sketch of my defense of philosophy. In a way, this book is an attempt to articulate what I might say about political philosophy to a sincerely interested companion on a very long flight. That is, I seek here to provide a sense of what political philosophy—as a living, breathing, and dynamic enterprise—is all about. More formally, this book aspires to give readers a state-of-the-art introduction to the leading questions, issues, and problems of political philosophy. Accordingly, its orientation is decidedly not historical. Although there will be occasion to mention the great ideas and texts that have shaped current thinking, one will not find in these pages extended treatments of the major books and figures in the grand historical tradition of political philosophy. Nor will one find in-depth exegeses of the major political philosophers of today. Once again, although there will be discussion of the ideas of those contemporary philosophers who have shaped—and continue to shape—the discipline, one will not find detailed commentary on their books and essays. This is because the aim of this book is not to provide an *overview* of political philosophy as an academic discipline, but rather to introduce readers to political philosophy. The objective is to acquaint readers with the same puzzles, problems, questions, and concerns that exercise professional political philosophers and stimulate their work today. The aspiration is to introduce readers to political philosophy as a kind of *activity*, an area of inquiry whose most fundamental questions are still very much open and thus in need of further investigation.

Using the vocabulary of the textbook publishers, one might say that this book is *problems-driven* rather than *figure-oriented* or *text-based*. Hence the title, *Engaging Political Philosophy*, is not a puffed-up description of the book's contents; the title does not claim that this book features only the kind of political philosophy that engages and leaves aside what is boring (though my hope, of course, is that the book will be engaging in this sense). The book instead seeks to engage its readers in political philosophizing, to get them involved in philosophical thinking about the political world. Or, to put it in a way that is somewhat hackneyed, the goal is not merely to *tell* readers about political philosophy, but rather to *do* political philosophy with them. For this reason, it might be better to regard the book as a *primer* in political philosophy rather than an *introduction* to the subject.

The book proceeds in a way that might strike those already familiar with the field as peculiar. Rather than starting with a summary of the leading positions and theories, and then proceeding to outline the main lines of critique, I begin instead by identifying the phenomena that provide the instigation for philosophical thinking, and then try to formulate the plausible responses that one might give to them. Along the way, the great ideas from the tradition of political philosophy (both historical and current) will be brought to bear on the problems under consideration, and of course the lines of objection and rejoinder that constitute the leading debates will be reviewed.

Other professionals might find this book peculiar in a different way. It will be noted that my discussions do not begin where most contemporary political philosophy begins, that is, with the groundbreaking work of John Rawls and his many commentators and critics. It is true that no one working today in political philosophy gets far without having to grapple seriously with Rawls's philosophy. And this is as it should be; in my judgment, Rawls's work is indeed *that* monumental. Yet, again, the present book is not an introduction to political philosophy as a professional sub-field within the academic discipline. The aim is not to acquaint the reader with the main thinkers and texts in the contemporary debates among professional political philosophers.

To put the point more broadly, the main texts and figures will not be presented as the *subject matter* of political philosophy. After all, the subject matter of political philosophy is *not* the texts and systems of the great political philosophers. If it were, we would instantly confront the absurd result that Plato, Aristotle, Hobbes, Locke, Mill, Rawls, and other luminaries in the field were not political philosophers at all, as their works are not about the tradition of political philosophy, but about justice, freedom, authority, citizenship, democracy, and so on. Furthermore, the view that the subject matter of political philosophy is the great works of the past has the similarly absurd implication that whereas Hobbes is not a political philosopher (because he did not write mainly about preceding political philosophers), someone who writes a book about Hobbes is a political philosopher. The point can be generalized to any approach that takes its proper focus to be great philosophical figures and texts; the approach is parasitic on the fact that those figures did *not* do philosophy in that way and their texts are *not* commentaries on their predecessors. In fact, one could plausibly argue that what makes the great figures and texts *great* is precisely that they are not primarily aimed at commenting on other figures and texts. It is better to affirm straightaway that the subject matter of political philosophy consists in the enduring perplexities and problems that political philosophers attempt to address. The towering figures of political philosophy are our fellow travelers on the long road of inquiry, and their great books can at times serve as guides; but ultimately our task is not that of mastering their ideas. The task is to figure out what is true, or, if that goal seems too lofty and distant, to figure out what views we have the best reasons to accept.

The aspiration to involve my reader in the activity of philosophy explains my tendency at certain points in the text to address you, my reader, directly by means of the second-personal pronoun, and to occasionally use the plural first-personal pronoun. I know that some will at least initially find this disrupting. But it is not employed as an affectation or a gimmick. Instead, it represents what I take to be a kind of methodological by-product of the aim of the book. To be more specific, the particular objective of the book requires that at points I take a *dialectical* or *conversational* tone. This is because, truth be told, there are several key junctures in the ensuing discussions where it is not clear to me what to think. A fancy way of saying this is that I find the deepest issues in political philosophy to end in *aporia*, an impasse or stand-off. In fact, it seems to me a mark of wisdom to recognize that with respect to the most central questions of political philosophy we are still at a loss. However, I do not see this as a skeptical result. The point is merely that there is still plenty to wonder about and thus a lot more political philosophy to do. The dialectical tone reflects this lingering puzzlement.

However, it must nonetheless be acknowledged that what is represented in the following pages is indeed one political theorist's view of things. Although I have tried to present an accurate depiction of the state of play regarding the central problems in political philosophy, the reader should keep in mind that this depiction is how things look to the author, who in this case is a participant in and contributor to the ongoing debates in professional political philosophy. Although it would be too strong, I think, to say that this book has an "agenda" or reflects my philosophical "biases," it cannot be denied that the account of political philosophy that is presented in these pages reflects only one way of conceptualizing the field. More importantly, as I try to indicate at the relevant points in the text, the conclusions reached along the way represent my own views, which (to say the least!) are not universally shared among political philosophers. In short, then, this book aspires to provide a reliable and evenhanded overview of political philosophy, but the reader should not lose sight of the fact that a different author would present this material differently.

Given the kind of book I have aspired to write, I have had to confront many difficult questions regarding the topics the book should cover. The field of political philosophy, perhaps especially at present, is uncommonly broad. In other areas of philosophy there is a fund of historical material that provides the necessary background to the current debates. The field of ethics is like this, for example. Although there is great variation in how introductory ethics is taught, almost any introductory course can be counted on to include discussion of key texts by Aristotle, Kant, and Mill. These texts provide the touchstones from which more current developments proceed. Indeed, it is difficult to conceive of how one could teach an introductory course in ethics without including this material. This is why it is almost impossible to find a textbook in introductory ethics that does not include substantial readings from, or discussions of, these thinkers.

Political philosophy is not unified to this degree. Even when it comes to the content of introductory-level courses, there is little agreement among political philosophers regarding what constitutes the "core" of the field, and thus no consensus about what material must be included in an introductory course. Some take an historical approach, seeking to introduce students to the great figures and texts; they are faced with the problem of having many more important texts than could be fit into a single semester. Others seek to introduce students to the most current developments, and hence at most mention in passing the historically influential texts and figures; among these, there is great variation concerning which of the current trends and tendencies it is most important to cover. Still others attempt to strike a judicious balance of historical and contemporary material; they thus inherit the challenges of both of the other models. In all cases, there are hard choices to make about what to include and what to leave aside.

The table of contents of this book is the product of several hard choices. It is likely to strike many political philosophers that the core chapters are fixed on topics that are old-fashioned, "traditional," or worse. There is no denying that liberty, authority, justice, and democracy are among the most overworked topics of the field. At the same time, other topics seem to be rising to the forefront of the discipline; professional journals are at present replete with articles about terrorism, sovereignty, immigration, environmentalism, colonialism, punishment, identity, race, gender, and much else. Certainly these are issues worthy of sustained philosophical attention. Yet it strikes me that discussions of these matters always presuppose specific views concerning more fundamental questions about the topics considered here: the nature of liberty, the scope of political authority, the demands of justice, and the value of democracy. For better or worse, these topics strike me as the nuts and bolts of political philosophy rather than a collection of antiquated concerns.

Although the central chapters of this book have been written so that they could be read independently of the others, the book has a clear trajectory and the chapters are probably best read in the order in which they appear. The two chapters composing the book's first part provide a broad introduction to the book by introducing some of the basic terminology and concepts that are employed throughout. The Conclusion attempts to draw a few philosophical lessons from the discussions that precede it, and so serves as a kind of summation of the book. The chapters that make up Part II tend to build on material presented in Part I. However, I have also attempted to write in a way that makes the book flexible and thus useable in a variety of contexts. To this end, I have added orientating remarks whenever referring to a crucial point made in an earlier chapter; I hope to have avoided excessive repetition. I believe that this feature will help instructors who may want to use this book alongside other readings. I have also added at the end of each chapter a brief discussion of some central texts that might be read by those who would like to explore further; though these discussions most certainly are not intended to be exhaustive.

Acknowledgments

This book took far longer to complete than I initially anticipated. Without going into the details, my work was delayed at several junctures because life kept intervening, in some ways pleasant and in others not. In the long process of completing this book, I incurred many debts, some of which I acknowledge here. First, I recognize the forms of institutional funding I received in connection with this project. Vanderbilt University granted me a Summer Research Award for 2013 and a year's sabbatical for academic year 2014–15; this support was crucial in helping me complete this book. I thank Carolyn Dever (Dean of Vanderbilt's College of Arts and Science) and Dennis Hall (Dean of Vanderbilt's Graduate School and Vice Provost for Research) for this support. Several people generously commented on drafts of the chapters, others engaged in lengthy conversations with me about various issues that arose along the way, some simply allowed me to talk to them about the manuscript and the issues discussed in it, and others offered support of a more personal kind. I am not able here to specify the contributions made by each of the following colleagues and friends, so I hope it is sufficient simply to thank them for their kindness, generosity, friendship, and assistance: Brooke Ackerly, Jody Azzouni, Michael Bacon, James Bednar, William James Booth, Thom Brooks, Adam Burgos, Mary Butterfield, Ann Cacoullos, Steven Cahn, Mike Calamari, Gregg Caruso, John Christman, Caleb Clanton, Alan Coates, Matthew Cotter, Josh Crites, Becky Davenport, Elizabeth Edenberg, David Estlund, Matthew Festenstein, Liz Fiss, Gerald Gaus, John Goldberg, Lenn Goodman, Dwight Goodyear, Carol Gould, David Miguel Gray, Michael Harbour, D. Micah Hester, David Hildebrand, Michael Hodges, Brad Hooker, Gary Jaeger, Angelo Juffras, David Kaspar, Chris King, John Lachs, Dave McCullough, Emily McGill, Amy McKiernan, Jose Medina, Vincent Minervini, Cheryl Misak, Paul Morrow, Emily Nacol, Jonathan Neufeld, John O'Connor, Jeanie Palomino, Fabienne Peter, John Peterman, Philip Pettit, Yvonne Raley, David Reidy, Dan Rosenberg, Steve Ross, Michael Santasiero, Luke Semrau, Peter Simpson, Andrew Smith, Edward Taylor, Rob Tempio, Jeffrey Tlumak, Chris Vigorito, Betty Villanueva, John Weymark, Tony Wong, Julian Wuerth, and Tyler Zimmer. Andrew Beck, Laura Briskman, and the editorial team at Routledge were especially patient and helpful throughout the longer-than-expected process of completing this book. I also benefitted greatly from the detailed and generous reviews provided by two anonymous referees of the manuscript; I have tried in earnest to accommodate their recommendations. Additionally, the manuscript benefitted greatly from Nicole Heller's stylistic expertise and good sense. Andrew Forcehimes provided essential research assistance and plenty of sound advice along the way. My trusty philosophical confidants Scott Aikin and Mason Marshall stepped in on short notice to provide valuable counsel regarding the final chapter. My parents, Pat and Bob Talisse, were as encouraging as ever. My longtime friend Theano Apostolou deserves special recognition for graciously hosting me on two separate occasions in her (mostly) quiet home while I was writing. And my wife, Joanne Billett, was, as usual, a source of sustaining inspiration.

PART I
Setting the Task

1 Some Preliminary Considerations

- The Social World
- What Is Political Philosophy?
- How We Will Proceed
- A Final Preliminary about Philosophy
- For Further Reading

1.1 The Social World

It may sound overly dramatic to say so, but each of us is born into a world that is not of our own making. This is obviously true of our physical environs. Upon arriving on the scene, we quickly confront several brute facts, such as that fire burns, unsupported objects fall, ice melts, and glass shatters. We simply find ourselves within a world of objects and forces, and there is not much we can do about it but learn how to work with what we have. According to a common view of these matters, the natural sciences are devoted to the task of learning how to work with our physical surroundings. There is no denying that these sciences have been quite successful; for instance, science produces various forms of technology, and we now are able to control, harness, and direct many of the features of our world.

Yet our world is not exclusively physical in this sense. We are each born into a *social* world as well. This is a world populated by other people, and here too we must learn how to work with our surroundings. But the social world into which we are born is not simply a world of other humans; it is also a world that features institutions that produce rules and practices that structure, and sometimes define, our interactions with others. Consider that each of us comes into the world already standing in relation to certain other people, and these relations are defined by social institutions. To point to a few obvious examples, each of us is somebody's biological child, some of us are born into siblinghood, and some are born into more complex familial relationships. The family is a social institution—perhaps the most basic social institution—and it is by reference to the family that we can identify certain others as our parents, grandparents, aunts, uncles, cousins, siblings, and so on.

Although the family is perhaps the most obvious example of a social institution into whose structures we are born, it is not the only one. We are often also born as members of communal entities beyond the family, such as neighborhoods, villages, towns, cities, and geographical regions. Hence in the United States some people identify themselves as New Yorkers, others as Southerners, still others as Midwesterners, and so on; these designations are often taken to have significance beyond the merely autobiographical information that they impart. That is, New Yorkers tend to have views about what people from the South are like, just as Southerners tend to have views about New Yorkers. And even within these broad categories, there are further classifications of the same kind. For example, I know firsthand that many Nashvillians tend to consider themselves to be living in the "New South"; they hence regard other cities in Tennessee as belonging to the "Old South," and see inhabitants of these cities as importantly different from themselves. There's a similar phenomenon among people who live in New York City; those living on the Upper West Side regard those who live in lower Manhattan as significantly dissimilar from themselves, and those living in Manhattan typically turn up their noses at those who live in the City's other boroughs. Of course, this is to say nothing about the view commonly held by those who live anywhere in New York City of those who live in New York State (that is, the parts of New York that are not New York City). Further, some Manhattanites view those who live in neighboring New Jersey as utterly alien and sometimes contemptible, too.

These phenomena are highly complex, often confusing, frequently just silly, and sometimes instances of plain bigotry. My point in mentioning them is neither to condemn nor condone. Instead, I note that although the facts of where and when one is born are matters of chance, we, for better or worse, often take them to be relevant in deciding who we (and others) are. This is because the circumstances of one's birth are typically closely tied to facts about how one was raised, what customs one has adopted, how one was educated, what religion one practices, what values one holds, and much else. And these facts tell us something important about a person. It is crucial to see that these facts are all products of social institutions.

Things get more complex, and decidedly less silly, when we consider that individuals are often born into membership in various religious communities, economic and occupational classes, as well as ethnic, gender, and racial groups. Consider first membership in a religious community. Religious communities set an expansive range of life-affecting rules and expectations for their members. These involve matters ranging from what foods one eats and what clothes one wears to more intimate matters, including who one can marry. For those who are members of a religious community, membership (at least initially) is often non-voluntary. Individuals are typically born into a religious community; they are "raised" in a given religion, and the religious community often serves as the social center of individuals' lives, especially during their more formative years.

Consider next membership in economic classes, and the frequently inter-twined matters of ethnicity, race, and gender. It is far less common these days, but it used to be the case that trades were passed down from parents to their children. For example, the son of a farmer would be a farmer him-self, and the daughter of a seamstress would learn the craft of sewing from her mother. Consequently, the family into which one was born would fix much of the course of one's subsequent life by determining one's occupation and thus one's economic class. Note that we still see informal remnants of this kind of phenomenon in certain professions, including among lawyers, physicians, musicians, and police officers. Furthermore, although great progress has been made in the last century, there are still significant respects in which various occupational, economic, and social roles are fixed by ethnicity, race, and gender. I am not (yet) an elderly man, but I can still remember a time when non-male non-white physicians, female accountants, and African American lawyers were markedly rare, if not totally unheard of. I am also old enough to recall a time when my mother was deemed ineligible for a credit card because of her gender; she was told that she would need to have her husband as a co-applicant. And I distinctly remember an episode over a family holiday dinner when a male guest confidently and proudly declared—in a room mostly of women and young girls, no less!—that women should not be allowed to vote because such an arrangement gives their husbands (or fathers, or boyfriends) two votes; his assumption was that women would naturally defer their political judgment to the men in their lives. I should note that this holiday dinner occurred in the mid-1970s, more than fifty years since the Nineteenth Amendment was introduced into the US Constitution.

I hope these events from my youth strike you as unbelievable, the stuff of a dark and thankfully distant history. But, in fact, episodes like these were commonplace not too long ago. We have made great strides in eliminating many of the most overt forms of institutional support for practices that determine an individual's social position and opportunities on the basis of such things as ethnicity, race, and gender. However, practices of this kind undoubtedly persist in our society. Women still tend not to get paid as well as their male equivalents in the workplace, and although legal racial segregation in the United States was eliminated by the Civil Rights Act of 1964, there remains unofficial but nonetheless socially enforced racial segregation in the United States. Whether the progress we have made is sufficient from the point of view of justice will be addressed in Chapter 5. For now, the point, again, is that our lives are undeniably and appreciably shaped by social institutions, and these institutions are not of our own making.

As a further example of the deep impact of institutions on our lives, consider that most individuals are born in a particular country, a fact that commonly renders them *citizens* of particular states. States are large-scale social entities, and though there are philosophical controversies concerning what precisely states are, we could say for now that states are social insti-tutions that govern or preside over all other social institutions within their territory or jurisdiction. States regulate, structure, and monitor the other facets of our social world. For starters, they make and enforce laws, they imprison people and punish them in other ways; they regulate commerce, they raise and maintain armies, and they can declare war on other states. States are massively powerful.

States of certain kinds wield their power in ways that terrorize, dominate, and oppress their citizens. In fact, in the case of certain states, it is not clear that the term *citizen* even applies properly to those who live within them; those who live under the governments of tyrannical and authoritarian states are perhaps better characterized as *subjects* of the state rather than citizens. In cases of extremely brutal tyranny, we might prefer to speak of those living within the state's territory as among its *victims*. Of course, there are states of other kinds that aspire to govern for the sake of the people living within their borders; they exist and rule *for* their citizens, on their *behalf*. These states also create and enforce laws, punish people, make war, and the rest. But they do so with the express purpose of *serving* their citizens, typically by sustaining a social order in which all could thrive or flourish.

We will have occasion in later chapters to examine a range of questions concerning the nature and power of states. Let us now note that the state into which one is born largely fixes an expansive range of features of one's life. The languages one will speak, the food one eats, the religion one practices (if any), the education one receives, the art to which one is exposed, the occupations that one may pursue, and much else—including the likely length of one's life—are all largely a matter of where one is born. Furthermore, what might be called one's overall worldview—one's general understanding of human history, science, the nature of the universe, the meaning of life, and what it is to live well—is largely a product of the country into which one was born.

But this is not the end of the story. Importantly, citizenship also carries with it obligations to one's state. For example, that one is a citizen of the United States entails that one owes allegiance to its laws and its government. This is why a citizen of, say, Canada cannot commit an act of *treason* against the United States. As a US citizen, one also arguably has a duty to vote and to participate in the shared task of democratic self-government. It is also commonly held that one has an obligation to one's state to contribute to its *protection* in times when it is threatened; consequently, in many states some form of military service is required, or at least under certain circumstances *expected*, of citizens. So one's citizenship determines, or strongly influences, a great deal concerning how one's life will go. And the status of *citizen* is acquired typically at the moment of one's birth. The world of states and citizens, and our own place within it, is something we simply inherit.

Thus far I have been laboring a single simple point, namely, that we are born into an array of social roles and relations and these in turn are defined by their corresponding social institutions: the family, the neighborhood, the city, the religious community, the economic class, the ethnic, racial, and gender group, the state, and so on. And each role we occupy carries with it various kinds of moral, social, and legal significance. Our place in the social world, though largely not a product of our individual choices, nonetheless establishes for us certain central duties, obligations, and expectations. It also plays a considerable role in determining the range of opportunities and benefits available to us throughout the course of our lives. The impact of social institutions is so pervasive that we may begin to wonder whether human lives really are that much different from the law-governed paths of falling heavy objects. Maybe our lives are merely the effects of all the physical and social forces at work at the moment of our birth.

We have as yet only scratched the surface. Hence we should avoid drawing any distinctively philosophical conclusions at this early juncture. There is much more to say about the nature of social institutions and the roles that they play in our lives. In fact, this entire book is devoted to examining various facets of this very issue. But the little that has been said suffices to show that the social world has at least as much impact on our lives as the brute facts of our physical environment. That fire burns and unsupported heavy objects fall are facts that we all do well to take account of in our everyday knocking about in the world. It is nonetheless important, though, to keep in mind the facts of our social existence. That some given action to which we are inclined is a crime or is harmful to others, for example, is something worthy of note in our day-to-day lives.

Still, what has been said thus far also brings into focus one crucial respect in which the social world is fundamentally different from the physical world. Although neither is of our own making, the social world exists *because* of us. The total disappearance of human beings from the world would not change the fact that fire burns, but it would cause governments, laws, families, and the rest to vanish. Were all human beings to disappear suddenly, the social institutions, roles, and practices that we have been discussing would be things that *used to exist*, but no longer do. So we may say that although the social world is not of our own *individual* making, it exists and persists because we *collectively* sustain it. This means, in turn, that even though we are born into a social world that we did not create, we nonetheless play some role in shaping it. As we know from even very recent and local history, the character of social institutions can change, and along with these changes come alterations in the relationships we have with each other and the rules that govern our interactions. More importantly, we know that *we* can change the institutions and rules by which we live together. So although we do not *create* the social world so much as *inherit* it, it is nonetheless *ours* in that we maintain it by engaging in social relations, and through our participation, sometimes things change.

That the social world is partly our own doing helps to explain one of its central features. Thus far, we have been speaking as if institutions, and the rules or laws that they produce, are detached from us, as if the forces that structure our social interactions could be ultimately of the same kind as the laws that govern falling objects. To be sure, there are some political philosophers who have defended the view that there are laws of politics that are as fixed and stable as the laws of gravity. But even according to views of this kind, social institutions are not quite as distant as the forces of nature. Institutions are collections of roles and offices that are occupied by people. Unlike physical laws, which all by themselves govern the motion of bodies, the rules and practices that govern our social lives get their force from us. That is, we *enforce* the rules; we hold each other to them.

Of course, not all enforcement is of the same kind. As was mentioned above, states enforce laws by means of the exercise of their power; they enact laws that incentivize or encourage certain kinds of behavior, and they punish those who fail to comply. But there are more subtle and ordinary forms of enforcement that are *direct* in that they do not invoke the power of the state. Consider the familiar phenomenon of line-cutting. When there is a sizeable line of people waiting for coffee at the local café, the social rule says that the person who has most recently arrived on the scene joins the line at its very end. When someone elects to violate this rule by cutting in line, there is often an outcry from the others. Of course, the enforcement of the rule against line-cutting rarely involves anything like a physical removal of the cutter, yet nonetheless the cutter is typically subjected to various signals of disapproval, and sometimes is confronted by others who demand that she take her proper place at the line's end. Similar phenomena prevail with respect to traffic laws. The person who drives recklessly, or who "cuts off" another driver, is often subjected to a protracted horn-blowing. This is a mild form of punishment; it is an expression of condemnation that is intended to shame or chastise the perpetrator. Other examples are easy to formulate.

We might be inclined to view cases of line-cutting or aggressive driving as more on the order of bad manners than rule-violation; we would then see the consequent social signals of disapproval amounting to little more than an expression of dissatisfaction. But this view misses something important about these phenomena. After all, the line-cutter is sometimes reprimanded even by those who are not adversely affected by his cutting; bystanders frequently protest along with those who are impacted by the bad behavior. Indeed, we often go *out of our way* to express disapproval of those who break certain social rules, and we do so at a cost to ourselves. That is, these ordinary reactions to mild forms of social rule-breaking are attempts to affect changes in the behavior of others. When we blow the car horn at a careless driver, we do not simply seek to express our disapproval of his driving; the point of expressing our disapproval is to attach a social cost to careless driving, and thus to encourage the careless driver to drive in accordance with the rules.

These commonplace instances of informal rule-enforcement are in some ways of the same *kind* as the official enforcement enacted by the state. To be sure, a police officer who issues a ticket to a careless driver is acting in a way that differs from your horn-blowing in the severity of the punishment imposed on the violator. The officer acts on behalf of the state in ways that are designed to encourage compliance with traffic laws and to punish those who violate them. At more complex levels, of course, the state organizes official processes and procedures for making, enforcing, and interpreting laws; these include an expansive court and legal system, a series of representative bodies responsible for making legislation, a broad arrangement of institutions that enact punishment, and much else. But, like car horns and informal rules about queues at cafés, all of this exists for the sake of maintaining a social order. And maintaining a social order involves acts that incentivize, encourage, urge, or even force people to behave in ways that they otherwise would not. Again, the social order is one that we *impose* on each other. As it turns out, this fact provides the primary material for political philosophy.

1.2 What Is Political Philosophy?

Let's take a moment to review. After discussing the impact that the social world has on our lives, we highlighted two of its main aspects. First, we noted its malleability. The social world is a complex of rules, roles, and institutions that give rise to a social order, and there are many different kinds of social order. Moreover, the institutions of society can change, and can be changed by us. Second, I pointed out that the social world exists because we sustain it by imposing its rules on each other; that is, the social world involves the making of *demands* that people act in some ways and refrain from acting in others.

The combination of these two features of the social world occasion a range of decidedly philosophical questions, including those questions that are distinctive of political philosophy. Before we begin to pose these, however, it might be helpful to take a step back and say something about what makes a question philosophical. This will, in turn, enable us to say what political philosophy is.

It is obvious that all areas of inquiry ask why. For example, physicists ask why unsupported heavy bodies fall, and chemists ask why ice melts. These sciences seek *explanations* of these phenomena. Formulating good explanations enables scientists to make predictions about natural events; this in turn enables them to manage and exert control over our natural surroundings. Philosophers also ask why. And they, too, seek explanations of the kind sought by the sciences. For example, philosophers who work in the area known as metaphysics are concerned to explain the most basic features of the world; they ask questions like, "What does it mean for something to exist?," "What is time?," and "What is the nature of causation?" Philosophers of mind ask questions like, "Why does consciousness exist?," "How does perception work?," and "Why do we dream?" In asking questions like these, philosophers attempt to build accounts of the phenomena under consideration; they seek an accurate picture of the world. Accordingly, many areas of philosophical inquiry are tightly partnered with relevant fields of science; for example, contemporary metaphysicians follow closely developments in physics, and philosophers of mind often work alongside psychologists and cognitive scientists.

But philosophers also ask questions of a different kind. In addition to explanations, philosophers also seek *justifications*. That is, they ask not only how things are, but how things *ought to be*, and whether the way things are is acceptable. This is to say that philosophers investigate *normative* matters, not only descriptive ones. Of course, the endeavor to find out how things ought to be often requires one to begin from an accurate picture of how things are, so the two kinds of investigation are certainly not unrelated. However, when we ask for an accurate description, the standard for correctness is *how things are*; if we have a description of the world according to which there are three hydrogen atoms in a molecule of water, and then discover that there are only two, we conclude that our description is incorrect and must be revised. By contrast, the standard of correctness in a normative account is not how things in fact are. Thus if we develop a normative account of the social world according to which eating fish is unjust, and then discover that fish-eating is extremely widespread, we do not take this fact to prove that our normative account is mistaken; we may, rather, conclude that the world contains a staggering degree of injustice. In other words, descriptive accounts must fit the world in order to be correct, but normative accounts need not fit the world in order to be correct. Their standard of correctness lies elsewhere.

These are highly simplified accounts of the differences between descriptive and normative claims, not to mention the differences between science and philosophy. But what has been said will serve our current purposes well enough. The point is that political philosophy is the normative enterprise of seeking justifications for various aspects of the social world.

This definition of political philosophy is surely insufficient. A little more precision can be gained by introducing a distinction within the social world between the *social* and the *political*. It is worth noting straightaway that any such distinction will be artificial and contestable. But, again, for our present purposes we can distinguish between social institutions that are more or less informal, such as the family and the neighborhood, and the institutions that are centrally elements of the state. One way of drawing the distinction is to recall the point made above that states regulate and thus help to define the other social institutions. They accomplish this by making and enforcing laws and policies. To be sure, all social institutions make rules to which those within the institution are expected to adhere. But it is generally thought that the state's laws are rules of a special kind, as they are enforceable in ways that go far beyond what other social institutions are capable of. To put the point bluntly, only *states* can rightfully imprison those who violate its rules. Consequently, only states can assemble official bodies for the purpose of enforcement, such as a police force and an army. Citizens may certainly band together for the sake of stopping or preventing crime, but citizens as such cannot rightfully act as a police force. They cannot rightly arrest, apprehend, or handcuff those who break laws. Your neighbor cannot build a jail in her garage and hold criminals there. Only states and their appointed officers can do things of this kind.

Contrast the state's power to make and enforce laws with the power that other social institutions exercise over their members. Consider first the family; there is no denying that families do impose rules on their members, and some of these rules can be very strict and demanding. We can also concede that families wield various kinds of power to encourage compliance; in many families, the consequences of breaking its central rules can be pretty extreme. But the important point about families is that, at least once one reaches an age that the state identifies as adulthood, one can simply declare oneself to be no longer a member of one's family; one can extricate oneself from the family and its rules at will. At the very least, one can create a sufficient amount of emotional and geographical space between oneself and one's family members so as to weaken the rules. This kind of extraction is of course not always emotionally pleasant or easy, but it is possible.

Next take the example of a religious community. As we noted above, such communities impose a broad range of rules on members. Members of religious communities are expected to uphold and live by the community's rules, and there are, again, various kinds of enforcement mechanisms in place that enable the community to secure compliance (or at least discourage defection). As with families, the cost of noncompliance with the religious rules sometimes is rather high. Indeed, for many, their religious community serves as something like an extended family. Accordingly, removal or extrication from the community can bring grave social costs; those who leave their religious communities frequently report losing many of their friends and other forms of social support. But the point, again, is that your religious community cannot rightfully *force* you into membership; it cannot *lock* you inside a church and hold you there against your will, at gunpoint for example. Even though religious communities can arrange things so that the social cost of defection is extremely high, voluntary extraction is always possible, at least legally.

Notice further that in cases where there is reason to suspect that a social organization—religious or otherwise—is indeed holding people against their will or engaging in other extreme forms of compulsion, the state rightfully may get involved. That is, the state demands that other social institutions provide a viable *exit option* for their members. Social institutions such as families and religious communities can decide their rules internally (within broad constraints), and they are given some latitude for enforcing those rules, but they cannot force individuals to be members, and they cannot impose extreme punishments on those who break the rules. They may shame, browbeat, blame, and disenfranchise rule-breakers, but they may not inflict physical punishment or imprison them. The state itself, however, does claim the right to impose such punishments on its members; the state, after all, puts some of its citizens in cages and forces them to stay there, sometimes in nearly complete social isolation, for what remains of their lives. Unlike those who violate the rules of the family or the religious community, those convicted of breaking certain laws imposed by the state are not able to evade the prescribed punishment by simply disassociating. To put the point in a way that is common among political philosophers, what is distinctive about states is that they hold a monopoly on certain forms of power. Whereas other social institutions hold various kinds of power that enable them to encourage compliance with their rules, only states claim the right to take away your most basic freedoms as punishment for breaking its laws. States can *force* you, against your will, to comply with their rules. We can say, then, that states claim a monopoly on *coercive power*, the power to force you to do what you otherwise would not do, and the power to *threaten* you with the exercise of such force. Yet, crucially, states claim even more than this. In addition to claiming to have a monopoly on coercive power, states claim to be *entitled* to hold a monopoly on coercive power. To introduce some terminology that will be further discussed later, states claim not only the *power* to force you to follow the rules, but the *moral right* to do so; that is, states claim for themselves *authority*.

The point is worth dwelling upon for a moment longer. We can say that power is an empirical thing. Who has power and how much power they have are both matters that can be decided by empirical investigation, roughly in the way that scientists can investigate the temperature at which ice melts. A powerful person is one that has the ability to compel others to do what she wants them to do; accordingly, if we want to discover who has power, we simply look to see who "calls the shots" or gives the orders that are likely to be complied with. Philosophically speaking, *authority* is importantly different from *power*. Authority is the *entitlement* to power, the *right* to hold and exercise power; it is therefore a *moral* thing. Consequently, a person in authority might in fact be powerless or out of control; similarly, someone in power might have no authority. Hence in order to discover who has authority, we cannot simply look to see who successfully wields power; we must ask who—if anyone—has the moral right to power. Put a little differently, someone who has authority is *entitled* to call the shots and give orders; correspondingly, those who are subject to that authority are obliged to do as he or she says.

States often indeed have the power to force their citizens to follow their rules. States command large armies and law enforcement agencies, and they have other instruments of control at their disposal, including prisons, jails, clinics, asylums, as well as a nearly inexhaustible supply of weapons of various kinds. But states also claim for themselves authority over their citizens. That is, your state claims to be *entitled* to your compliance. Suppose for a moment that the state is indeed entitled to your compliance. It follows then that you are obligated to comply with its orders, including (though perhaps not limited to) its laws. In breaking a law, then, you not only act imprudently (in that you risk getting caught and hence subject to punishment), you also do something *immoral*; in breaking the law, you violate an obligation.

Hence you not only make yourself liable to punishment, you make yourself *deserving* of it.

Now, at last, we are able to say something more determinate about what political philosophy is. Whereas social philosophy is the area of philosophy that examines and normatively evaluates the social world in its various aspects, political philosophy, as we will understand it in this book, is the part of social philosophy that is concerned particularly with normative investigation into the state. Political philosophy is the attempt to identify the principal aspects or elements of the state and to assess them normatively. It asks whether there should be states at all, and, if so, how states should be organized. It must be emphasized that the two instances of the word "should" in the previous sentence are both to be understood as normative. That is, political philosophy is not the attempt to figure out whether states are particularly efficient or effective instruments for achieving certain ends; nor is it the attempt to determine which policies or institutional designs are best able to deliver some specified social result or outcome. Questions of that purely empirical kind lie within the domain of political science. Political philosophy, rather, is the enterprise of figuring out whether states have any rightful claim to our allegiance, whether states are ever right in punishing individuals who break their laws, whether a state indeed could be entitled to a monopoly on coercive power, or, in short, whether any state has authority. If the answer to these questions is affirmative, then political philosophy next attempts to figure out how states should be organized by determining the nature and limits of state power. If these matters can be worked out, it remains for political philosophy to ask whether any possibly existing or real-world state could be entitled to that kind of power. If actual states are so entitled, then political philosophy asks about the relations between states, and whether states can rightfully exercise power over other states. As one would expect, political philosophy gets complicated quickly. For now, though, we can say that political philosophy seeks a *justification* for the state.

1.3 How We Will Proceed

This book will proceed according to the understanding of the nature of political philosophy that was just set out above. Our investigation is thus focused on the relation between individuals and states; in other words, we will be engaged in an exploration of the philosophical issues pertaining to the justification of political authority.

As I emphasized earlier, our lives are always embedded within preexisting social networks of norms, rules, and institutions. It should come as no surprise, then, that our examination of the state and its justification cannot begin from scratch, as it were. Rather, our explorations must begin from the particular social and political contexts in which we happen to find ourselves. Just as we find ourselves living within a social and political order that is not of our own making, our ideas about social and political matters originate with that order. To be sure, this does not mean that we are helplessly entrenched in the commonplace norms and principles of the societies into which we are born (most likely, modern Western democracy), thereby doomed merely to parrot the conventional pieties and traditional platitudes of our respective societies. The aim, after all, is largely to achieve a critical perspective on the social world we inhabit. But in order to gain that kind of intellectual distance from our everyday social environment, it helps to begin with a view from within that environment.

Accordingly, Chapter 2 develops a philosophical articulation of our starting place, our political-philosophical home. The objective there will be to draw a familiar image of our social world. That image will be drawn with the tools of political philosophy, so there may be much that is unfamiliar. However, if the chapter is successful, there will be little in the resulting picture that is foreign; indeed, the image developed in Chapter 2 should strike you as little more than a new way of describing the things you already know.

In describing our political-philosophical starting point, we will have occasion to note several junctures where distinctively philosophical questions reside. Beginning with Chapter 3, we examine many of these questions. In Chapter 3, we explore issues concerning the nature of individual liberty, and then in Chapter 4 we examine the nature of the kind of authority that is claimed by the state. One result of these chapters is that if the state is to be justified at all, its justification depends upon establishing clear *constraints* or *limits* on its authority. And this requires us to devise a conception of what the state's proper role is. It is nearly vacuous to say that the state's primary job is to secure justice, but it is important to note that an *unjust* state is a failed state, no matter what other positive attributes it may manifest. So it is crucial to our inquiry to examine what justice is. This is the topic of Chapter 5.

But even if we figure out what justice requires, there still may be a question of what *authorizes* the state to do what is necessary to secure justice. These days, we are likely to think that a society ruled by a benevolent king who always enacts the right laws would be nonetheless unjustified. This is because we are inclined to think that part of what justifies the state is not simply what laws it enacts, but the way in which it decides what laws to enact and the way in which it regards those living under its jurisdiction. In other words, we tend to think that the state must in some way be *accountable* to those over whom it claims authority; we tend to think that democracy is necessary. This raises a long series of questions about the nature of democracy that is the subject of Chapter 6.

In the Conclusion (Chapter 7), I attempt to tie together all of our results and identify some areas in need of further investigation.

1.4 A Final Preliminary about Philosophy

In the Preface, I suggested that philosophy is in large part the activity of questioning, examining, and arguing for the sake of finding out what's true, and guarding ourselves against false but comfortable consensus. This renders philosophy squarely out of step with current modes of popular politics. Today's political environment prizes line-toeing, party loyalty, and doctrinal purity, sometimes explicitly without concern for reasons. Our political leaders often profess "moral clarity" and tout the allegedly consequent ability to act "without blinking." They similarly criticize those who change their minds about political questions for "flip-flopping" and "waffling." They tend to overtly dismiss the very thought that fundamental questions of politics and public policy are worth asking; this denial is accompanied by the claim that anyone who opposes, or even questions, the political ideas that they favor is thereby ignorant, foolish, disingenuous, and sometimes even traitorous. The prevailing thought among politicians and popular political commentators is that the truths about politics are not only well known, but so obvious and simple that only the depraved or dishonest could go on examining such matters.

A cursory pass through your local bookstore's collection of politics titles confirms this. Although they are written from different and opposing political perspectives, titles like *Liberalism Is a Mental Disorder, The Republican Noise Machine, How to Talk to a Liberal (If You Must),* and *Lies and the Lying Liars Who Tell Them* assert the very same political message, namely, that there is no political argument worth having because there is no intelligent and rational political opponent to the author's favored viewpoint. This common refrain is resolutely anti-philosophical. Arguably, it is also profoundly antidemocratic. Philosophers adopt the view that the most important questions are also the most difficult and complicated questions. This in turn means that one should expect such questions to permit a wide range of intellectually responsible and philosophically defensible answers. In fact, the basic premise underlying the activity of philosophy is that rational disagreement is possible, and this means that it is possible for two people who are each intelligent, sincere, well informed, and earnest to nonetheless *disagree* about deep and important matters.

Crucially, the philosopher's commitment to the possibility of rational disagreement is not a commitment to relativism, which is the view that says that no one's opinion about political matters is better (or worse) than anyone else's. That kind of position can easily be shown to be absurd. After all, the relativist position *itself* asserts a position, which it claims is better than the opposing positions; that is, the relativist claims that relativism is *itself* better than non-relativist views about political matters. But that's precisely the kind of claim that relativism is supposed to oppose or disallow. In the parlance of philosophers, relativism is thus *self-defeating*. Again, the philosopher's commitment to the possibility of rational disagreement is not relativism; rather, it is the commitment to the idea that, when it comes to highly complex and difficult questions, we humans are fallible, even when properly exercising our rational faculties. Consequently, the philosopher draws a distinction between the *truth* of a claim and the *rationality* and *intelligence* of the person making it. The philosopher contends that sometimes there are well-grounded falsehoods and honest errors. Sometimes impeccably conducted research, reasoning, and argument nonetheless leads to falsehood, just as sometimes a lucky-guesser arrives at the truth. The philosopher holds, then, that even though there is but one true answer to any difficult and complex question, there are many different answers that are false and yet consistent with being rational. To put it in a slogan, the philosopher insists on there being a difference between being *wrong* and being *stupid*.

The billion-dollar industry devoted to producing popular political commentary is unified against this simple idea. The pundits, authors, radio hosts, made-for-television 'experts' are unanimous in thinking that anyone who they deem to be wrong about politics is *therefore* stupid, irrational, ignorant, incompetent, wicked, or worse. They consequently reject the idea that lies at the heart of political philosophy (and this book), namely, that we owe it to our most cherished ideals to subject them to rational scrutiny, to relentlessly test the grounds upon which we hold the beliefs that we hold, and to give a cogent voice to those who oppose those beliefs. As we proceed in this book, then, we will try to give our own political commitments the kind of respect and reverence that they deserve by critically examining the reasons and arguments that underwrite our loyalty to them.

It should be recognized at the start that philosophy can be risky. This seems especially true in the case of political philosophy. In the course of philosophically examining our political views, we could discover that some cherished commitment is in need of revision, refinement, or supplementation. We could also find that a deeply held and important idea is false or inadequate and thus must be abandoned altogether. That is, political philosophy is an activity that sometimes requires us to change our minds about things that we may have grown accustomed to regarding as fixed, firm, and finished. Similarly, we could find that some opposing idea that we have long reviled as mere silliness is in fact a cogent alternative to our own view. Or we may find that even though a long-reviled opposing view is indeed silly, some proponents of that view nonetheless have proposed a serious and difficult objection to our dearly held view. When doing philosophy, we set ourselves up for a kind of disorientation; we invite the destabilization of our beliefs.

Some argue that this disorienting and destabilizing aspect of philosophy is what makes it objectionable. They claim that philosophers try to lead people astray by introducing confusion and uncertainty, in effect diverting people away from tried-and-true traditions while having no positive alternative to offer. It is added that this kind of confusion is especially dangerous when it comes to moral and political matters. These charges against philosophy enjoy a long history going back at least to the trial and execution of Socrates in ancient Athens. And perhaps there is something to them; philosophy may indeed be dangerous.

Yet those who press this kind of critique of philosophy rarely consider the dangers that come with the alternative, namely, an uncritical acceptance of tradition and unquestioning adherence to the past. There is undeniable danger in these, too. Most obvious among them is the danger of uncritically adhering to traditional ideals that are in fact deeply harmful and unjust. We need not catalogue the famous cases of horrific acts committed simply in the name of tradition and conformity to (what was at the time taken to be) common sense. Of course, critics of philosophy will readily concede that flawed traditions and mistaken ideals should be subjected to unrelenting scrutiny and challenge; they will hold simply that in the case where proper traditions and worthy ideals are in place, philosophy can only mislead. But this, too, seems to be mistaken. When philosophical examination is rejected for the sake of protecting allegedly tried-and-true traditional commitments, we resolve to opt out of the processes by which we could demonstrate to ourselves their enduring value. Proper traditions and worthy ideals should be able to withstand philosophical scrutiny, and the activity of scrutinizing such traditions and ideals should leave us with an ever firmer grasp of their value. By contrast, when we decline to subject our traditions and ideals to philosophical examination, we risk losing our grasp of the reasons and considerations that favor them, and therefore we risk losing our allegiance to them.

So our question is this: To philosophize or not to philosophize? There are risks in either case. But notice that to give any answer to the question is to commit an act of philosophy. Philosophy is risky, but it is also inevitable; we must do it. Our choice is between trying to philosophize self-consciously and deliberately, or instead haphazardly. The aim of this book, then, is not to defend any particular philosophical theory of liberty, authority, justice, or democracy. The aim instead is to attempt to *philosophize well* about these matters.

For Further Reading

The broad themes discussed in this chapter concerning the nature of philosophy in general, and political philosophy in particular, can be explored further by consulting Bertrand Russell's 1947 lecture "Philosophy and Politics" (reprinted in his *Unpopular Essays*, New York: Simon and Schuster, 1950), Isaiah Berlin's 1961 essay "Does Political Theory Still Exist?" (reprinted in his *Concepts and Categories*, Second Edition, Princeton: Princeton University Press, 2013), and Robert Nozick's "The Zigzag of Politics" (reprinted in his *The Examined Life*, New York: Simon and Schuster, 1989). Some skeptical views about the abstractness of political philosophy can be found in Bonnie Honig's *Political Theory and the Displacement of Politics* (Ithaca: Cornell University Press, 1993) and Raymond Guess's *Philosophy and Real Politics* (Princeton: Princeton University Press, 2008).

Those looking to examine further the idea that political philosophy is centrally concerned with the normative evaluation of the state and its claim to authority may consult the classical anarchist writings of Mikhail Bakunin (collected in *Bakunin on Anarchy*, New York: Knopf, 1972), Peter Kropotkin (collected in *Anarchism: A Collection of Revolutionary Writings*, New York: Dover Publications, 2002), and Emma Goldman (collected in *The Writings of Emma Goldman*, New York: Red and Black Publishers, 2013). For more recent treatments, see Robert Paul Wolff's *In Defense of Anarchism* (New York: Harper and Row, 1970), A. John Simmons's *Moral Principles and Political Obligation* (Princeton: Princeton University Press, 1979), and Margaret Gilbert's *A Theory of Political Obligation* (New York: Oxford University Press, 2008).

2   Beginning Where We Are

- Where to Begin?
- Liberalism in Political Philosophy
- Liberalism and Popular Politics
- Varieties of Liberal Theory
- Conclusion
- For Further Reading

2.1 Where to Begin?

The aspiration of this book is to explore the terrain of political philosophy from the ground up. There is a sense, however, in which what was said in Chapter 1 already has committed us to a particular viewpoint within political philosophy. We have defined political philosophy as the normative project of evaluating the state, specifically of seeking a philosophical justification for its claim to authority. This is already to presume, at least to some degree, that states are the kinds of things that stand in need of a justification. Recall the point made earlier that we do not seek a justification for the laws of gravity; we rather look for an explanation of why unsupported heavy bodies fall. In conceiving of political philosophy as the attempt to see whether the state can be justified, we implicitly affirm that states are fundamentally different from, say, the laws of gravity; we affirm that states are, at least in principle, entities that need not be as they are, and could be changed or abolished altogether. A related point is worth emphasizing. In defining political philosophy as inquiry into whether states can be justified, we implicitly affirm that we are *entitled* to such a justification. At the very least, in pursuing political philosophy in the manner set forth above, we implicitly take ourselves to be *permitted* to ask whether our state—or any other state—is justified, properly ordered, worthy of our allegiance, and authoritative.

These ramifications of our conception of political philosophy are important because throughout much of human history political philosophy in the sense we mean was forbidden. It used to be widely accepted that states were ultimately not especially different from the laws of gravity; it was held that states exist by nature, and they were taken to be a fundamental fact of the natural order of the world. Kings and rulers of other kinds claimed to have been appointed by God. Hence it once was the norm for states to claim for themselves an authority beyond question and hence not subject to examination, let alone challenge. And even those states that took their power to require justification saw themselves as answerable only to *some* of those living within its borders; under such arrangements, political philosophy was not for just *anyone* who might pick up a book on the subject, but only for the few, usually a privileged class of clergy or propertied aristocrats. Of course, there still are states in the world that embrace this kind of view of their authority.

Notice the following implication. That you are now reading this book is, in a way, remarkable. Moreover, that I am able to write a book that has at its core the question of whether states are justified is a kind of political accomplishment, as is the fact that the book's publisher is able to print, publicize, and distribute it. Chances are that you are now reading this book without any fear at all of being persecuted for doing so. I am at this moment writing this sentence without any fear of being prosecuted for sedition or treason. The publisher openly intends to publicize and distribute this book widely, and sees no danger in it. These facts may strike you as obvious and mundane, as we often simply take for granted the basic freedoms to read the books we wish to read, to make up our own minds about matters of interest, to openly express our thoughts on any issue we see fit, and to freely question, or even overtly criticize and challenge, existing social and political arrangements, including our government and those who hold office within it. But it is important to keep in mind that such things are possible only within a very particular kind of political order, one that is relatively new on the stage of human history.

To drive the point home, consider the following claims:

1. George W. Bush, Dick Cheney, and Donald Rumsfeld are war criminals.
2. President Barack Obama is a traitor and a fraud who was not born in the United States, and so is in fact ineligible for the presidency. His entire administration is illegitimate.
3. Supreme Court Justices Roberts and Scalia are ignorant bigots who have no business sitting on the Court.
4. Citizens of the United States should arm themselves heavily in preparation for an imminent large-scale war against the current government.
5. The United States Government orchestrated the horrific attacks of September 11, 2001; it thereby murdered its own citizens and hence must be overthrown immediately.
6. The United States is a despotic and genocidal globally oppressive force, responsible for the murder, enslavement, and misery of billions of people worldwide; its destruction is morally imperative.

Some of these claims might strike you as odd, problematic, off-putting, or even mildly offensive; others might strike you as obviously false, unserious, or just silly. But there are two things worth emphasizing. First, in reading the above assertions, you probably experienced no worry concerning the *legality* of your doing so. Moreover, having read the assertions above, you have no fear of being arrested for being in possession of this book. You likely have no concern at all that this book or your possession of it is in any way criminal. Second, your judgment that there is nothing criminal in writing, publishing, or reading the assertions above is bolstered by the fact that in public forums such as the Internet, street corners, local parks, and in print media, it is not uncommon to find US citizens making assertions like those above, and they do so without any fear of legal reprisal. Indeed, it is easy to encounter citizens who make public renunciations of the US government and its office holders that are far more extreme than those printed above. Though these facts may strike you as commonplace, they are remarkable.

Let me put the point in a different way. If you are reading this book, it is highly likely that you are a citizen of a state of a specific kind, one that is officially bound to a series of commitments much like the following: It treats its citizens as equals; it recognizes a collection of individual liberties, codified as individual rights; it takes itself to be accountable to its citizens, and sees its job as that of providing a fair and stable social framework within which each individual may live as he or she sees fit, within the broad constraint that each individual respects the freedom of the others to live by their own lights. Filling in a few more details, it is likely that you are a citizen of a state that officially takes its purpose to be that of *serving* its citizens. What's more, the state sees its authority as deriving from the citizens themselves, typically by way of their freely given consent to be governed. Accordingly, the state sees its authority as *contingent* upon the authorization of its citizens, who could withhold it or withdraw it and, under certain conditions, rightfully rebel against the state. Perhaps most importantly, the state understands all of this to entail that its authority is not all-encompassing, but limited in very particular ways. More precisely, the state sees itself less as a parent or a moral instructor, and more like an impartial umpire or judge, a neutral keeper of political order, and a protector of individual liberty.

This is, of course, only a very rough and preliminary sketch. Much more needs to be said about what it means for the state to regard its citizens as equals, what our individual liberties are, what the state's accountability amounts to, and so on. Additionally, it is important to note that the sketch depicts an *ideal* regarding the relations between states and citizens; we are all too aware of the many respects in which actually-existing states—even those officially committed to upholding the views we have just set out—fall short. Yet this sketch sufficiently conveys the general shape of what is likely to be a familiar image of the political world. To be sure, the familiarity of this picture is no guarantee of its philosophical defensibility, but that it is familiar makes it a good place from which to begin.

2.2 Liberalism in Political Philosophy

In political philosophy, the general picture we have just been describing is called *liberalism*. The term is admittedly a bit confusing because in popular political discourse in the United States liberalism is used to refer to the political policies associated with the Democratic Party. In this popular usage, liberalism is contrasted with *conservatism*, which in turn is associated with the policy platform of the Republican Party. Much of popular politics in the United States is focused upon the conflict between liberals and conservatives; in fact, political commentary that revolves around this conflict is currently a billion-dollar industry. However, in political philosophy liberalism is the name of a particular way of conceptualizing the world of politics; it is what I will call a *framework* for political thinking rather than a particular collection of public policy commitments. Democrats and Republicans, in the popular senses of those terms (in the United States, at least), are all *liberals* in this philosophical sense. This is not to say that deep down Republicans and Democrats do not really disagree about anything; nor is it to suggest that conservatives are just confused liberals (in the popular sense of that term). The claim, rather, is that liberalism in the philosophical sense provides the common field within which policy debates among Republicans and Democrats are conducted. We could even go so far as to say that Republicans and Democrats are able to disagree about policy precisely because they share a common conception of the political world. Again, this is what I mean by calling liberalism a framework for political thinking.

All of this calls for further explanation. Liberalism in the philosophical sense (which is the sense in which I'll be using it as we proceed) is a family of commitments, each of which is subject to multiple philosophical interpretations. Yet it is possible to identify a set of ideas that are characteristic of the liberal framework. Let us begin, then, by trying to get a clearer view of these characteristic commitments. Then we will be able to see how opposing views in our popular politics can be understood as competing interpretations of a shared framework.

2.2.1 Three Core Commitments of Liberalism

Our analysis of liberalism begins with three core commitments. These are ideas that are almost uniformly affirmed by anyone identifying with liberalism as a framework for political analysis. Later on, we will have occasion to question whether one could be a liberal and nonetheless deny any of these three commitments; for now, we will proceed as if all liberalisms agreed on at least these three claims.

First and foremost, liberalism holds that individuals, taken as such, are the primary units of political-philosophical analysis. Liberalism is thus fundamentally contrasted with views that take some social unit or other—the family, the tribe, the ethnic group, the economic class, the nation—to be basic. In other words, the liberal holds that, for the purposes of political philosophy at least, social entities and institutions are to be understood as variously organized collections of *individuals*. Many varieties of non-liberalism explicitly deny this; they hold some version of the thought that individuals are always to be understood in terms of their membership in some social group. In fact, it is not uncommon for non-liberal approaches to hold that social membership is *prior to* or *constitutive of* the individual, that *what you are* is a member of this or that social group, and consequently that your membership in some or other social group *defines* you. Accordingly, non-liberal views sometimes affirm that the very idea of an asocial individual is a kind of contradiction; to be an individual is to be a member of some social unit, they say. Liberals deny this. They hold that no matter how important our varied social relations may be, and no matter how deeply we identify with the social groups of which we are members, for the purposes of political philosophy we are to be understood as fundamentally individuals who are in principle detachable from those relations. The cornerstone of liberalism is the claim that political philosophy begins from this idea of the individual as fundamentally detached from his or her social relations.

Call this fundamental liberal commitment *individualism*. It is important to keep in mind precisely what kind of commitment it is. Individualism is not the claim that individuals are intrinsically egotistical or selfish. Nor is it the claim that social relations do not matter or are always disposable. And, furthermore, individualism does not affirm that the best or healthiest kind of person is one who conceives of himself as a loner, a "free agent," or a Robinson Crusoe. Individualism, rather, is a claim about where political philosophy begins. To repeat, it is the claim that, for the purposes of political philosophy, we should understand individuals as separable from their particular social entanglements. Whether individuals are in fact separable in this way is not at issue; the claim of individualism is that when we are doing political philosophy we begin from the assumption that they are.

Individualism is closely tied to a second plank of liberalism, what we will call *moral egalitarianism*. Later, we will encounter a view distinctively about justice that we will call egalitarianism; for now, we are using the term more broadly. Naturally enough, moral egalitarianism is the view that individuals are to be regarded as moral equals. Again, it is important to be clear about what this means. Moral egalitarianism is not the claim that each individual is equally good, nor is it the view that the schoolteacher and the thief are to be given the same treatment by society. It is rather the assertion that, at least as far as the state is concerned, each individual is entitled to equal moral regard. This means that the state must see each individual life as equally important, equally worthy of protection, and deserving of equal respect and concern. Or, to put the point in a different way, moral egalitarianism means that the state must recognize no *natural* hierarchies among individuals; it must affirm that no one is by birth the political subordinate of another, and correspondingly it must treat each individual as an equal *citizen*. Moral egalitarianism is thus inconsistent with practices that determine a citizen's political standing on the basis of his economic class, caste, nobility, race, gender, ethnicity, or religious affiliation. Accordingly, the liberal state cannot rightfully declare that central political offices are open only to men, or the wealthy or well born, nor can it enact laws that apply only to women, or to members of some specified racial or ethnic group. The state must treat us as equals.

The denial of natural hierarchies among citizens entails that, from the point of view of the state, no one's life is intrinsically more important than yours; but it also means that no one is by nature your boss, supervisor, or master. This brings us to a third core commitment of liberalism. Given that we are moral equals, we are also in some fundamental sense *free*. Now, freedom is a multifaceted concept that invokes many considerations across several distinct sub-fields of philosophy, from metaphysics and philosophy of mind to ethics and political philosophy. We do not want to get embroiled in these difficulties here. We will use *liberty* and *freedom* interchangeably, and we will use these terms to denote something distinctively political. Our third core commitment of liberalism is liberty.

As we will see in Chapter 3, there is considerable controversy among liberal political philosophers over the precise nature of liberty. Consequently, what we say here can be only a prelude. In most of its standard formulations, liberalism is committed to the view that liberty consists in the absence of external constraint or interference. In other words, our liberty consists in the ability to act without obstruction from others. In this sense of the term, then, the fact that I cannot leap tall buildings in a single bound is not a limitation on my freedom, though the fact that I cannot (rightfully) drive your car without your permission is. On this standard view, liberty is reduced whenever others impose constraints on my action, that is, when the range of actions that I could perform is diminished by the obstruction or interference of others. As a preliminary, we can say that liberalism is committed to a view of individual liberty according to which liberty consists in the *absence* of something. To be a little more precise, we can say that liberalism is traditionally committed to the view that liberty is always the *freedom from* external obstruction. This thought is captured by the claim that liberalism is most frequently wedded to a *negative* conception of liberty.

2.2.2 Liberalism and the Challenge of Anarchism

These three commitments—individualism, moral egalitarianism, and liberty—form the core of liberalism as a framework for political philosophy. Our discussion thus far might suggest that liberalism is a simple (perhaps simple-minded) approach to politics. However, liberalism is in fact a very complicated view. We can begin to appreciate this by noting two features of the negative conception of liberty that complicate liberalism significantly. First, the negative conception entails that a castaway stranded alone on a desert island enjoys perfect liberty. He is, after all, completely free from the interference of others and may, in that sense, do whatever he pleases. More precisely, as there are no constraints on his action that are imposed by others, the castaway's liberty is therefore complete. Second, the negative conception of liberty means that as laws and rules always constrain the range of actions that an individual may (rightly) perform, they always reduce freedom. In other words, as the state power is coercive power, states fundamentally reduce individual liberty.

We take special note of these two ramifications of the negative conception because they reveal an important feature of liberalism, namely, that liberalism is a framework for thinking about the political world that deliberately puts into question the moral appropriateness of the state. Consider: As liberals, we are committed to viewing ourselves as fundamentally morally equal and free citizens, and this seems to entail that no one has the right to simply push others around. But, as we just reiterated, states claim for themselves the exclusive right to coerce us by means of laws, and, as we just said, laws reduce our liberty. That is, not only do states push us around, they claim to be exclusively entitled to do so. How, then, is the liberal constellation of individualism, moral egalitarianism, and liberty consistent with the existence of states?

We are now able to see clearly how the conception of political philosophy set out in Chapter 1 is implicitly committed to a distinctively liberal view of the political world. In placing the *justification* of the state at the heart of political philosophy, we assume that states are the kinds of entities that *require* justification. To invoke once again the distinction drawn earlier between explanation and justification, we do not seek a *justification* of the Atlantic Ocean, for example. We take the Atlantic as something to be *explained*. And there may be social entities—possibly the family, for instance—whose existence is properly seen as something to explain rather than to justify. But states are different in that it seems worth asking not only for an explanation of how they function and why, but also for a justification, an account of why they should exist at all. Our ordinary conception of political philosophy, then, presupposes a broadly liberal view of the state in that it takes seriously the possibility that, morally speaking, there should be no states, that no state is justified.

We are now also poised to make an additional point about liberalism. Given what we have said thus far, liberalism looks a lot like a view that is called *philosophical anarchism*. To clarify, *philosophical* anarchism is to be distinguished from anarchism as a political platform, ideal, strategy, or tactic. That is, the philosophical anarchist is not necessarily committed to the overthrow of the state; in fact, many philosophical anarchists hold that states *should* exist. Philosophical anarchism is, rather, the distinctive claim that no state has the moral entitlement to our obedience and loyalty. That is, philosophical anarchism is the thesis that no state in fact has *authority*. Arguments for philosophical anarchism frequently rely on the characteristic liberal commitments we have discussed thus far. Very roughly stated, the philosophical anarchist argues that relations of authority cannot exist among free and morally equal individuals; put otherwise, the argument is that authority always involves some unjustifiable violation of equality or liberty. But liberalism is not anarchism; in fact, liberalism is opposed to philosophical anarchism. We might even say that liberalism is the attempt to take seriously the philosophical anarchist's objection to the state, and to attempt to defend the state despite the fact that it is primarily in the business of reducing liberty. So there must be more to liberalism than what we have identified thus far.

2.2.3 Further Commitments of Liberalism

Indeed there is more to liberalism than our core trio of individualism, moral egalitarianism, and liberty; these additional commitments set liberalism apart from philosophical anarchism. One further commitment follows closely on the heels of the negative conception of liberty. Liberals tend to hold that liberty means not only that we are not to be interfered with; it also means that we are in some sense the authors of our individual lives, that our lives are in some important sense *our own*. Call this the liberal commitment to *autonomy*.

Liberal autonomy is the claim that it is the prerogative of each individual to determine for himself how to live. This means that each of us must decide for ourselves the answers to what we might call Life's Big Questions: What is truly valuable? What is worth achieving? What is the meaning of life? To what should my life be devoted? What is worth dying for? Is there a God? What makes a life a success? How should I live my life? In the course of determining how to live, we must also assess our own potential, estimate our individual capabilities, figure out what possibilities are open to us, and attempt to set reasonable expectations for our lives. In short, autonomy means that in addition to having a life to live, we each have a life to *plan*.

The commitment to autonomy imposes significant limits on what the state is permitted to do. Consider: The commitment to autonomy entails that it is not the job of the state to assign life-plans to citizens. Your occupation, your aspirations, your hobbies, and how you spend your day and with whom you spend it are all, for the most part and within certain constraints, up to you. Moreover, as noted above, the commitment to autonomy means that the state cannot impose upon you answers to Life's Big Questions, and this means in turn that it cannot (rightfully) require you to attend a church, to worship, to pray, or to refrain from praying and worshiping. Nor can the liberal state compel you to live according to some specific philosophy of the good life. In fact, the state cannot oblige you to reflect on your life at all. Similarly, it cannot compel you to read great literature, develop an appreciation of Modern Art, study higher mathematics, meditate, exercise, plant a garden, practice the piano, or watch less television. Nor can the state require you to develop your talents, get married, pursue a career in public service, or give up your ambition to become a concert pianist. Liberalism's commitment to autonomy means that these are all matters that are ultimately up to you, the individual.

Of course, liberal autonomy does not deny that you may seek advice from others about how to live, and you may even choose to live your life according to a plan provided by your parents, a text that you regard as sacred, or the advice of a therapist or life-coach. Indeed, you may elect to become a subservient disciple of some guru, and live unquestioningly according to her instructions. Moreover, the liberal commitment to autonomy is consistent with the idea that it would be *good* for you to seek advice on how to live life, or even that you ought to live entirely according to another's directions. Liberalism does not require you to live a life of nonconformity or moral self-exploration; liberalism rather claims that the state cannot require you to conform to its own conception of how your life should be lived. To put the point in a different way, autonomy means that the state is not your moral tutor; its job is not that of making you a good person. Again, that's up to you.

Hence we see that liberal autonomy has an important further dimension, namely, that your life is ultimately your *responsibility*. As your life is yours to *live* and *plan*, it is also yours to *manage*. Your success in life, then, is largely up to you. This means that it is not the job of the state to make your life good or to ensure that you achieve whatever it is that you find to be most worth achieving. To be sure, its commitment to moral egalitarianism entails that the state must regard each citizen's life as equally morally important, and this is frequently understood to entail that the state must provide equal *opportunity* for each citizen to succeed at whatever he determines to be most worthy of pursuit, provided of course that he is pursuing a life-plan that falls within a broad range of what is permissible; the liberal state need not provide equal opportunity to those who aspire to a life of crime. But when it comes to executing one's life-plan, the state simply sets the conditions that would permit one to succeed; it does not take on the additional job of ensuring success.

To be sure, it is plausible to think that autonomy is or involves a kind of *skill* that individuals must develop, exercise, and maintain. Autonomy, it seems, is a kind of *achievement* rather than a condition in which individuals simply find themselves. After all, we do not simply pop into the world as competent planners and managers of our lives. In order to live lives of our own we must *make* our lives our own. And this ongoing process of planning and managing is obviously not automatic, but requires effort and resources. Consequently, a commitment to individual autonomy might entail that the state secure the social and material conditions by which citizens could come to be autonomous. Hence it is common to think that the liberal state must provide, at the very least, a sufficient degree of education and material security to all citizens, for it is obvious that an individual that lacks a basic education cannot responsibly manage her life. Similarly, the individual under constant threat of physical harm cannot develop within herself the skills required for responsibly planning her life according to her own ambitions and goals.

Yet this intuitive thought complicates what was said a moment ago about the limits to what the state may do. We will all agree that the state may *require* individuals to achieve a certain level of education. Again, we tend to think that the state may require this precisely because a certain level of educational achievement is necessary for autonomy. But this gives rise to an important question about the limits to what a state might do in the name of promoting autonomy. Some think it obvious that individual autonomy is served by exposure to fine painting, classical music, and great works of literature. Encounters with high art, they say, open the mind and stimulate the imagination, allowing individuals to envision new possibilities for their own lives. Suppose for the moment that these claims about the impact of exposure to certain forms of art are correct. Would there then be a case for thinking that the state could require citizens to visit museums, symphony halls, and theaters? Now consider the question from the other end. Suppose it is true that exposure to a certain kind of music, activity, or hobby reliably *stunts* or constrains an individual's conception of his life and its possibilities or strongly encourages in individuals servile conformity. Would that fact supply an argument for a state prohibition on that music, activity, or hobby? Finally, consider that it is likely that a certain degree of physical health is required for autonomy. After all, the profoundly unhealthy person is a lot like the person who lives under constant threat of physical harm: neither can devote cognitive and other resources to responsibly planning a life; both are consumed by the need to thwart threats to their very survival. Does it follow, then, that the state may require citizens to maintain a certain level of physical health? Could the state be justified in mandating a certain amount of daily exercise? Might it instate a law requiring citizens to join gyms?

Perhaps some of these examples strike you as silly. But the philosophical question is serious. Once we recognize that autonomy is, at least in part, a kind of skill, we confront the question of what the state is permitted to do in the name of promoting autonomy. And this question gives rise to a divide among liberal theorists between those who hold an expansive view of what the state may do in order to promote autonomy, and those who hold a constrained view. The expansive view is sometimes called *liberal perfectionism*; it holds that the state is *prima facie* justified in requiring any activity that promotes autonomy (and prohibiting any activity that diminishes it). *Antiperfectionists*, by contrast, hold that there are some autonomy-promoting activities that the state may nonetheless not require, even if it could do so efficiently and without cost. At the risk of oversimplifying, the liberal perfectionist holds that a certain level of moral and psychological cultivation on the part of the state is simply the entailment of its commitment to autonomy, whereas the anti-perfectionist contends that certain political measures are *paternalistic*, even though they may be indeed beneficial to citizens, and the liberal state must avoid paternalism.

It should be emphasized that this debate between liberal perfectionists and anti-perfectionists occurs *within* liberal political philosophy. In this way, the liberal perfectionist is to be distinguished from the non-liberal perfectionist. The contrast here is intuitive. The non-liberal perfectionist holds that the state may require any activity that it has reason to judge is good for citizens to engage in, whether it be kale-eating, yoga, or religious observance. That is, according to the non-liberal perfectionist, the state's job is indeed to make citizens good. The liberal perfectionist rejects the idea that the state has this all-encompassing moral remit, holding instead that the state may require of citizens that which is necessary specifically in order to develop their autonomy. Accordingly, the liberal perfectionist recommends moral interventions on the part of the state only when they are necessary from the point of view of the liberal value of autonomy. The disagreement between the liberal perfectionist and the anti-perfectionist lies within liberalism, as they both accept the importance of individual autonomy, but disagree only about what the state is permitted to do in the name of promoting it. It seems that the liberal perfectionist and the non-liberal perfectionist have a deeper disagreement than this, as the latter denies the liberal value of individual autonomy.

Having said this, I note that the debate between liberal perfectionists and anti-perfectionists is complex and currently rather active. In order to get a firm handle on its central contours, one would need far more background than I have been able to provide at this point. So let's pick up the thread we had been following. We are trying to contrast liberalism and philosophical anarchism. To this contrast we now return.

Thus far, we have spoken of liberalism as a set of four interlocking commitments that are primarily focused on how the state regards and treats its citizens. We can summarize our results by saying that liberalism is the view according to which the state must see its citizens as morally equal, free, and autonomous individuals. We have noted how this view of citizens poses constraints on what states can (rightly) do. And so we confront once again the anarchist's questions: What is the state for? What is its purpose? What justifies the state?

We now have the resources for giving a preliminary reply. Liberalism holds that states exist for the sake of maintaining a social order in which each citizen—again understood as a free and equal autonomous individual—can live well given the fact that, to put it bluntly, we are stuck with each other. By means of its laws, institutions, rules, and processes, the liberal state endeavors to create a system of social interaction that preserves as far as possible the liberty and equality of each citizen while providing space for each to exercise his autonomy, to live a life of his own. To speak bluntly again, according to liberalism, the state exists to keep us out of each other's way while treating us as free equals and recognizing our autonomy.

As this formulation indicates, liberalism concedes to the philosophical anarchist that the state coerces, and that coercion always involves the reduction of individual liberty. The distinctive claim of liberalism against the philosophical anarchist is that the reduction of liberty by means of political coercion can be morally justified, provided that certain conditions are satisfied. To be a little more precise, liberalism proposes that political authority can be justified to free and morally equal autonomous individuals when it is exercised *impartially* and by institutions that are *accountable*. These are the final two features of the liberal framework that we will discuss here.

The liberal holds that although the state cannot avoid reducing individual liberty, it can do so in a way that nonetheless respects individual equality. It does this by imposing the very same rules on every one of its citizens. In the liberal state, there is not one set of rules for, say, the well born and noble, and a different set for the commoners or the underclass; in deciding and enforcing policy, the state does not rely upon invidious comparisons among its citizens. In this sense, impartiality consists in the equality of all citizens before the law. This is what is commonly meant when people speak of the "rule of law."

There is a second and related dimension to impartiality as well. Impartiality also means that when the state coerces, it must do so not for the sake of making us virtuous men and women, but rather with the aim of providing a framework within which all citizens can pursue their ends as equals. To be sure, this imposes on each of us a significant constraint: No one is permitted to pursue a way of life at the expense of the moral equality, liberty, or autonomy of others. In other words, the state must not only regard each of us as free and morally equal autonomous individuals; it must also require us to regard *each other* in this way. This is captured by the familiar idea that we may do as we please up to the point where our actions prevent others from doing as they please. This principle indeed reduces everyone's liberty, but the vital flipside is that we are each protected by the state from infringement of our liberty, equality, and autonomy by others. Bringing these two aspects of impartiality together, then, we can say that, according to liberalism, the state must provide equal protection for its citizens, and when it coerces us it must do so for the sake of sustaining a social system within which each of us can pursue our own autonomously adopted ends.

In addition to a commitment to state impartiality, liberalism affirms a principle of state *accountability*. This means that states must maintain channels by which citizens can question, challenge, oppose, and direct state policy and action. Accountability in this sense means that states must govern in ways that are *representative* of the views and concerns of their citizens. But states must also be *responsive* to their citizens, and this responsiveness has two principal elements. First, a state is responsive to its citizens when it satisfies the requirement to *justify* its coercive acts to them. In other words, liberalism holds that when the state coerces, it *owes* to its citizens reasons for its actions. Crucially, this justification cannot be of the kind that parents sometimes offer to their children; in response to a call for the justification of some law or policy, the state cannot say to its citizens, "Because we said so," or "Just do it." The state must justify its acts to its citizens in a way that respects their moral equality; "Because we said so" implicitly denies that equality. Hence when the state acts, it owes its citizens reasons that are consistent with their status as morally equal and autonomous individuals. Second, in order to be responsive to its citizens, a state must feature institutions and processes by which citizens can *hold the state responsible* for its actions. This means that there must be ways for citizens to impose costs on their states for bad behavior, or to force the state to correct its errors.

2.2.4 Liberalism and Democracy

Now we can say that, given the general character of its commitments, and especially in light of its view of state accountability, liberalism is committed to a *democratic* state. That is, liberalism holds that democracy—and perhaps *only* democracy—can render the authority of the state consistent with the freedom, moral equality, and autonomy of individuals. Consequently, democracy is liberalism's response to the philosophical anarchist.

Of course, there are deep philosophical controversies concerning the precise nature of democracy. We will examine these issues in detail in Chapter 6. At present, it suffices to say that liberalism is committed to democracy in that it upholds a state in which citizens collectively govern themselves. But there's more. Liberalism is committed to a particular form of democracy, what is sometimes called *representative constitutional democracy*. To explain: In liberal democracies, self-government is mediated by complex systems of representation in which the citizens govern themselves largely by electing people to political offices of various kinds. Crucially, these offices—including the powers invested in them—are carefully defined and delineated in a public constitution. Elections select citizens to occupy public offices, and are conducted by means of transparent processes by which each citizen commands an equal share of decision-making power, and some fair rule for decision (such as majority rule) determines the collectively binding outcome.

Moreover, the state must introduce procedures and processes by which its officers can be subject to popular oversight, and its laws and policies can be scrutinized, meaningfully challenged, and even revised if necessary. And this in turn means that the state must allow for and support certain individual liberties that are necessary from the point of view of accountability, including the liberty to speak and assemble freely, even when—especially when—one seeks to criticize the government or object to its policies. It must, for similar reasons, also recognize liberties pertaining to the publication and distribution of ideas and opinions, especially those pertaining to politics, the state, and the collective lives of citizens. And it may have to introduce special measures to protect would-be critics and dissenters from informal sanctions aimed at encouraging their silence.

Finally, and arguably most importantly, liberalism holds that the state must recognize limits on what it has the authority to legislate. That is, the state must acknowledge that there are some things that even an overwhelming democratic majority cannot get the state to do. For example, in a modern liberal democracy, a majority cannot vote to enslave a tiny minority. To take another example, even if the entire democratic citizenry except for you is agreed that some variety of Christianity is the true faith, they cannot impose a law requiring you to worship their God. In a liberal democracy, then, majority rule is constrained by the liberal commitments to equality, liberty, and autonomy. This is often expressed by saying that liberal democracy is not a purely majoritarian form of democracy; rather, it is democracy understood as constrained by the *rights* of the individual, and these rights are entitlements *against* certain forms of interference from the state and from other citizens, including large groups of citizens.

2.3 Liberalism and Popular Politics

We have traveled quite a long way in trying to articulate a view of the political world that I claimed should be utterly familiar to you. In case the familiarity is not obvious, notice that the liberal framework is asserted in the Declaration of Independence, where it is affirmed that governments exist for the purpose of protecting the "unalienable rights" of their citizens, and that, consequently, a government that refuses or is unable to serve that purpose no longer has authority and should be dissolved. Liberalism is also at work in the Bill of Rights of the US Constitution, where, among other things, are affirmed very precise, and in many cases sweeping, protections of citizens against the state, including protections against vast democratic majorities. It should be noted further that the Bill of Rights also affirms individual entitlements designed to enable individual autonomy; the First Amendment prohibition against establishing a state church and its guarantee of freedom of speech and the press are clear manifestations of liberalism. Indeed, the US Constitution as a document is mainly devoted to specifying the limits to state authority. It is not incorrect to say, then, that the United States was founded on the principles of liberalism.

Liberalism is also presupposed in many of the controversies of contemporary popular politics. Debates over pornography, for example, often involve disagreements over whether the production and consumption of such materials constitutes *harm* to women; the claim made by those who seek legal prohibitions on pornography is that pornography does, indeed, harm women. The argument on the opposing side typically takes the form of denying that the production and consumption of pornography harms anyone. Notice that both sides agree with the fundamental liberal view that the state's job is to protect individuals from various kinds of harm. The debate concerning abortion rights makes for an instructive further example. Here, pro-life arguments tend to focus on the rights of the unborn, claiming, incontestably, that the state must protect the lives of all people living within its borders, and, contestably, that fetuses are persons in the relevant respect. Pro-choice arguments typically attack the claim that fetuses are persons, but they also raise an additional consideration in favor of abortion rights, namely, that the autonomy of women depends upon their right to govern their own bodies. Notice how both positions invoke lines of argument that appeal to characteristically liberal commitments.

Now imagine someone arguing that pornography should be legally prohibited because viewing it is sinful. Imagine another person arguing that pornography should be permitted because it is a mark of the sexually liberated to enjoy pornographic materials, and we should all live sexually liberated lives. Or, imagine a pro-life proponent arguing that abortion should be prohibited because no woman could be happy unless she is a mother. Alternatively, imagine a pro-choice argument that rested on the claim that the human race is morally required to pursue its own extinction, and so we each must take voluntary action now to prevent there from being future generations. These arguments might strike you as odd in themselves, and it is important to note that within the liberal framework one may base one's political views upon whatever grounds one sees fit. But, crucially, arguments like these should strike you as *of the wrong kind*. That is, it should seem to you that the state may not adopt laws on the basis of claims about, for example, the joy of motherhood or the positive value of viewing pornography.

This is as it should be, because these arguments all presuppose some version of a non-liberal conception of the political world. As liberals, we are inclined to say that even if it were true that motherhood is the key to happiness for women, it is no reason to enact pro-life legislation. We are inclined to say this because we are committed to the idea that the state is not in the business of making us happy or of enshrining in its laws some particular conception of what makes life worthwhile. As liberals, we instead hold that the state's job is that of providing a political environment within which individuals can decide for themselves where happiness lies, and then pursue it.

Now, as we saw above in the brief discussion of perfectionism and anti-perfectionism, the waters of liberalism can be muddied by claims to the effect that, say, exposure to pornography inhibits an individual's capacity for autonomy, or motherhood is essential to a woman's autonomy. But at present we are considering arguments of a different kind that do not pro-voke the debate concerning perfectionism. We are considering specifically arguments that claim that motherhood is essential to a woman's happiness, and viewing pornography makes life worthwhile. Such arguments should strike us as entirely beside the point. We tend to think that the question of what the state may do lies elsewhere.

Note that this stance does not require us to claim that it is *false* that a woman's happiness lies in motherhood; nor do those defending the right to produce and consume pornography need to affirm any view according to which pornography is good for those who view it. We need to take no view at all about the value of pornography or motherhood. In fact, the point of the liberal framework is to enable citizens and states to *avoid* such pronouncements altogether when deciding policy.

There is certainly much more to say about all of these matters, and nothing that has been said thus far is intended to be the final word. In fact, we have only just begun, and many of these issues will reemerge in the course of this book. At present, though, what has been said enables us, at long last, to see how the liberal framework is the shared ground that underlies opposing programs in our popular politics. We can see liberalism (in the popular sense of the term) and conservatism as competing *interpretations* of liberalism (in the philosophical sense). Speaking very roughly now, liberals (in the popular sense) take the commitment to individual liberty, equality, and autonomy to license the state to do what is necessary to provide the social conditions under which all individuals can meaningfully *exercise* their liberties. Accordingly, liberalism (in the popular sense) is associated with state intervention designed to redistribute social and economic goods and opportunities in a way that more fully realizes equality. We would not go too far wrong in saying, then, that given the range of commitments characteristic of liberalism (in the philosophical sense), liberalism (in the popular sense) prioritizes equality. Conservatives, on the other hand, tend to see the state as a primary threat to individual liberty; they consequently seek to limit state intervention as far as possible while maintaining social stability. Conservatism is also typically committed strongly to the responsibility element of liberal (in the philosophical sense) autonomy. The conservative, that is, sees the role of the state to be confined to providing and maintaining a free and fair system for individual interactions; consequently, efforts to redistribute social and economic goods beyond what is produced by fair interactions among citizens is looked at with great suspicion. We can say, then, that within the liberal framework, conservatives prioritize individual liberty, and see it as tightly connected with individual responsibility. They therefore favor greater constraints on state action.

This depiction of the terrain of our popular politics is admittedly drastically underdeveloped. But if it strikes you as even remotely on target, then the claim made at the beginning of this section—that liberalism in the philosophical sense is the framework within which popular politics is conducted—has been vindicated. And now that we are able to see liberalism as a framework that admits of a broad range of interpretations, we are able to make a different kind of claim: Modern democratic states are all liberal states of one kind or another.

2.4 Varieties of Liberal Theory

We now have before us a broad picture of liberalism as a framework for thinking about the political world. We have also understood the ways in which liberalism admits of various interpretations. And, again, we have said that our aim in doing political philosophy is to see whether the state can be justified. We may then pose the question that guides this entire book as follows: Is there an interpretation of liberalism that allows us to formulate a conception of the state that could be philosophically justified?

Let us get clear about what this question means. We are asking whether there could be a state such that it could be justified to individuals conceived as free, morally equal, and autonomous. Justifying the state involves showing to free, morally equal, and autonomous individuals that a state of a particular description *should exist*, that it is at least *permissible* for such a state to exist. And this requires us to see whether it is possible to devise an argument to the effect that were there a state that satisfied certain conditions, then free, morally equal, and autonomous individuals should live under its authority. As we have already noted, philosophical anarchism is the thesis that no state could be such that free, morally equal, and autonomous individuals would be required to live under its rule. Liberalism, as we have been discussing it thus far, is the philosophical project of trying to show that the philosophical anarchist is wrong; that is, liberalism is the ongoing attempt to devise a conception of the state that could be justified.

Thus we can identify several distinct types of *liberal theory*, each type representing a distinct attempt to justify the state. Often liberal theories divide over what a successful justification would consist of. Accordingly, one kind of liberal theory holds that justifying the state requires the political philosopher to formulate a description of the state such that free, morally equal, and autonomous individuals would be *morally* required to submit to its authority. Another kind holds that justifying the state requires the political philosopher to show that there could be a state such that such individuals would be *rationally* required to submit to its authority. These are both instances of a more general class of liberal theory that is known as *contractarianism*. Contractarian views take the justification of the state to lie in the demonstration of its *choice-worthiness* among free, morally equal, and autonomous individuals.

Another broad category of liberal theory can be called *consequentialist*. Consequentialist liberal theories hold that the state is justified if it can be shown that it is *necessary* in order for individuals to satisfy certain important moral duties or realize important moral goods (or avoid serious moral bads). Imagine a view according to which we are each morally required to do what we can to maximize human happiness. One who holds this view might then attempt to justify some version of the liberal state on the grounds that it is markedly better than its competitors at enabling individuals to satisfy that moral obligation. Or, imagine a view according to which there is a moral imperative to maximize liberty; someone might believe that, even though the liberal state necessarily reduces liberty to some extent, some version of the liberal state best maximizes overall liberty. Finally, imagine a view according to which some version of the liberal state is thought to be the best available political arrangement for securing social stability and avoiding violent rebellion and social discord; someone might argue on these grounds that that version of the liberal state is justified. All such views would count as consequentialist liberal theories.

There are additional kinds of liberal theory, and many nuances within each kind. But the main varieties of liberal theory are either contractarian or consequentialist. To be sure, there are various ways in which the considerations typical of each approach could be mixed. There could be, for example, a contractarian view according to which the consequentialist benefits of a particular kind of liberal state provide the moral reasons that free, morally equal, and autonomous individuals should agree to submit to its rule. Similarly, a consequentialist could affirm that the only kind of state that could deliver a moral result that would suffice to justify it would be one that satisfies some contractarian requirement for choice-worthiness. So, once again, matters are complicated. However, these approaches are distinguished by their different conceptions of *what does the justifying*. Contractarians hold that a certain kind of *agreement* or *consent* to the state's authority on the part of the citizens is required in order for the state to be justified. Consequentialists deny this; for them, justification does not require a demonstration that a certain act of will on the part of free, morally equal, and autonomous individuals would be required. Consequentialist views hold instead that the overall good consequences of the liberal state suffice to justify its authority.

2.5 Conclusion

In this chapter and the one preceding it, we have developed a broad portrait of the political world that we inhabit. We have also begun to lay out the philosophical underpinnings of that world. We have seen that we live within a broadly liberal political order, and that we consequently tend simply to take for granted a range of philosophical commitments that until quite recently in the history of human societies would have been seen as highly implausible, if not positively seditious. That we are equal and autonomous individuals, whose liberty can rightfully be curtailed only when it would be justifiable to do so, that the body that governs us must *serve* us (and derives its authority from us), and that consequently the government must represent us and be accountable to us are all radical ideas. In spelling out the general contours of the liberal political framework within which we live, we have noted several of its complexities. We have noted, at times only very briefly, that the constituent concepts of the liberal framework—individual liberty, authority, justice, and democracy—are fraught with philosophical difficulty. In order to get a firm grasp on the liberal political philosophy that we live, we will need to delve into the details regarding each of liberalism's elements. If liberalism is to meet the challenge posed by the philosophical anarchist, the liberal theorist must be able to provide philosophically defensible accounts of each of liberalism's core commitments. We turn, then, to an examination of liberalism's central components.

For Further Reading

For further examination of topics discussed in this chapter, the classic texts in the history of political philosophy should be consulted; the writings of Plato, Aristotle, Augustine, Thomas Hobbes, Niccolo Machiavelli, John Locke, Jean-Jacques Rousseau, Immanuel Kant, Mary Wollstonecraft, Karl Marx, and John Stuart Mill are particularly central, and most historically oriented political philosophy anthologies contain adequate selections from their major works. Those looking for recent assessments of the modern tradition of political philosophy (beginning roughly with Hobbes) should consult C. B. Macpherson's *The Political Theory of Possessive Individualism* (Oxford: Oxford University Press, 1961), Jean Hampton's *Hobbes and the Social Contract Tradition* (Cambridge: Cambridge University Press, 1986), and the essays collected in Christopher W. Morris's (ed.) *The Social Contract Theorists* (Lanham, MD: Rowman and Littlefield, 1999). Critiques of the social contract tradition can be found in Virginia Held's "Non-Contractual Society" (*Canadian Journal of Philosophy*, Volume 17, Number 1, 1987), and Carole Pateman and Charles Mills's *Contract and Domination* (London: Polity, 2007).

The contemporary literature on liberalism is expansive. John Rawls's two major works, *A Theory of Justice* (Cambridge, MA: Harvard University Press, 1971) and *Political Liberalism* (New York: Columbia University Press, 1993), have set the agenda for liberal political philosophy. See also Jeremy Waldron's "The Theoretical Foundations of Liberalism" (reprinted in his *Liberal Rights: Collected Papers 1981–1991*, Cambridge: Cambridge University Press, 1993), Ronald Dworkin's "Liberalism" (reprinted in his *A Matter of Principle*, New York: Oxford University Press, 1985), and Will Kymlicka's *Liberalism, Community, and Culture* (New York: Oxford University Press, 1989). Jean Hampton's "Should Political Philosophy Be Done without Metaphysics?" (in the journal *Ethics*, Volume 99, Number 4, 1989) should also be consulted. Contemporary critiques of liberalism can be found in Michael Sandel's *Liberalism and the Limits of Justice* (Cambridge: Cambridge University Press, 1982), Charles Taylor's "Atomism" (reprinted in his *Philosophical Papers, Volume 2: Philosophy and the Human Sciences*, Cambridge: Cambridge University Press, 1985), and Iris Marion Young's *Justice and the Politics of Difference* (Princeton: Princeton University Press, 1990). For liberal assessments of these criticisms, see Amy Gutmann's "Communitarian Critics of Liberalism" (in the journal *Philosophy and Public Affairs*, Volume 14, Number 3, 1985) and Martha Nussbaum's "Feminist Critics of Liberalism" (reprinted in her *Sex and Social Justice*, Cambridge, MA: Harvard University Press, 1999). A difficult but rewarding defense of a distinctive kind of liberalism can be found in Gerald Gaus's *Justificatory Liberalism* (New York: Oxford University Press, 1996). Those wishing to investigate perfectionist liberalism should consult Joseph Raz's perfectionist masterpiece *The Morality of Freedom* (New York: Oxford University Press, 1986). Alan Ryan's *The Making of Modern Liberalism* (Princeton: Princeton University Press, 2012) provides a nuanced account of the development of liberalism from the Enlightenment to the present.

PART II
Fundamental Concepts

3 Liberty

3.1 The Concept of Liberty

As anyone who supervises children will readily acknowledge, we humans bristle against physical restraint from the time we are very young. Belts, straps, cuffs, ropes, and other implements that restrict our movement tend to make us markedly uncomfortable. There is a distinctive kind of distress, frustration, or, perhaps, vulnerability that one feels when one's capacity for physical movement is hindered; this is especially so in cases in which we cannot control when we will be released. But the feeling is not restricted to cases in which we are not in control of the restraints. For example, to this day, my father refuses to wear a seatbelt simply on the grounds that he cannot stand the feeling of being strapped into place. The general resistance to constraint is evident in other contexts as well. Many people deliberately avoid small enclosures, even when there is an easy way of exit. And I know several people who will not fly because they find being in an airplane too claustrophobic, even though on most flights the actual restrictions on bodily motion are fairly minimal.

In our ordinary ways of talking, we sometimes employ the idea of liberty or freedom (we will treat these as synonymous) to describe the condition of being bound. We say that handcuffs restrict one's *freedom* of motion, and that being restrained means that one is not *at liberty* to perform certain kinds of actions; similarly, we *free* or *liberate* someone from restraints. Of course, in the everyday run of things, it seems overwrought to describe a seatbelt as an enemy of freedom. But still, there is something intuitive about the thought that one's freedom is in some way closely connected to one's ability to move one's body as one chooses.

This intuitive thought is far from being a philosophical analysis of liberty; as it stands, it is far too simplistic. Notice the range of philosophical questions that come to the fore once we say, as we just have, that freedom is in some way closely connected to bodily movement. For example, one might ask why the ability to move one's body as one chooses seems so important to us. It seems that we do not normally value the ability merely to move our limbs as we like; rather, we value the ability to perform the *actions* that we choose, and this typically requires the capacity to move our bodies at will. It seems, then, that restraints distress us because we think it important to be able not merely to *move* as we wish, but to *act* as we wish. Is this correct?

Imagine two cases. First, Betty has locked Alfred in a room. Ordinarily, we would think that this would constitute a serious assault on Alfred's liberty. But now imagine that the room happens to be one that Alfred does not want to leave; even if the door to the room were unlocked, he would stay where he is. Of course, should Alfred come to desire to leave, he would not be able to do so. But, luckily, and for the time being, his desires remain unaltered and he does not want to leave. What should we make of this? Alfred is locked in a room, yet he is not prevented from acting as he wishes. Is he free?

Consider a second case. Imagine that Carl is addicted to a potent drug that is very harmful to his health. His addiction causes in Carl protracted episodes of uncompromising and overwhelming desire for the drug, but at other times he wants to be rid of his addiction. In a sober moment, Carl admits himself into a treatment center that restrains him in various ways, preventing him from acquiring his drug. Imagine now that Carl's addiction kicks in, and he wants nothing more than the drug. In that moment, Carl is forcibly prevented from acting as he wishes. Is he free?

These two cases are interesting because they suggest ways in which it is at least arguable that one could be constrained and yet free. In fact, some are attracted to the idea that, in the second example, Carl's restraints actually serve to *liberate* him. Perhaps being free and being constrained are quite distinct after all?

3.1.1 Liberty: Metaphysical and Political

Human freedom lies at the core of two longstanding philosophical issues that we should try to keep distinct (if possible). One concerns what is called *freedom of the will*, and it belongs centrally to the area of philosophy known as metaphysics. The concern with liberty in this metaphysical sense has to do with the query of whether human actions are causally determined by prior physical conditions. Here, a fundamental question is whether it is ever true to say of some act *x* performed by an individual *S* that *S* could have done something other than *x*. Metaphysical *determinists* say no, while *indeterminists* say yes, and *compatibilists* also say no but deny that the ability to have done otherwise than what one in fact does is a necessary condition for having free will.

Many philosophers see an obvious and tight connection between meta-physical liberty and central questions in moral philosophy; their thought is that if, indeed, all human actions are (as the determinist alleges) causally determined, then no one could be morally responsible for what he or she does. The intuitiveness of this view is easy to grasp: Dennis steals a car. If determinism is true, he could not have done otherwise. But if Dennis could not have done otherwise, then morally *blaming* him for stealing would be like blaming a man for not being able to breathe under water. The same would go for moral praise as well: Edie heroically saves a child's life. If determinism is true, Edie could not but have done that; thus morally *praising* her seems misplaced. It seems, then, that free will is necessary for moral responsibility. Consequently, determinists often hold that the very idea of moral responsibility is spurious. Indeterminists reject determinism, sometimes arguing that since our conception of moral responsibility is indispensible, determinism must be false. And, against both the determinist and the indeterminist, compatibilists contend that free will (and moral responsibility) can be reconciled with the idea that human actions are causally determined.

The metaphysical issue of free will is complex, as is the question concerning the relation of the metaphysical issue to moral philosophy. It may seem natural to think that because free will and moral responsibility seem so intimately tied, the metaphysical sense of freedom is also at the heart of the second longstanding philosophical issue I mentioned earlier, namely, the issue of what might be called *political* liberty. If indeed the answer to the free-will question fixes our conception of moral responsibility, then it seems natural to think that our view of freedom in the political realm should similarly be dependent upon our view of metaphysical freedom.

Yet there is reason to think that the political and metaphysical questions are distinct. Recall that metaphysical freedom primarily concerns questions regarding whether an individual could have done something other than what he in fact did. As we will see, political liberty primarily concerns the relations between individuals and social and political bodies. An individual's political liberty is partly a matter of what she is *permitted* or *able* to do in light of the social and political order within which she acts. In this respect, the political question is about the character of an individual's action rather than the metaphysical availability to an individual of alternative possibilities for action. To be sure, in the ultimate analysis, the metaphysical, moral, and political issues might have to be taken together; the distinctness might prove illusory or unsustainable, and entanglement might prove unavoidable. But for now we will proceed on the premise that the metaphysical and political issues are different. Still, from here forward, we will use *liberty* (and *freedom*) in the political sense. And now, you may ask, just what sense is *that*?

3.1.2 The Concept/Conception Distinction

As you may expect, there are several competing conceptions of liberty that are worth our consideration. But before launching into our examination, we must first make explicit an important philosophical distinction between a *concept* and a *conception*.

The concept/conception distinction is necessary in order to make sense of the difference between a case in which two philosophers are using the same word to talk about different things, and an instance in which two philosophers are proposing distinct and opposing accounts of the same thing. When we talk of there being several distinct philosophical conceptions of liberty, we mean to say that there is a dispute about how to best understand it; the competing ideas are distinct *conceptions of* the same concept, namely liberty. That these conceptions are conceptions of the same concept explains how it is possible for philosophers who favor different views about liberty to *disagree* about liberty rather than simply "talking past each other," as we sometimes say. When two people talk past each other, they speak of different things, but take themselves to be proposing opposing views of the same thing. To employ our distinction, those who talk past each other speak of different concepts, yet take themselves to be asserting distinct conceptions of the same concept; they hence are not actually embroiled in a disagreement, though they may think that they are. In order for there to be a disagreement, there must be some concept of which the disputants propose opposing conceptions.

This is unduly abstract, so let's consider an example. I sometimes teach a course in formal logic at my university, and, in the most general sense, logic is the study of *argument*. On the first day of class, I often assert this definition of the subject-matter of the class by saying, "In this course we will be studying argument." But I have learned to quickly follow that announcement with a clarification; I specify that formal logic is the study of argument, and *argument* is understood as a formal relation between declarative statements, where some (the premises) are alleged to provide support for, or demonstrate the truth of, another statement (the conclusion). I learned to introduce this clarification because, very early in my teaching career, a student once criticized my class as follows (I paraphrase loosely from a student evaluation):

> This class was interesting, but it had nothing to do with *argument* at all. We never actually got to argue with the professor about anything. It was all just variables, symbols, and proofs with nothing to disagree about. I took the class because the description said it was a philosophical study of argument. I wanted to learn how to win arguments. This class didn't help. It seems like false advertising.

Here, the complaint draws upon a different *concept* of argument than the one that the discipline of Formal Logic studies. In fact, there is another discipline called Rhetoric that examines argument in the student's sense, the sense in which argument is an attempt to persuade interlocutors and audiences to believe what you say. Logicians and rhetoricians do not offer different theories of argument so much as they study two different things, both of which are called 'argument'. It should be noted that within formal logic there are different *conceptions* of argument; different theories of the nature of successful arguments, opposing accounts of how arguments work, disputes over the proper analysis of certain logical functions, and so on. That is, there are disagreements among logicians. And there are, to be sure, many disagreements among logicians and rhetoricians, but they do not propose different conceptions of the same concept (namely argument); rather, they employ different concepts, both of which are called 'argument'.

3.1.3 Identifying the Concept

As I have said, there are different and competing conceptions of liberty, different ways of thinking about what liberty really is. And we now know that this means that there must be a common *concept* of liberty with respect to which the distinct conceptions differ. So you may ask once again what that is. We may seem to have made little progress. But note that we are now in a better position to know what question we should be asking. In asking for the concept, we are looking to identify an idea of liberty shared by the different conceptions of liberty and over which those conceptions disagree. So, if we are going to explore the philosophical disagreements about liberty, we must look for a way to identify the concept of liberty that does not invoke any particular conception to the exclusion of the others.

Identifying a concept in a way that does not seem to privilege one of the conceptions in contention is a notoriously tricky business in philosophy. The fact that we can draw a distinction between the concept of liberty and the competing conceptions of it does not mean that it is *easy* to identify the concept with respect to which the conceptions differ. Indeed, it is difficult to avoid mistaking the concept for one's favored conception, thereby ensuring that no philosophical dispute can be engaged; this is, of course, to be avoided. Moreover, there is reason to be suspicious of the very claim that there is a *single* concept of liberty. Some philosophers have argued that concepts are always names for *families* or *clusters* of ideas, with no single core among the members. And in any case, one might raise a range of philosophical questions about the very idea of a concept: "What are they, anyway?"; "What kind of entity is a concept?"; "How do we come to know concepts?"; "Where do they reside?"; and so on.

As we are centrally concerned with the philosophical disputes over the nature of liberty, we should like to avoid entanglement in these other deep philosophical matters. So let us say that in looking for the concept of liberty, we are only looking to identify a few undisputed *examples* of liberty. That is, for our purposes, it will suffice to begin from a few cases upon which all of the conceptions agree. If we can find at least one such undisputed example, we can then begin by comparing the competing conceptions according to the different analyses they offer of the example.

In looking for noncontroversial examples or instantiations of a concept, sometimes it is easier to identify non-contested examples of its *absence*. And in the case of liberty, there is, understandably, widespread agreement that *slavery* is a paradigmatic case of unfreedom. According to almost any conception of liberty, slaves are unfree. In fact, were there a proposed conception of liberty that did *not* regard slavery as a condition of profound unfreedom, we would have good reason to reject that conception as nonviable. After all, if anything should count as an example of the near-total absence of liberty, it is slavery. We can make some progress in thinking about liberty, then, by looking at this noncontroversial instance of liberty's absence.

Think for a moment about what it is to be a slave. To keep matters simple, let us think about slavery only in the strict sense. That is, think about slavery as a social and political institution, such as was practiced in the United States prior to 1865. Of course, we sometimes speak of slavery in an extended sense, as when we describe someone as being a slave to his possessions. But, at least for now, think only of the non-extended sense of the term. More importantly, think about slavery as a purely descriptive matter; we, of course, take as granted that slavery is a morally horrific phenomenon. Our aim here is to try to make sense of what it is in the slave's condition that makes slavery such a profound condition of unfreedom. A description, separate from the moral condemnation, is what is called for here.

To begin, slaves are legally property; they are human beings that legally *belong* to other human beings. Slaves are owned by masters, and, accordingly, are under the control of their masters. This means, among other things, that the slave's activities are constrained and directed by the master; the slave is chained or bound, and hence unable to escape from the master. Moreover, the master issues orders to the slave and the slave must comply or else suffer punishment. Consequently, there are many things a slave is able to do, and might want to do, that he is prevented from doing on account of the constraints imposed by his master. In this sense, the slave's actions are not his own. More importantly, the slave's life is not his own. The slave is, as Aristotle put it, a human tool, an instrument of the master's aims and purposes. The slave thus does not live according to his own judgments and does not live on his own terms; he is consequently not the author of his own life. He does not live his life "from the inside," so to speak, but his aims and projects are imposed upon him by the master.

Now, nearly everybody, and certainly all liberal political philosophers, regards slavery as obviously a grave injustice. In fact, many regard it as the most extreme kind of wrongdoing imaginable. This is because slavery seems to embody a strikingly broad range of evils. Where there is slavery, slaves are subjected to violence, intimidation, pain, suffering, torture, rape, humiliation, degradation, sorrow, desperation, and vulnerability, among much else that is undeniably exceedingly bad. Where there is slavery, there is also a full range of serious social evils, including institutionally codified inequality, hierarchy, subjugation, oppression, and exploitation. But where there is slavery, there is also an extreme loss of liberty. This is the core concept with which our examination can begin: Liberty is that which the slave profoundly lacks. The different conceptions of liberty disagree over the precise nature of the freedom-violating element in the slave's condition.

To be sure, this identification of the concept of liberty is pretty sparse; in fact, one might say that it is bordering on uninformative. But, at least for now, this is as it should be. Recall that we were looking to characterize the concept that the opposing conceptions of liberty held in common. We can now see how the debate among proponents of the different conceptions of liberty could proceed. Each conception that we will examine proposes a different analysis of the slave's unfreedom, a different interpretation of precisely what in the slave's condition renders him unfree.

3.2 Three Conceptions of Liberty

Let's begin by noting a few obvious and intuitive ways in which one might think of the slave's condition. Consider the following three possibilities:

1. The slave's lack of freedom lies in his bonds. He is unfree in virtue of being chained, or otherwise confined. Removing his chains increases his freedom.
2. The slave's lack of freedom lies in his lack of self-control. He is unfree in virtue of being under the control of another person. Enabling him to control himself would render him free.
3. The slave's lack of freedom lies in his lack of civic standing relative to his master. He is unfree in virtue of being subordinate to others, regarded as property, and hence socially powerless against them. Recognizing his equal civic status renders him free.

These three intuitive thoughts will find philosophical expression in the conceptions we are about to examine. They might at first seem roughly equivalent, merely different ways of saying the same thing. But note a few contrasts: According to the first view, freedom consists in the *absence* of something, whereas the other two views seem to hold that freedom is the matter of the *presence* of something. Now note the difference between the second and third views: According to the second view, freedom consists in the presence of something *internal* to the individual, whereas on the third view, freedom is a matter of the presence of something *external* to the individual, namely civic standing relative to others. We can summarize these contrasts between the three interpretations above as follows:

1. Freedom is the absence of something external to the individual.
2. Freedom is the presence of something internal to the individual.
3. Freedom is the presence of something external to the individual.

3.2.1 Negative Liberty

We'll begin with the intuitive thought that the slave lacks liberty in virtue of his bonds. One might think, then, that slavery is so extreme an evil because it is an extreme case of imprisonment; just as prison inmates are trapped in their cells with cuffs, bars, concrete, and armed guards, slaves are even more *absolutely* imprisoned than inmates. The liberty of prison inmates is, of course, greatly reduced, but even prisoners serving life sentences have legal rights, and this means that *some* degree of freedom is preserved. The slave, by contrast, is abjectly unfree; he is, in every respect, *chained*.

This thought lies at the core of the negative conception of liberty, which was briefly discussed in Chapter 2. According to the negative conception, freedom consists in the *absence* of constraints. Of course, there are constraints of different kinds. Physical laws constrain my action; there is a sense in which they prevent me from being able to run at the speed of light, jump tall buildings in a single bound, breathe under water, and so on. But it seems perverse to say that these reduce my liberty. Similarly, natural occurrences including blizzards, tornadoes, avalanches, and the like can interrupt my plans and block my actions. Yet these are not the kinds of constraints with which we are concerned. Instead, the negative conception identifies liberty with the absence of constraints *imposed by others*. That is to say, one is free just to the extent one can act *without interference from others*; one's freedom is lessened when one is *prevented by others* from doing what one could otherwise do.

We can see why, on this view, the slave is incontrovertibly unfree. For, as we have said, the slave lives under the near-total imposition of his master; there is no area of the slave's life that is not vulnerable to the master's impediments. Of all the things that the slave wants to do, there are very few that he is, in fact, able to do without the master's interference. He lacks liberty precisely to this extent. Accordingly, as external constraints are removed and interference is blocked, his liberty expands.

The negative conception of liberty has many obvious virtues. Chief among these is its apparent simplicity. If liberty consists in the absence of external constraint, it is easy to measure the extent of one's freedom; roughly, one simply needs to count the number of constraints one faces. Moreover, the negative conception can easily account for the commonsense view that there are degrees of liberty; one is more (or less) free than another, depending roughly upon the frequency with which one encounters external obstruction. For similar reasons, the negative conception enables us to judge the degree of freedom that prevails in a society, and it enables us to say what it would mean for a political policy to *enhance* (or *diminish*) liberty. And finally, the negative conception seems *non-judgmental*; in calling an individual free, we do not thereby assess her or the quality of her choices in any way. That is, the negative conception can recognize that irrational, foolish, and morally dubious individuals can nonetheless be free.

The negative conception does indeed look simple. Alas, looks can be deceiving. In fact, we have already seen one complication in the case mentioned earlier involving Alfred and Betty. If liberty consists in the absence of external interference, then it seems that a man locked in a room that he does not wish to leave is nonetheless as free as he would be were the door not locked; further, locking the door to Alfred's room would have no impact at all on his freedom. Consider a similar kind of case. Imagine that Betty is a cook, and she presents Alfred with a large menu of dishes, asking him to choose what he'd like to eat. Alfred looks through the menu and orders the hamburger. Soon thereafter, Betty presents him with his burger, which Alfred proceeds to enjoy immensely. But here's the rub: Unbeknownst to Alfred, Betty will cook him only a hamburger; thus, regardless of what he ordered, Alfred would have been served a hamburger. Although it seems to Alfred that he has several options from which to choose, he in fact has no options; he will get a hamburger no matter what.

Reflection on this kind of case prompts a distinction between two different interpretations of the idea of freedom from others' interference. One interpretation says that Alfred is indeed free. He wants a hamburger and he gets a hamburger—no one obstructs him. We can call this interpretation of negative liberty the *non-obstruction* interpretation. According to this view, one is free just insofar as nobody stands in the way of one doing what one wants. The number of options that are open to an agent is irrelevant to the question of his freedom; all that matters is that he is able to act as he in fact chooses.

The non-obstruction interpretation retains the virtue of simplicity that we mentioned above. Yet it looks like a flawed vision of freedom. For one thing, it makes an individual's freedom depend entirely upon what he happens to desire. Indeed, it looks as if the non-obstruction view renders freedom consistent with being a slave; were slaves simply to learn to *want* to be in chains, they would be free. This thought looks perverse. One might say that a slave who comes to want to be in chains is not liberated, but *all the more* enslaved, and the fact of his enslavement *all the more pernicious*.

This thought about the slave can be generalized to more common cases. Consider, first, the *sour-grapes phenomenon*, in which, like the fox in Aesop's fable, one trains oneself to not want whatever one is blocked from getting; one simply attunes one's desires and ambitions to one's prospects and, in doing so, one frees oneself from frustration. In many instances, this looks like a good policy. But there are cases in which this policy is troubling, and definitely not liberating. For example, there are what are known as *adaptive preferences*. Adaptive preferences are preferences one develops, often unconsciously, in light of one's oppressive circumstances. It is, in fact, a common psychological phenomenon among people who are oppressed or deprived; as they cannot get what they want, they come to want what they get, even when (perhaps *especially* when) what they get is discomforting and humiliating but seemingly inescapable. In short, the non-obstruction interpretation of negative liberty sees liberation where we would be more inclined to see only submission, degradation, and resignation.

There is a different interpretation of the idea of freedom as non-interference that looks more promising. It holds that non-interference consists in the ability to act without obstruction given the presence of a range of *opportunities for action*. We can call this second interpretation of negative liberty the *opportunity* interpretation. According to the opportunity interpretation, a man locked in a room that he chooses not to leave is nonetheless unfree; his unfreedom consists in the fact that there is but a single option that is open to him, namely staying in the room. That Alfred happens to want to stay in the room may be a stroke of good luck, but it does not render him free.

The opportunity interpretation is more promising than the non-obstruction interpretation because it allows us to give the intuitive answers in sour-grapes and adaptive-preferences cases; it allows us to say about socially oppressed people that they are not free, despite the fact that they may have unconsciously adjusted their preferences according to their oppressive circumstances. Similarly, the opportunity interpretation can maintain that slavery is a condition of severe lack of freedom, regardless of how an individual slave happens to regard his bonds. But this improvement over the non-obstruction interpretation comes at a price. The opportunity interpretation loses a lot of the simplicity that looked like one of the negative conception's core virtues.

To explain: The opportunity interpretation introduces into the idea of negative liberty a *modal* component. This is a philosopher's way of saying that on the opportunity interpretation we must think about "what ifs" or non-actual possibilities; we must be concerned not only with what an agent in fact does and whether she in fact faces obstacles, but with what she is *able* to do and with what *would have happened* had she done something else. That is, on the opportunity interpretation, in order to determine the degree to which individuals are free it is not enough to see how frequently the actions they perform are met with external interference; we must consider the range of actions it is possible for them to perform and determine how many of those actions *would be* met with interference were they to be performed. Accordingly, a man who wants a hamburger but would be blocked from any other meal he might choose is not free in virtue of the range of options that are closed, even if those options are, in fact, unattractive to him.

"What ifs" are notoriously thorny, and there is a great deal of philosophical dispute over how precisely to understand statements of the following sort:

1. Had he ordered the spaghetti, he would have been served a hamburger; and
2. Were he to order the spaghetti, he would be served a hamburger.

Contrast these statements with this one:

3. Alfred ordered a hamburger.

To get a feel for the puzzlement, notice that it seems obvious that when a statement like (3) is true, it is because of some *fact* about what Alfred actually ordered. We might say that the fact that Alfred ordered a hamburger is what *makes* statement (3) true. We might also say that the fact that Alfred ordered a hamburger is what makes the statement "Alfred ordered pizza" false. But now ask yourself about statements (1) and (2). What could make these statements true?

Putting this complication aside, one might still wonder whether negative liberty, now understood in its opportunity interpretation, is acceptable. Negative liberty holds that the extent of one's freedom is equivalent to the range of options for unobstructed action from which one may choose. Recall that one of the attractions of the negative conception is that it is *non-judgmental*. In determining the extent of an individual's freedom, one need assess neither the rationality nor the morality of the agent's choices or aims; rather, one needs only to count the individual's opportunities for unobstructed action. In assessing freedom, that is, we need not consider the question of what an individual's opportunities for unhindered action are *opportunities for*, and we do not need to know anything about the soundness of the individual's decision-making.

Could this be correct? Consider a few cases. First, take an instance in which Alfred is presented with a full menu and Betty will prepare any dish he may order. But Alfred is in the grip of an irrational fear of eating anything other than hamburgers, and so orders the hamburger. Alternatively, imagine that Alfred orders the hamburger but has been brainwashed into believing that eating anything other than hamburgers is fatal; or, imagine that Alfred feels intimidated by Betty, who he knows wants him to order a hamburger. It seems natural to say of Alfred in any of these examples that his psychological state constrains the range of actions available to him, and thus that his ordering of the hamburger is not free. Thus the negative-liberty theorist should want to include psychological blocks of various kinds to the list of things that can hinder an individual's liberty. Accordingly, interference from others looks as if it can have an internal aspect.

Another example derives from the nineteenth-century philosopher John Stuart Mill. Imagine that you stand near the base of a bridge that crosses a river, and you know that the bridge has very recently been damaged and is now unsound. The damage is recent enough that there is no warning yet posted about the unsoundness of the bridge. Along comes a man, clearly intending to step on the bridge, and you do not have the time to verbally warn him of the fact that the bridge is unsafe. Mill alleges that in putting your hands on the man and physically stopping him from stepping on the bridge, you do *not* lessen his freedom. Mill reasons that as the man wants to cross to the other side of the river rather than fall into the river, he really does not *want* to step on the bridge, but only (incorrectly) believes that he does. Consequently, in preventing the man from stepping on the bridge, you assist him in doing what he wants to do, thereby actually *serving* his freedom. It seems, then, that certain kinds of *ignorance* can defeat freedom, rendering one incapable of acting as one wants. Mill thinks that interfering with the actions of those in the grip of such ignorance can further their liberty. If Mill is correct, then, at least in certain cases, determining the extent of an individual's liberty will sometimes require us to assess his or her rationality.

The contemporary philosopher Charles Taylor offers a different kind of case. Imagine two countries; call them A and B for short. Country A is nearly anarchic in that it has very few laws, and practically no laws governing automobile traffic. Drivers in Country A never experience the hindrance of red lights, speed limits, and stop signs. However, Country A does have strict laws against religious exercise. Although citizens of Country A move freely in their vehicles throughout the day, they are forbidden from attending religious services and they may not publically participate in acts of religious observance. Contrast Country A with Country B. Country B is much like your own country. It has a great many laws that govern the movement of traffic, and consequently there are many traffic lights, speed regulations, and stop signs. There are thus a large number of instances in which drivers must stop, slow, or yield when traveling in their vehicles; their day-to-day driving is fraught with staggering instances of interference. But Country B recognizes a robust freedom of religious exercise; citizens are free to attend religious services and to publicly express their religious convictions. Now, let us suppose that, strictly in terms of *occasions* of interference, citizens in Country B face interference far more frequently than those in Country A. But wouldn't it be absurd to conclude that the people in Country A are freer than those in B? It would seem so. But why?

Taylor alleges that freedom in part is a matter of the ability to do things that are *worthwhile* and *significant* from the perspective of human well-being. Freedom, then, would at least in part depend upon the nature of an individual's aims and ambitions. Unobstructed driving is, according to Taylor, trivial, and thus laws that regulate driving are insignificant from the point of view of human liberty. By contrast, the freedoms associated with religious exercise are decidedly momentous with respect to human flourishing; consequently, laws that constrain religious exercise are especially impactful, even if they result in fewer instances of interference than traffic laws. If you find Taylor's argument compelling, you will have to accept that freedom is not simply of *how many things* one can do, but of the *significance of what one can do*. To put the point differently, if Taylor is right, then in measuring freedom we cannot simply *count* instances of interference; we must *weigh* them.

As they call attention to the importance of assessing the rationality of the agent and the significance of her actions, the foregoing considerations point away from the negative conception of liberty. They suggest that in order to determine whether an individual is free, we must evaluate things internal to her. We have moved, then, in the direction of a conception that sees freedom as a matter of the *presence* of something internal to the individual.

3.2.2 Positive Liberty

As we mentioned earlier, one might think that the slave's unfreedom consists in the fact that his life is not his own; he belongs to his master and so his life is directed toward fulfilling the master's aims rather than the slave's own. When the master commands the slave to dig a ditch, the slave must dig, regardless of whether he finds digging a purposeful, fulfilling, or worthwhile action. The slave's own aims, goals, thoughts, and values play little or no role in guiding his actions; he is, as we mentioned earlier (and Aristotle observed long ago), the living tool of the master. According to the positive conception of liberty, one is free to the degree that one is in control of one's actions, and thus one's life. That is, the positive-liberty theorist holds that freedom is self-control or self-directedness, or, as some positive-liberty theorists like to put it, self-mastery. It is this that the slave lacks; that is his unfreedom.

This analysis of freedom looks promising, and it seems to be a decisive improvement over the negative conception. In light of the discussion above, it might occur to us that the slave's lack of liberty does not really reside in his chains or his inability to move his limbs, as the negative conception alleges. Of course, we might still see the bonds as the *manifestations*, *symbols*, or, perhaps *instruments* of his unfreedom, but the slave's lack of freedom seems to rest in some other feature of his condition. Consider: An unchained slave who through intimidation, humiliation, and habituation has nonetheless internalized the conception of himself as a mere tool of his master and so obeys should still be regarded as lacking freedom. The removal of external constraints does not suffice to render him free. Moreover, we might want to say that the slave who remains servile despite the absence of external constraints indeed may have vast opportunities for action available to him, but is nonetheless *all the more unfree*.

As it regards freedom as something depending upon matters *internal* to the individual, the positive conception does not see the removal of external obstacles as sufficient for expanding or restoring freedom. Again, the core claim is that freedom consists in the *presence* of something internal to the individual. But notice that what must be present in the individual in order for him to be free is a collection of cognitive and psychological capacities that *must be exercised*. To put the point in a way that punctuates the contrast with the negative conception, the capacities required for freedom do not exist merely as *opportunities* for self-control; the free individual is one who *exercises* the capacities and *therefore* is self-controlling. On the positive conception, an individual is free not in virtue of her *ability* to govern herself, but in virtue of the fact that she *in fact* is self-governing. Freedom lies in the *exercise* of one's internal capacities for rational self-control. So, when we describe the positive conception as holding that freedom consists in the presence of something internal to the agent, we must remember that what must be present is not merely the *opportunity* for self-mastery, but the *exercise* of that capacity.

Another kind of example will help to clarify this crucial "exercise" element of the positive conception. At the beginning of this chapter, we considered an addict named Carl. Recall that Carl is addicted to a very harmful and destructive drug and, in his sober moments, wants to be rid of his addiction. We might say of sober Carl that he not only does not want the drug, but he *wants not to want it*. Yet in the non-sober moments when his addiction is activated, Carl is compelled to feed the addiction; as is common with addicts, we might suppose that non-sober Carl is driven to act in ways that otherwise he would never even dream of acting. He is, as we tend to say, a slave to his addiction.

Just as the negative-liberty theorist tends to see the prisoner as the paradigm of the lack of freedom, the positive-liberty theorist sees the addict as exemplary of unfreedom. Given what has already been said, it's not difficult to see why. The addict is someone who is profoundly lacking in self-control; unlike the slave, whose lack of self-control partly is due to the control of another, the addict is under the control of forces *within himself* that are alien and not truly his own. In fact, much of the language we use in describing and discussing addiction highlights this feature of the phenomenon. For example, addicts refer to their drives and desires for their drug not as parts of themselves, but as their *addiction*; they thereby indicate that those drives and desires are something *foreign*, something to be *expelled*, and not part of who they truly are. More revealing is that the treatment of addicts is called *recovery*. The thought is that in expunging the addiction the individual—the *true* person—is restored.

We use similar language in discussing closely related psychological phenomena. For example, we sometimes speak of individuals being *gripped* by anxiety, *blinded* by ignorance, *overcome* by rage, *overwhelmed* by despair, and so on. This language is designed to indicate that the individual is out of control due to forces within him that nonetheless are not truly his own. That is, these psychological forces *assail* those they affect and (temporarily) take over, leaving the individual (momentarily) powerless. Revealingly, we describe an individual in the grip of such forces as "not himself."

These somewhat simplistic examples provide a fair representation of the core idea driving the positive conception of liberty: we are free when our lives—including our actions, aims, desires, attitudes, and aspirations—are *our own*. Freedom is a matter of living on one's own terms, and of having one's life—again, in the extended sense just described—be a manifestation of one's own exercise of one's internal capacities to plan, direct, and control oneself. Hence the positive conception is frequently characterized in the slogan *freedom is self-mastery*.

Importantly, the positive conception of freedom says that, in some cases, restraining people makes them free. This is likely to strike you as very odd, possibly contradictory. But think again of Carl, especially in his non-sober state. When we forcibly prevent Carl from taking his drug, there is a sense in which we contribute to his freedom. We help to free him from his addiction; we empower the sober Carl by oppressing the non-sober Carl. We might even say that by restraining (non-sober) Carl, we help to *liberate* (sober) Carl. In the striking words of the eighteenth-century philosopher Jean-Jacques Rousseau, we force him to be free.

The contradictory flavor of the idea of forcing someone to be free can be mitigated by taking note of the fact that in describing the core of the positive view we had to make reference to an individual's "true" self. We said of Carl that in his sober moments he desires neither the drug nor his desire for the drug, but in his non-sober moments he seems at least to want the drug. We hence employed a distinction between sober and non-sober Carl, and we associated the "true" Carl with the sober Carl. That is, in describing Carl's addiction as a force within him that is nevertheless alien, we affirm that Carl's "true" self is the non-addicted Carl; we identified Carl with the self that would be *recovered* were his addiction to be defeated, the self that is *liberated* when we suppress his addiction. We force Carl to be free when we constrain his non-sober self in order that his sober self might be liberated. This distinction between one's "true" self and the merely apparent, or distorted, self that prevails when we are in the grip of an addiction, compulsion, or obsession is a common feature of our everyday talk about ourselves and others. Yet it is philosophically curious.

Think about it: How could a desire be *yours*, be *within* you, and yet not really *belong to* you? We have said that Carl's desire for the drug is not really his; we attributed his drug-related drives to his addiction, as if the drug addiction were itself a different being that possesses its own aims and purposes that control Carl, not unlike the slave's master. This way of speaking makes sense, as far as it goes. But ultimately we know that the "two selves" talk is all metaphorical. Carl's addiction is not some foreign entity that has invaded Carl's body like a spirit does in a horror movie about demonic possession. The addiction is part of what Carl *is*. We employ the language of Carl's two selves as a handy way of describing the *struggle* within him. Fair enough. But note that we are not apt to say of Carl that his true self is the drug addict, and that the sober self is the enemy of (non-sober) Carl's freedom. That is, we associate Carl's freedom with the empowerment of what we take to be his *rational* self.

Contrast Carl with another addict, Dora. Like Carl, when Dora is in the grip of her addiction she goes to great lengths to get her drug, often hurting herself and others in the process. But, unlike Carl, Dora seems to have no desire to kick the addiction; when sober, Dora is merely sullen. She never expresses the desire to not have the desire for the drug. So there is no struggle within Dora between a "sober" and "non-sober" self; she is, we might say, *fully* an addict.

What is striking is that we are inclined to say that Dora is *all the more enslaved* by her addiction. Accordingly, we may even say that Dora's is all the more in need of intervention. When we forcibly prevent Carl from getting his drug, we impose sober Carl's will on non-sober Carl; we liberate the rational Carl from the irrational alien force within him. But when we prevent Dora from getting her drug, we simply impose on her against her will. Yet we would still want to say that we are forcing her to be free. This is because we identify Dora's "true" self as the unaddicted self that we believe Dora would want to be but for her addiction. In this case, we identify Dora's true self as the self *we want her to be*.

It seems, then, that according to the positive conception we need not only to assess the individual's internal states and processes in order to determine whether she is free; we will also need to discriminate among those internal states, deciding which of them are properly *her*. In Carl's case, this looks easy. We listen to Carl's sober self and coerce the non-sober self on (sober) Carl's behalf; we force him to be free in the sense that we suppress the false Carl as a way to restore the true Carl. But Dora's case is importantly different. In Dora's case, we must decide *for her* who she truly is, coercing her on behalf of a self that we project upon her.

This difference provides an indication of what many see as a serious problem with the positive conception of liberty. We noted above the oddness of the idea of forcing someone to be free. Then we saw that the oddness could be mitigated by drawing a distinction between an individual's "true" and "false" selves. Again, in forcing Carl to be free, it's the *false* Carl that gets pushed around, and the *true* Carl that gets freed. But notice what we have just said. The Carl that is subject to the force is not the *true* Carl, but the *false* Carl. *Who* is *that*? When we force Carl to be free, *who is being forced*? Here the metaphors begin to lead us astray.

This gives rise to a criticism championed by the twentieth-century philosopher and intellectual historian Isaiah Berlin. Berlin argued that the "two selves" idea at the heart of the positive conception of liberty is morally and politically dangerous. Here's why: As we saw, the "two selves" idea involves not just a separation of Carl into the sober and non-sober selves, but also an identification of Carl's sober self as the *true* Carl. That is, the "two selves" idea really involves the separation a "true" or "higher" self from a "false" or "lower" self, and this separation obviously invokes a *moral* judgment concerning the person Carl *ought to be*. Again, one furthers Carl's freedom by restoring his higher self. In fact, by suppressing the false self one really does not suppress *Carl* at all; one instead liberates (the true) Carl. Indeed, when Carl is chained, handcuffed, or placed in a prison cell, and is thereby prevented from getting his drug, we *free* him.

Something seems to have gone awry. According to the positive conception of liberty, Carl's freedom can be served by imprisoning him. Can prison really make someone free? Now, maybe this is not as counterintuitive as it may initially sound. After all, when he is sober Carl claims that he *wants* to be rid of his addiction but is powerless to resist his drug. It may be, then, that by imprisoning him we help him to do what he wants, namely, overcome his addiction. And, as we saw above when considering Mill's example of the broken bridge, it seems sensible to think that when we help someone to do what he wants to do we serve his freedom.

But think again of Dora. So deep is her addiction that she does not express any desire to be rid of it and indeed has no such desire. We tend to think that this depth supplies even *greater warrant* for intervention and obstruction. However, when we chain Dora in order to prevent her from getting her drug, we are not helping her to do what *she* wants. Rather, we are forcing her to do what *we* want, and presumably what we *want her to want*. Dora thus has become a tool for our purposes, purposes that she does not endorse (though we wish she would). Of course, in this case, our main purpose is to transform Dora into a different, and by our lights *better*, kind of person. But she's a tool nonetheless. When we chain her, we force her to submit to our plans for her. How, then, does Dora's condition differ from that of the slave?

That's the core of Berlin's objection. He alleges that the positive conception of liberty ultimately cannot keep liberty and submission distinct. The positive conception must regard as liberating any measure aimed at empowering the "true" self, no matter how constraining or (as in Dora's case) unwelcome. Furthermore, it must regard drug-addicted Dora as unfree, despite the fact that she has absolutely no desire to kick her addiction. Once freedom is seen as realization of the true self, and the overcoming of the false self, the door is open for governments to allege that the individual's true self is the compliant citizen, the unquestioning soldier, the constituent of a specific economic class, or a member of some political party. The diversity among individuals, the variety of choices they may make, and the lifestyles they pursue can then be suppressed in the name of freedom. This, Berlin argues, is a perversion of freedom, a transformation of liberty into *submission*.

Earlier, we criticized the negative conception on the grounds that it is unable to recognize that removing constraints is not sufficient to render a person free. We reasoned that the slave's unfreedom consists less in his inability to move his limbs and more in the fact that he is not in control of his life. Accordingly, the positive conception looked promising. But now we see that the positive conception is too comfortable with the idea that chains and other restraints serve individual freedom. In fact, history is riddled with cases in which tyrants have inflicted brutal force upon people, all in the name of "liberating" them. Whatever might be said for the positive conception of liberty as a model for understanding the ways in which we can be enslaved by forces within us, Berlin seems correct to think that it is dangerous when understood as a political ideal.

3.2.3 Freedom as Civic Standing

So let's explore the third intuitive view with which we began. Here the thought is that the slave's unfreedom consists in his lack of social status relative to his master and others. According to this view, the slave's unfreedom consists neither in that he is in chains, nor in that he is not in control of his life, but rather in that he is regarded as a subordinate and is thus subject to the control of another. Recall that we encapsulated this view as saying that freedom consists in the presence of something external to the individual, namely the civic status to block others' attempts to be his master. This encapsulation suggests that the civic standing conception is a hybrid of the negative view (freedom is the absence of something external) and the positive view (freedom is the presence of something internal), a "middle way" that attempts to harness and synthesize the virtues of the other two views while avoiding their vices.

The "middle way" strategy is understandably popular in philosophy. In fact, we encountered one earlier while discussing the metaphysical question of freedom. There, we said that the compatibilist stands in between the determinist and the indeterminist, holding ultimately that causal determinism is compatible with freedom of the will. The problem facing "middle way" views should already be apparent: Such views often *sound* internally conflicted or at least unstable. Think again of the metaphysical compatibilist. Her view is that one has free will despite the fact that all of one's actions are causally necessitated. It makes good sense to wonder *what the compatibilist means* by "free will" if she thinks it is consistent with determinism. *How* could I have free will and yet be unable to do otherwise than what I in fact do?

To be sure, metaphysical compatibilists tend to have sophisticated views about what exactly freedom of the will amounts to, and why it matters. That is, they have arguments aimed at dispelling the initial dissonance that their position arouses. Yet philosophically sophisticated opponents of compatibilism press a telling critique. They argue that compatibilism is *either* not a "middle way" at all, but simply a clever version of one of the other two views, *or* it is indeed distinctive but not really a view of metaphysical freedom. Note the two "prongs" of this criticism. The first says that compatibilism is collapsible into one of the other views; the second says that the compatibilist has in effect changed the subject by theorizing a different *concept* than the concept that divides determinists and indeterminists. In short, the criticism tries to characterize compatibilism as either *nothing new* (collapsible into one of the standing views) or *not relevant* (examining a different concept altogether); we can characterize these, respectively, as the *old news* and *who cares?* responses. In reply, the compatibilist must argue for the distinctiveness of her "middle way" while also demonstrating that it is indeed an alternate conception of the very same concept over which the two other views disagree.

This argumentative pattern with respect to "middle way" views is found throughout the discipline of Philosophy. And in the present case, it may be especially easy to anticipate how critics respond to the idea that freedom consists in civic standing: Some say that the civic-standing view either collapses into one of the other views (*old news*) or offers an analysis of a different concept altogether (*who cares?*). But before we examine these critical maneuvers, we need to look more closely at the civic-standing view.

We have already said that, according to the view to be considered, the slave's lack of freedom lies in his official status as a subordinate. He is unfree because he cannot be his "own man"; as a matter of the social order, he has a master or a boss. He is, we might say, "under the thumb" of another person and is powerless to extricate himself from his subordination. Now, we are all sometimes "subordinate" to others in the way that employees are subordinate to their bosses and athletes are subordinate to their coaches. The crucial thing to notice about these cases is that the subordination is *limited* to particular roles that have been voluntarily adopted. The slave's subordination is not restricted to some particular task or sphere of life, and is certainly not voluntary. The slave is subordinate to his master partly *because* he is socially regarded as subordinate, and his social subordination involves a lack of power to change his status. In order to free him, it is not sufficient that we remove his chains; nor will it do to develop in him the powers of self-mastery. To be free, he must be rid of the mastery of others; he must gain the social status of a non-subordinate.

The idea of freedom as the presence of a kind of civic standing has a few obvious attractions. First of all, this conception of freedom seems most decidedly *political* in that it treats freedom as something that could be enjoyed only within a certain social structure. Recall that according to the negative conception, Robinson Crusoe—a man alone on a desert island—is the paragon of freedom; there is no one else around to obstruct him, so his freedom is complete. The positive conception, too, has a kind of asocial flavor. Although it might be that the powers of self-control can be developed by human beings only within a certain kind of social structure, one's freedom does not *reside* within that structure; society might be *causally* necessary for freedom, but it is not *conceptually* necessary. According to the positive conception, Robinson Crusoe could be free, provided that he has the requisite capacities of self-mastery. The civic-standing conception is unique in that it treats an individual's freedom as *intrinsically* a matter of the social relations he or she bears to others; on this view, one *cannot* be free except within a society. According to the civic-standing view, Robinson Crusoe *cannot* be free. To be sure, Crusoe cannot be unfree, either; as he has *no civic status at all*, the civic-standing view would say that Crusoe is neither free nor unfree.

That is an intriguing thought. Freedom and its opposite exist only within societies, only within socially structured interpersonal relations. We can understand this idea in two ways that are worth distinguishing. The first holds that because freedom resides only within societies, societies are the entities that are free or unfree in the primary sense. That is, on one interpretation of the civic-standing view, the individual is free only if she is a member of a *free society*; so in order to determine whether some person is free, we first need to determine whether her society is free. This view, which we shall call the *communitarian* interpretation of the civic-standing conception, holds that individual freedom consists in *citizenship* within a free society, and a free society is necessarily a *democratic society*. Roughly, the idea is that one is free only if one is a democratic citizen.

The communitarian interpretation of the civic-standing view can be easily shown to collapse into the positive view, which means that it inherits all of the difficulties with positive liberty that we discussed above, for the communitarian interpretation is simply the self-mastery view writ large: The self-mastery that is constitutive of freedom is *collective* self-government. This view hence adopts the *exercise* aspect of positive liberty; it holds that the freedom of an individual rests in *acting* in her role as citizen. As the nonparticipating citizen does not actively contribute to the government of her society, she is failing to be free. Consequently, by forcing an individual to act as a citizen—or, by forcing her to act as we believe a citizen should act—we contribute to her freedom.

This looks unacceptable. So let's turn to a second and more promising interpretation of the civic-standing view. This interpretation is championed by the contemporary philosopher Philip Pettit. As it locates its inspiration in the early Roman republic, we can call it the *Neo-Roman* interpretation.

The Neo-Roman view begins with a critical thought aimed at the negative conception of liberty. You will remember that the negative-liberty theorist holds that freedom consists in the absence of others' interference. Now, imagine the case of the "lucky" slave. This is a slave who is fortunate enough to have a benevolent and undemanding master. Although the slave is indeed the master's property, luck has it that he is nevertheless wholly free of the master's intrusions, and so he lives as he wishes. It seems that the negative conception would have to say that there is nothing in the slave's condition that renders him unfree; he is a slave, but his freedom nevertheless is intact due to the fact that his master is disinclined to interfere or make any demands of him. He is a slave, yet free. How could this be correct?

The Neo-Roman contends that the lucky slave case shows a deep flaw in the idea that freedom is the absence of interference. It is, the Neo-Roman contends, blind to the nature of the slave's lack of freedom. Holding steadfastly to the idea that there could be no such thing as a slave who is nonetheless free, the Neo-Roman provides an analysis of the lucky slave's unfreedom. The core idea is that one's freedom is undermined when one is *subject* or *vulnerable* to another's interference, even if no actual interference takes place. In this way, the slave lacks freedom not in virtue of his chains, but rather in virtue of the fact that he is *liable* to be chained, that someone may at will chain him. Even the lucky slave, then, will count as unfree; despite his good fortune in having a non-interfering master, he nonetheless could at any time be chained, beaten, or killed should his master's disposition suddenly change.

We can see clearly now how the Neo-Roman interpretation of the civic-standing view is a kind of hybrid of the negative and positive conceptions of freedom. Like the negative conception, the Neo-Roman interpretation sees freedom partly as a matter of freedom from others' interference. But, unlike the negative conception, the Neo-Roman view does not require any *actual* interference in order for there to be a violation of freedom; on the Neo-Roman view, merely the *possibility* of interference suffices for unfreedom.

Surely the view that freedom consists in the *impossibility* of interference is implausible; we are all unavoidably subject to *possible* interference. So the Neo-Roman view must say more than this. And here is where the Neo-Roman incorporates a bit of the positive conception. Strictly speaking, the Neo-Roman holds that the lucky slave's lack of freedom consists in the master's ability to interfere *at will* and *with impunity* in the slave's affairs. That is, the Neo-Roman holds with the positive view that freedom requires a kind of control over one's life. But, unlike the positive-liberty theorist, the Neo-Roman does not identify the requisite control in the internal rational capacities of the individual, but rather in the *social power* of the individual to *block* or *resist* others' intrusions. In other words, according to the Neo-Roman, the freedom-making capacity is not the "rational self-control" of the positive theorist, but the kind of control over one's life that is achieved when one has the power to prevent others from taking control. However, with the positive view, the Neo-Roman holds that unfreedom lies not only in the loss of control, but in a kind of powerlessness in the face of alien controlling forces. Recall that according to the positive-liberty view these forces are within the agent; they take the form of addictions, obsessions, anxieties, and vices. By contrast, the Neo-Roman holds that the alien forces vying for control over your life are *other people*, particularly those others who wield forms and degrees of social power against which you cannot defend yourself.

To get a firmer sense of how this combination of elements from the negative and positive conceptions works, consider a different kind of case that is often discussed by Pettit. Call her the *traditional wife*. The traditional wife lives in a society where there are almost no laws governing the treatment of wives by husbands in the home; such matters are officially considered "private" and therefore out of the reach of the state and its laws. Now, the traditional wife is married to a husband who is well tempered, kind, considerate, and thoroughly reasonable. They share a happy marriage as equals. Yet recall that were her husband to turn abusive or violent, the traditional wife would be *socially* powerless to defend herself; as domestic affairs are regarded by her society as "private," she could not call the police or seek legal action against her husband's abuse. Her sole recourse would be to kowtow to her husband, attempt to placate him, or act toward him in ways designed to not provoke his anger. In short, she would have to either assume a subordinate role in her marriage or endure his abuse.

It is, of course, worth noticing that this description is an accurate depiction of the way domestic affairs were regarded in the United States until quite recently. The Neo-Roman's point is that, like the lucky slave, the traditional wife is rendered unfree simply in virtue of her *vulnerability* to spousal abuse. And this vulnerability exists even in cases, like hers, in which a woman is married to a non-abusive man. But notice what we mean here by *vulnerability*. The thought is not that the wife is rendered unfree simply in virtue of the fact that it is possible for her husband to interfere with her; again, we are all "vulnerable" to others' interference in *that* sense. The operative sense of "vulnerability" for the Neo-Roman lies in the traditional wife's *powerlessness* to protect against abuse were her husband's disposition to change. This powerlessness is *social*. She is powerless not in the sense that she cannot physically defend herself in an altercation, but rather in the sense that she lacks the *social standing* to seek *legal* protection against abuse, and *legal* redress against her husband should he abuse her.

Notice how this sense of vulnerability incorporates part of the flavor of the positive-liberty view. As was said, were the traditional wife's husband to turn abusive, she would have no legal or social recourse to defend herself. She must either suffer his abuse or else modify her behavior so as not to provoke his ire. Either way, her life is in the control of her husband and thus no longer hers. She must live under the gaze of another who has the power to punish and abuse her, wholly at his own whim. She simply must bend her life to his will, and she has no social means of escape from his control. Not unlike the addict, she is trapped.

It seems, then, that the Neo-Roman gets the best elements of both of the other conceptions. Yet, as we said earlier, there are two characteristic difficulties that hybrid views tend to attract: *old news* and *who cares?* In fact, we have already deployed a version of the old-news charge against the communitarian interpretation of the social-standing view; it was suggested that the communitarian view is simply a variation on the positive-liberty conception. So now let's consider the worry that the Neo-Roman interpretation is old news in the other direction. That is, let us consider the possibility that the Neo-Roman is really just a proponent of negative liberty.

As we saw, the Neo-Roman begins from the objection that negative liberty is blind to, and hence cannot adequately account for, the fact that the lucky slave is unfree. But is this really the case? Consider the fact that the Neo-Roman incorporates into his account the fact that the lucky slave must kowtow to his master in order to keep him benevolent; the slave must stay in the good graces of his (luckily) benevolent master or else suffer interference. Similarly, the wife under traditional arrangements with a husband that has abusive tendencies must bend her life to her husband's will to keep him from abusing her; indeed, even the wife who is luckily married to a well-tempered husband might nonetheless see fit to adjust her behavior to avoid occasions where abusive tendencies *could* be provoked. All of this looks to the negative-liberty theorist like interference, albeit of a complex kind. To be sure, in discussing the negative conception, we relied nearly exclusively upon the simplistic example of chains and handcuffs as paradigm restraints. But the negative-liberty conception need not reject the thought that there are more sophisticated means of interference, such as intimidation, fear, browbeating, disapproval, and threats. It is open to the negative-liberty proponent to say that, under some circumstances, intimidation can be every bit as opportunity-closing as physical bonds. Consequently, the negative-liberty view could concede that the lucky slave and traditional wife are indeed unfree by claiming that they are also interfered with in especially subtle—but no less freedom-lessening—ways. The Neo-Roman view consequently looks like old news; it is merely a dressed-up negative conception.

The Neo-Roman might here insist that her view is distinct from the negative conception. She might remind us that her view is an *inherently social* conception of freedom. Unlike the negative conception, which would regard Robinson Crusoe as paradigmatically free because he is free of all social bonds, the Neo-Roman view contends that one's freedom resides *only* within one's relations with others. To be specific, the Neo-Roman holds that an individual is free only if he is *socially equal* to those with whom he lives. The negative-liberty theorist's view that one is most free when in isolation from others looks to the Neo-Roman incoherent.

This does look like a distinctive feature of the Neo-Roman view. But in emphasizing this feature of her view, the Neo-Roman now invites the old-news criticism that faces the communitarian interpretation of the civic-standing view; that is, in striving to avoid the charge that she is offering merely a new fangled version of negative liberty, the Neo-Roman has cast her view in a way that makes it look like the positive conception.

Here's how this argument could run: By emphasizing the idea that one's freedom consists in being a social equal, the Neo-Roman concedes that coercion and force are not freedom-lessening when exercised under conditions of equality. When one social equal (Emma) exerts force against another equal (Frank), she may indeed obstruct or block him from acting as he wishes. But given that Emma and Frank are social equals, Frank has the civic standing to socially retaliate against Emma for her intrusion. Frank's social ability to pursue redress against Emma means, on the Neo-Roman view, that although he has suffered wrongful interference, he is nonetheless not *vulnerable* to Emma's intrusion; he can, after all, strike back as a social equal. And *that* is sufficient for Frank's freedom. As a result, it looks as if the Neo-Roman view must hold that Emma's obstruction of Frank did not lessen Frank's freedom. Recall that the positive conception holds that it is possible to force someone to be free; in fact, as we saw, the positive view contends that in some cases chains, jails, and straitjackets might actually *serve* freedom. To be sure, the Neo-Roman might not go so far as to say that by forcing Frank, Emma might have rendered him free. But the Neo-Roman does say that by forcing Frank, Emma might not have *lessened* his freedom. The negative-liberty theorist argues that this suffices to render the Neo-Roman view merely a variation on the old positive-liberty conception. At the very least, it seems, then, that the civic-standing view is unstable.

3.3 Conclusion

In this chapter, we have briskly traveled a great philosophical distance, and it should be mentioned that the debates among the three conceptions of freedom that we have discussed continue to rage among contemporary political philosophers. So we should remind ourselves that nothing we have said should be regarded as the final word concerning any of the matters we have examined. But I want to bring this discussion to a close by suggesting a resolution of sorts, even though I think it will strike many philosophers as unattractive. Roughly, I want to propose a modified version of the *who cares?* objection. See what you think.

When philosophers have been locked in a long philosophical debate, it sometimes makes good sense to step back and consider the possibility that they actually have been talking past each other. This is to say that they have been using the same words to talk about different concepts; they have mistakenly thought they were offering opposing conceptions of the same concept, while in fact they have been talking about different concepts. Now, different and distinct concepts can certainly be *closely related* to each other, and, accordingly, conceptions of distinct concepts can bear relations to each other as well. So, to the debates between the three views of liberal that have been discussed, one might propose a *so what?* response without thereby asserting that the negative-liberty, positive-liberty, and civic-standing views are wholly irrelevant to each other. Indeed, in claiming that the negative-liberty, positive-liberty, and civic-standing views are capturing *different concepts*, one allows for the possibility that they might all be correct and non-rivalrous. Perhaps they are mutually supporting. This is roughly what I want to suggest.

It looks as if the positive conception is adequately capturing a concept very closely related to liberty, namely *autonomy*. The civic-standing view seems to be tracking a different but also closely related concept, namely *social equality*. In saying that only the negative view captures the concept of liberty, one of course proposes the *who cares?* reply to the positive-liberty and civic-standing accounts. But this is not necessarily to say that the thoughts driving the positive-liberty and civic-standing views are *irrelevant* to thinking about liberty. It is only to say that the positive-liberty and civic-standing theorists are conceptualizing a distinct concept. The accounts offered by positive-liberty and civic-standing theorists might yet be relevant to our thinking about liberty proper.

Here's how. Let's stipulate that liberty is what the negative-liberty theorist claims: the absence of others' interference. We may then say that although autonomy is a distinct concept from liberty, it is nonetheless true that cases in which individuals are rendered non-autonomous tend to be cases in which individuals are unfree. This may be because non-autonomous individuals are especially prone to others' interference. Their lack of autonomy may be strongly causally correlated with their unfreedom, even though autonomy is autonomy, and liberty is something else. A similar thought can be run with respect to the civic-standing view. It offers a conceptualization of social equality, not liberty. Yet the lack of social equality is in obvious ways causally correlated with the presence of others' interference.

Given this, we may even say that furthering individual autonomy and securing social equality might suffice to enhance liberty. Thus we could incorporate into our negative conception of liberty some reference to what looks most attractive in the other views. Perhaps we should go so far as to say that freedom is the absence of interference among autonomous social equals. Freedom, then, would be the absence of something in the presence of other things. That may sound promising. But, alas, it also is not especially informative. In order to theorize freedom, one would have to also defend particular conceptions of autonomy and equality. Moreover, the result would be yet another hybrid view. And it accordingly will have to face the usual charges. Still, there is something valuable in the thought that although they are three distinct concepts, a proper understanding of liberty must invoke plausible conceptions of autonomy and equality.

For Further Reading

The major works in the history of political philosophy recommended at the close of Chapter 2 (p. 36) provide a good background to the current debates concerning liberty. One might also consult the historical and contemporary selections anthologized in *Freedom: A Philosophical Anthology*, edited by Ian Carter, Matthew Kramer, and Hillel Steiner (Oxford: Blackwell, 2007). In any case, one should read an unabridged version of Isaiah Berlin's duly influential 1958 essay "Two Concepts of Liberty" (reprinted in his *Liberty*, New York: Oxford University Press, 2002). One might also consult Friedrich Hayek's 1944 *The Road to Serfdom* (Chicago: University of Chicago Press, 2007), Richard Flathman's *The Philosophy and Politics of Freedom* (Chicago: University of Chicago Press, 1987), and Amartya Sen's *Development as Freedom* (New York: Anchor Books, 2000). For current articulations of the negative conception of liberty, see Matthew Kramer's *The Quality of Freedom* (New York: Oxford University Press, 2003) and Ian Carter's *A Measure of Freedom* (New York: Oxford University Press, 2004). Charles Taylor's criticism of negative liberty can be found throughout his works, but is the focus of his essay "What's Wrong with Negative Liberty" (reprinted in his *Philosophical Papers, Volume 2: Philosophy and the Human Sciences*, Cambridge: Cambridge University Press, 1985). John Christman's *The Politics of Persons* (Cambridge: Cambridge University Press, 2009) is a book-length defense of one kind of positive conception of liberty. See also Nancy Hirschman's *The Subject of Liberty* (Princeton: Princeton University Press, 2002). A contemporary version of the social-standing view can be found throughout Philip Pettit's work. See especially Pettit's highly influential *Republicanism* (New York: Oxford University Press, 1997); his *A Theory of Freedom* (New York: Oxford University Press, 2001) has the added virtue of attempting to provide an integrated theory of metaphysical and political freedom. For a rich overview of contemporary theories of freedom, see Katrin Flikschuh's *Freedom* (London: Polity, 2007).

4 Authority

4.1 Some Initial Distinctions

On television last night, a newscaster was interviewing someone she introduced as an "authority on cyber-security," who in turn proceeded to claim that the cyber-security at Target stores is markedly lax. The copy of Mark Twain's *Adventures of Huckleberry Finn* that sits on my bookshelf has a cover that features the claim that it is "the only authoritative edition based on the complete, original manuscript." Sometimes we encounter doors bearing signs that say "Authorized Personnel Only." On the back of your credit card, there is a space for an "authorizing signature." At weddings we hear a pronouncement that begins with the words "by the authority vested in me." In airports, there are public announcements instructing us to "alert the authorities" should we witness suspicious behavior. There is a lot of talk within politics about things like "police authority," "state authority," "the authority of the President," and "the authority of law." In these latter cases, the discussion seems to focus on the *bounds* or *limitations* of the authority in question. And there is a car in my neighborhood bearing a bumper sticker that directs us to "question authority."

Talk of authority is widespread. But what do these various employments of the term amount to? On the face of it, there seem to be several concepts in use, and not all of them are relevant to political philosophy. So it is worth beginning our examination with a few distinctions.

4.1.1 Expertise and Permission

First, we should identify the *expertise* sense of the term. One is an authority in this sense in virtue of one's *expert* or *uncommon* knowledge. Accordingly, the expert interviewed on the news program is an authority *with respect to* some specific topic, in this case cyber-security; his authority consists simply in his expertise regarding that topic. By calling him an authority, the newscaster was indicating that her guest's pronouncements about cyber-security should be taken by her viewers to carry a special kind of *epistemic* weight. She was affirming that her guest's assertions about cyber-security should be taken as true, or at least warranted and highly likely to be true, especially by non-experts. Accordingly, although I have no first-hand information about Target's cyber-security, and do not know anything about how one might go about assessing the cyber-security standards of a large national retailer, I now have a justified belief that Target's standards are lax. My belief is justified simply in virtue of the fact that the expert said that Target has lax cyber-security standards.

This looks like the kind of authority that physicians have. When your doctor says, "Take two of these pills with breakfast every morning," you take the fact that she prescribed this course of action to be strong evidence that you should, indeed, take two of those pills with breakfast every morning. After all, she has had special training and has proven to have expert knowledge about health, and, moreover, she is bound by her profession to treat your illness. Unless you are also a health expert, *you* do not have any special insight directly into how you should treat your illness, yet under the normal range of circumstances it would be foolish to disregard her prescription. You are justified in holding that you should take the pills with breakfast each morning, even if you cannot explain why that course of action will produce the needed effect; your justification lies simply in the say-so of the medical authority.

But note a difference between the physician and the cyber-security expert. The cyber-security expert made a *claim* that something is the case with respect to Target's security, whereas the physician issued a *directive*; she told you to do something. The idea of a *directive* will prove crucial when we examine another form of authority. But for now, we can simply note the distinction and then set it aside, for just as we could imagine the cyber-security expert issuing a directive ("Do not trust the cyber-security at Target stores!"), we can reinterpret the physician's directive as a kind of claim ("It would be good for you to take two of these pills with breakfast each day"). That is, the difference between the security expert's and the physician's utterances are not presently at issue. Our point thus far is simply that when an authority in the expertise sense of the term makes a pronouncement, the rest of us should take the fact that *he or she has said it* to be strong evidence of the truth of what was said. To put the point more generally, when an authority (in the expertise sense) speaks on the matters about which he or she is an expert, we generally ought to believe what he or she says. *That* the authority has made the assertion serves for us as sufficient reason to adopt what was asserted. This, of course, is not to say that the say-so of an expert is sufficient for the *truth* of what the expert says; authorities in the expertise sense surely can be mistaken. The idea, rather, is that by asserting some claim the authority *gives us* (non-experts) strong evidence for believing that claim. *Our* evidence for believing what the authority has said is *the fact that* the authority said it; in many cases, that kind of evidence provides sufficient warrant for our belief.

The idea of an *authoritative* edition of a great novel is closely related. By calling a particular edition of *The Adventures of Huckleberry Finn* "authoritative," the publisher is saying that Twain experts have reviewed and endorsed the edition in question; the edition is authoritative in virtue of having met with the approval of authorities regarding Twain's writings. In declaring it an "authoritative" edition, the experts on Twain have in effect said that it is an *authentic* and complete version of the text that Twain wrote. Accordingly, were there to be some dispute among Twain's readers about, say, the number of times that a particular character mentions the Mississippi River, disputants should consult the authoritative text rather than some other edition. Here the authoritative status of the edition of Twain's novel *derives* from the endorsement of those who are authorities (in the expert sense) on Twain. *Their* declaration of that edition as authoritative *makes it* the authoritative edition and, again, those of us who are not Twain experts ought to *accept* that edition as the authoritative one. As we are not Twain experts, we do not know *why* this particular edition has been deemed authoritative, and we might not have any idea at all about how to evaluate different Twain editions for their authoritativeness. But this is no matter. Again, the say-so of the Twain authorities alone suffices as strong evidence for us to accept what they say.

It should be repeated that in both cases those with authority have it in virtue of their expertise. The fact that they have had special training and have special knowledge is what accounts for their ability to speak *authoritatively* about certain topics. And when they speak authoritatively, their pronouncements carry a special kind of epistemic weight. *That* the expert has said that Target's cyber-security is lax counts as strong evidence for us to believe that Target's cyber-security is lax. Part of *our* evidence (as non-experts) is the *very fact that an expert has said so*. Contrast this with the pronouncements offered by a non-expert. I, for example, have no special knowledge of cyber-security; I am no authority on that subject. When *I* declare that Target has lax cyber-security standards, my declaration carries no special force on its own; it *at best* carries a derivative weight in virtue of the fact that I am *reporting* what an authority has declared. When I repeat what the expert has said, I in no way *add* to the epistemic quality of the original pronouncement. And if I—again, a non-expert—instead declare that Target has especially stringent cyber-security standards, I have given no one any *evidence* for adopting that view. In other words, my say-so is *not authoritative*.

When you think about it, this is precisely as it should be. Most of what we claim to know about the world around us is, at least in part, derived from the say-so of others. In fact, the world around us is so complicated that we cannot help but rely on the cognitive resources of others—their knowledge, experiences, evidence, data, findings, and so forth. We must *defer* to others when forming our beliefs about the world; we must treat the mere say-so of others as sufficient evidence for our beliefs. Indeed, when we are pressed to articulate our reasons for holding a belief about, say, the causes of global climate change, we inevitably cite the testimony, findings, and research of others. *We* do not conduct such research ourselves; instead, we rely on others to do the research, and accept their testimony as our evidence. Such deference is inescapable. But of course it is also hazardous. One could defer to the wrong person to the wrong degree, and thereby arrive at a wide array of false and unjustified beliefs about the world. One could rely on professed experts who in fact have no expertise at all. One could be conned or duped by people who *seem* to speak authoritatively, but in fact are simply smooth talkers.

Questions about epistemic deference and trust are philosophically deep and difficult. These questions lie beyond our present concern. Here we note again that the authority of the expert does not require him to be *infallible*; experts can err and yet remain authorities with respect to their area of expertise. But still, their authority rests in their expertise, and their status as *expert* depends on their ability to *demonstrate* their special knowledge. Consequently, there are certain kinds of errors that are sufficient for revoking an expert's authority. Sometimes the revocation is formal—as when a physician loses her medical license due to malpractice—but in other cases its process is simply one in which people stop treating the pronouncements of the expert as authoritative. The point is that authority in the expertise sense is *conditional* on the expert's *reliability* with respect to his or her topic of expertise. When the fact that he has asserted something no longer provides a reliable guide to what we (non-experts) ought to believe, the authority recedes.

Contrast this with another employment of the term: the door bearing the sign that says "Authorized Personnel Only." That sign indicates that only select persons have permission to enter, and others must stay out. Like the authoritative edition of Twain, those who are authorized to enter have had that status *conferred* upon them by someone with the *authority* to grant and withhold permission to walk through the doorway. Again, it is in virtue of the fact that the person with permission-granting authority has *authorized* you to walk through the door that you are permitted to do so. However, in this case, the person with the authority need not be an *expert* in anything at all.

The authority to permit or forbid others to enter a room typically falls to whoever *owns* the room, simply in virtue of their ownership. If you own a house, you typically therefore have the authority to permit or forbid persons from entering it. There are limits to that authority, of course; for example, under certain circumstances you may not forbid police, fire, or rescue personnel from entering your house. But generally, you have the authority to permit and forbid entrance simply in virtue of the fact that the house is *yours*. You need not demonstrate expert knowledge, or even good judgment, in order to have and maintain the authority to grant and withhold permission for others to enter your home. In fact, you need not have any particularly good reasons to grant permission to someone to enter your home; you may open your house to strangers and indigents if you choose. Similarly, under typical conditions, you may refuse entry to almost anyone for any reason at all, no matter how silly or objectionable. Your pronouncement that "left-handed persons who have brown hair are not allowed in my home" suffices to make it the case that leftie brunettes are not permitted to enter. If it's your home, you make the rules concerning who may enter. Your status in this respect is not contingent on your ability to demonstrate good (let alone expert) judgment.

This type of authority is also at work in the case of your credit card. When you provide an "authorizing signature" on the back of your credit card, you are presenting an example of your signature so that when you use the card to make purchases your signature on the receipt can be compared to the signature on the card. By providing the authorizing signature on the card, you in effect authorize anyone who can duplicate your signature to incur charges to your credit account. Of course, the crucial thought is that only *you* can duplicate your signature. But the structure of the authorization is similar to the cases involving your house. By providing a duplicate of the authorizing signature on a credit-card receipt when you make a purchase, you make a kind of pledge; you authorize the retailer to charge your credit account for the indicated sum, and you promise to pay the indicated amount to your bank according to the terms of your credit agreement. In fact, most purchase receipts include an explicit pledge roughly of a form that says, "I hereby agree to pay the amount indicated above in compliance with my credit-card agreement." The authority to incur debt, as we know all too well, is not in any way tied to an individual's financial expertise or purchasing wisdom. To be sure, making foolish purchases repeatedly might result in your accruing unacceptable amounts of debt, and *this* might result in your bank *revoking* your credit card. However, your foolish purchases are not *themselves* marks against your authority to permit retailers from charging your credit account.

4.1.2 A Point about Oughts

To summarize the discussion thus far, we have identified two different senses of authority: *expert authority* and the authority to grant permission, what we might call *permission authority*. Both forms of authority involve the conferral of a status by means of an (implicit or explicit) communicative act (typically an act of speech). In the expertise cases, the authority confers on a statement a kind of epistemic justification, a reason for non-experts to believe what the authority has asserted. In the permission cases, the authority makes a declaration or signs a pledge which *grants* (or *withholds*) permission to others to act in specified ways.

This reveals an important difference between expert authority and permission authority, a difference concerning the force of the word *ought*. When we said that we *ought* to believe what an expert asserts, we were claiming that generally it would be *irrational* for us—non-experts—to disregard the expert's say-so. The *ought* at work in expert authority concerns our *rationality*. Generally speaking, one ought to believe what the expert asserts, or else one fails to be rational; hence we say that expert authority issues *rational oughts*. Contrast this with the *ought* that operates in the permission-authority cases. Let's imagine that, at your invitation, I have shown up to a party at your house, but have been behaving very badly. When you tell me that I am no longer welcome in your home and must leave, you thereby make it the case that I *ought* to leave. The *ought* here does not refer to what I must do if I am to be rational. Rather, the *ought* at play in this case is what philosophers sometimes call the *moral ought*. When you revoke my permission to be in your home, you make it that case that I must, as a *moral* matter, leave. If after being told that I am no longer welcome in your home, I refuse to leave, I am doing something *immoral*; to stay after you have revoked my permission is to *wrong* you. To be sure, when I reject my physician's prescription, I do something irrational, and I may *thereby* do something immoral with respect to, for example, my dependants who count on me to maintain good health. Yet in acting against the prescription, I in no way *wrong* my physician. The defiance against the physician's order is, again, foolish but it is not all by itself *morally wrong*. Things are different in the permission cases; except under special circumstances, to defy someone with permission authority is to do wrong.

It is worth emphasizing that although there is this difference in the character of the *ought* between the expert and permission cases, there remains the obvious similarity that both cases of authority issue *oughts*. That is, when you revoke my permission to be in your home, you do not (merely) threaten me, "Get out, or else!" And when the physician prescribes a medication, she does not (merely) attempt to induce me to take the pills. In both cases, the *authority* in question establishes something that I *ought* to do; hence authority is distinct from the *power* to compel compliance. A charismatic speaker might be able to induce in you the belief that Target's cyber-security is lax, but this does not make him an authority on cyber-security. A good-looking and eloquent speaker may be able to convince you to take a drug, but this does not make her a medical expert. The say-so of a non-expert charismatic speaker carries no *epistemic weight*; the fact that the non-expert has claimed that Target's cyber-security is lax does not constitute evidence for the truth of what he claimed. That he is charismatic only makes it more *likely* that he will be believed; it does not make it true that he *ought to be* believed. Likewise, a physically imposing person might be able to push you out of his house, but his power to physically eject you is not what accounts for his authority. A physically slight individual has the same authority to revoke your permission to be in his home; even though he poses no physical threat, and so perhaps cannot make it more *likely* that you will leave his home, he can nonetheless make it the case that you are morally required to leave.

All of this is to say that authority is something *normative*. When we fail to comply with an authority, we are in some way criticizable; exercises of authority are instances of creating *requirements*. Of course, sometimes these requirements may be quite weak. For example, imagine that an expert has declared that the cyber-security at Target is lax, but you never shop at Target; you now have evidence that Target's cyber-security is lax, but matters with respect to Target stores are simply of no concern to you. Similarly, someone might revoke your permission to be in a room that you intended to leave anyway; in this case, the requirement to leave has marginal impact. Still, in either case, the authority in question has introduced a requirement. In order to preserve your rationality, if you have any belief about Target's cyber-security at all, you should believe that it is lax. And regardless of your independent desire to leave the room, you are morally required to leave it in virtue of the fact that your permission to occupy the room has been revoked.

The force of the oughts that authority imposes is more clearly felt in cases in which what the authority requires of us conflicts with our inclinations. Imagine that you find the thought that Target employs only the most stringent cyber-security standards especially comforting. The expert has made it the case that you *ought not* sustain that comforting thought, and if you do maintain it you are rightly subject to criticism. Consider next a case in which you have been told by your host to leave his home, but you are having an especially good time there, and, moreover, think that your host is being rude in demanding that you leave. Perhaps the host *is* being rude. But that's no matter; you nonetheless are required to leave the party. Or consider a modified case in which you are told to leave the host's home because the host mis-takenly believes that you are the guest who clumsily broke his favorite lamp. Of course, you might insist to the host that you did not break the lamp; but if the host is unconvinced and still demands that you leave, you must leave. Again, his authority to grant or withhold permission does not diminish in cases where he is in error.

4.1.3 Political Authority

Now consider the remaining examples mentioned at the start of this chapter. These have a different character from those we have been examining. At weddings, there is an official who performs the act of legally marrying a couple by means of a proclamation; the official (a Justice of the Peace) utters words like: "By the power vested in me by the state of [for example] Nevada, I now pronounce you husband and wife." The official has the authority to perform the legal act of marrying people because he or she has been imbued with that authority by the state of Nevada. Similarly, we are told in airports to "alert the authorities" should we witness suspicious behavior because there are some people—soldiers, police officers, security agents, and other "authorities"—who have been authorized by the state to perform certain kinds of acts that no ordinary citizen could, including stopping travelers, frisking them, detaining them, interrogating them, searching their belongings, confiscating their property, and arresting them. Finally, when politicians and political theorists talk about the "authority of law" or the "authority of the President," they are frequently talking about the ability of the state and its agencies to impose requirements on citizens.

We see, then, that a distinctive element of these cases is that they invoke the state, its offices, its officers, and its rightful powers. That is, these claims regarding authority make implicit or explicit reference to the state and its institutions; absent a state, there could be no Justice of the Peace, no police officers, and no President, for these are roles within the state's institutions. Now, as we said earlier, the state has the ability to grant to individuals certain special powers that other individuals do not have. For example, I cannot perform the act of marrying a couple, nor can I arrest a suspicious person. Furthermore, I cannot marshal an army, declare war, print money, create a law, levy taxes, ratify an international treaty, issue a subpoena, sentence a criminal, build a prison, grant amnesty, stay an execution, declare a state of emergency, issue a liquor license, or establish a national holiday. Only states (and their officers) can do such things. More importantly, the state not only has the *power* to perform these actions, it also claims *the authority* to do so. Hence we can speak of *political authority* as that kind of authority that is claimed by states and, by extension, their officers, agents, and institutions.

To be sure, the claim that political authority is that kind of authority claimed by states is not very informative, so let's look deeper. In some ways, political authority seems akin to permission authority. When the state passes a law establishing a speed limit on Main Street, it in effect grants drivers permission to drive at that speed (or under); similarly, when the state grants a liquor license to a local restaurant, it permits that business to sell liquor. Much of what the state does has this general character. It sets a policy or establishes an institution that regulates individuals' behavior by identifying what they are permitted (and not permitted) to do. But the similarities between political authority and permission authority quickly give out once we consider a broader range of actions that states claim the authority to perform. States do not only grant permissions, they also make *demands* and issue *directives*; in many cases, these are accurately characterized as *commands*. For example, the state demands that you pay taxes; it does not merely permit an agency to extract money from your paycheck. In fact, in demanding that you pay taxes the state directs you annually to report your earnings. To take another example, the state can demand that you appear in a court of law on an appointed day; it does not merely withhold permission for you to stay at home on that day. It can *summon* you to court. Further still, the state can command you to don a uniform, take up a weapon, put your life in extreme danger, and even kill others; it does not merely grant you permission to do so. That is, states do not only grant and withhold permission. They do more than tell you what you *may* do; they also *tell you what you must do.*

Political authority, then, is a far more extensive kind of authority than permission authority.

Still, political authority is like permission authority in at least one respect. Like permission authority, political authority issues *moral oughts*. That is, when the state summons you to appear in a court of law, you are *morally required* to show up on the appointed day. Similarly, when a police officer commands you to pull your car to the side of the road, you are morally required to do so. In either case, to defy the state is to make oneself liable to various forms of state-sanctioned punishment. After all, states can also fine, penalize, imprison, and in other ways punish those who do not comply with their rules and directives. Consequently, to disregard or defy the state is to do something risky and perhaps irrational. However, it is also to do something *wrong*.

It should be noted that just as authority as such is different from power, political authority is different from what can be called *political power*. Political power is the capacity of the state to gain your compliance. The police officer's handcuffs, Taser, firearms, pepper spray, riot gear, and other weapons, along with the social standing to deploy them, are sites of political power, as are the state's prisons, jails, asylums, and detention centers. These are all rather impressive manifestations of the state's power to compel people to act according to its wishes. Not only can states punish, imprison, and in some places even kill people who refuse to comply, they can gain compliance by means of the *threat* they credibly pose to those who might resist. The mere fact that the state has the ability to exercise such expansive controlling power is *itself* a kind of power. But, again, power is crucially different from authority. And the state claims more than mere power.

What the state claims when it claims to have authority is the *moral right* to issue directives and commands and the *moral capacity* to impose moral requirements on citizens by means of its directives and commands. That is, if a state indeed has the authority it claims, when one of its police officers commands you to freeze you are thereby morally required to freeze; the moral requirement to freeze results *simply* from the fact that the relevant agent of the state has issued the command. That you do not want to freeze, or even that you know that the police officer has mistaken you for a fleeing bank robber, is irrelevant. When the officer commands you to freeze, you must freeze, and it would be morally wrong for you not to freeze. That's the distinctive nature of political authority.

We can better capture this feature of political authority by saying that it involves the moral ability to require *obedience*. Obedience is different from mere compliance in that when one obeys an order, one takes the fact that the order has been issued to be *sufficient* for being required to act as the order demands. When a police officer commands you to freeze, you may deem it to be in your best interest to freeze, because if you do not freeze the officer will arrest you. Or perhaps you decide to freeze when commanded to do so simply because you like to freeze every once in a while, and the officer's command provides a nice occasion for you to engage in an activity that you happen to enjoy. In either of these cases, when the officer commands you to freeze and you do in fact freeze, you have at least *complied* with his command. But obedience involves something in addition to compliance. To *obey* the officer is to take his command to be *all by itself* sufficient for freezing. A clear case of obedience, then, would be one in which you have no desire to freeze, and believe you could neglect to freeze and escape arrest, but nonetheless freeze when commanded. In such a case, you freeze *simply because of* the command. That you have been commanded to freeze gives you *sufficient* reason to do so, a reason strong enough to compel you to freeze regardless of other considerations that might apply. We might say then, that, in cases of obedience, one *submits* to another's will; one allows another's will to *preempt* one's own. The officer's will for you to freeze, as expressed in his command, morally *overrides* your own judgment about how you should act. Consequently, when the state claims to have political authority, it claims that (with the exception of some very special circumstances) when it commands you to do something you *therefore* are morally required to do that thing, even if you *correctly believe that the state is wrong*.

Although it might make us uncomfortable to admit it, obedience is a widespread phenomenon. We often act as others direct us simply because they have given the directive; in a wide range of contexts, we are prone simply to follow orders, to do as we are told. Advertisers bank on this tendency, which is why television commercials are composed mostly of commands. A quick survey of the commercials shown during mid-afternoon television is revealing: a sports-apparel company commands, "Just do it"; a soft-drink company orders, "Obey your thirst"; pitchmen selling a product that grows hair urges, "Act now"; and (my personal favorite) a company that sells an addictive nicotine product commands, "Take back your freedom."

Yet political authority involves more than the simple issuing of orders and the tendency on the part of citizens to act as those in authority command. Again, the state claims not only the *power* to make you comply, but also claims to hold the *right* to your obedience. In other words, it claims the *moral entitlement* to your submission. And, furthermore, the state claims that because it is morally entitled to your obedience, it is also entitled to *punish* your disobedience, and to *threaten* you with punishment in order to secure your obedience. Additionally, the state claims that it has the right to *force* you into compliance; it may *coerce* you to bend your will to its commands.

This provides a flavor of the distinctive character of political authority. Given what has been said, it is already apparent that political authority is deeply puzzling, perhaps even patently problematic. Yet, before moving forward to consider its puzzling and potentially problematic character, we should add one further aspect of the state's claim to political authority. States claim not only to have political authority, but to have a *monopoly* on this distinctive kind of authority. Your state claims an *exclusive* right to your obedience and a correspondingly exclusive right to coerce you. Consider a contrast with a run-of-the-mill social association. Imagine that you have joined a book club. The club has distinctive rules regarding how its meetings are to be conducted, the ways in which the various responsibilities are to be distributed, how collective decisions are to be made, and so on. Compliance with the rules is a condition of maintaining your membership in the club. If you routinely break the rules, you may be ejected from the club. Of course, the club is *not* permitted to impose more severe sanctions on rule-breakers than relatively mild ones, including ejection. And note, too, that that membership in the book club is entered into voluntarily; you may terminate your membership any time you choose. Moreover, if you grow to dislike the club's rules, you are at liberty to start your own book club with rules more to your liking.

Things are markedly different with states. When you break a law, you may be punished, perhaps severely; you cannot simply disassociate from your state and go on your merry way. If you are convicted of a serious crime, you will be imprisoned, perhaps for the rest of your life. Depending on the crime and the laws of your state, you may even be executed. And you cannot simply decide to create your own state. In short, when the state claims political authority, it claims an *exclusive* entitlement to certain *extensive* forms of power; it claims to be morally entitled to do things to you that *no other person or social entity* is permitted to do. In effect, the state can *force* you to be a member, *restrict* your exit from its jurisdiction, and prevent you from forming or joining another state. Indeed, the state claims not only a monopoly on the right to certain forms of power, it additionally claims that you have a *particular* set of duties to your state and no other. This is why, for example, you can commit an act of *treason* only against the state in which you are a citizen. Importantly, we seem generally to accept the idea that in virtue of its political authority the state is permitted to do things that no person or other institution is allowed to do. We tend to *accept* the state's claim to extensive, exclusive, and particular political authority over us.

The extent, exclusivity, and particularity of the political authority that the state claims for itself corresponds with the fact that special expressions and symbols of the state's authority are so pervasive. The state not only gives orders, forces compliance, and punishes offenders; it also establishes holidays devoted to celebrating its existence. It orchestrates commemorations, parades, parties, and other public events for itself. It issues special honors, statuses, medals, titles, and uniforms to those it deems worthy. It commissions works of art, including musical compositions, which extol the state's splendor. It builds monuments, buildings, and statues to itself. In its public schools, student-aged citizens are compelled to pledge allegiance to the state; at sporting events, we are called upon to sing collectively in praise of the state. And, furthermore, we acknowledge a distinctive moral virtue associated with manifesting the appropriate degree of loyalty and devotion toward one's state. We call it *patriotism*.

We have established that states claim to have political authority. We now have noted in addition that the state puts an enormous amount of effort into *convincing us* that it has, in addition to its vast power, political authority, and it goes to great lengths to foster within us the *acknowledgment* of that authority. In fact, we tend to *approve* of acts performed by the state that in any other case would count as megalomaniacal or otherwise deeply problematic. Just imagine what you would think of a neighbor who built statues to himself, produced special uniforms to be worn by those he deemed loyal, and organized parades celebrating his birth. Now imagine what you would think of a neighbor who claimed a moral right to your obedience!

A final point is in order before we move on. Just as political authority is that distinctive form of authority that states claim, states are those political entities that claim to be politically authoritative. But, of course, although every state claims to have political authority over its citizens or residents, not every state in fact has this authority. Some states are shams; they rule over their people without any moral right to do so. When a sham state issues a command to its people, it at best gives them a prudential reason to comply; roughly, "Do as we say, or else!" A sham state's commands are really only threats; they do not carry any *moral* force, and such states have no moral entitlement to obedience. In fact, we tend to think that in the case of certain kinds of sham state, such as especially brutal dictatorships, there is a moral requirement on the people to resist or even revolt. So, again, political authority is different from political power; a state that gains widespread compliance among its population nonetheless might not be politically authoritative. And the power of a politically authoritative state may prove insufficient to overcome a coup or invasion.

Hence we should distinguish those existing states that indeed have the political authority they claim from those that merely claim political authority but in fact have only power. One common way to mark this distinction is to distinguish between *de facto* and *de jure* authority. All states claim *de jure* authority, the moral entitlement to obedience. But some states have merely *de facto* authority: They have the power to compel compliance, but have no moral entitlement to be obeyed. States have *de jure* authority when they in fact have the moral entitlement to obedience. It is important to emphasize that just as a state can wield a degree of power sufficient to compel compliance but nonetheless lack *de jure* authority, so too could there be a state that lacks the power to compel compliance but nonetheless is entitled to obedience. Simplifying a bit, *de facto* authority is mere political power, and *de jure* authority is the moral entitlement to obedience. Our concern, of course, is with *de jure* authority, which is what we have been calling political authority. Our question is, does any state have *de jure* authority? Or, alternatively, are there any states that are in fact politically authoritative?

4.2 The Puzzle of Political Authority

Given what has been said thus far, it is clear that political authority is puzzling. A few key questions instantly arise. What accounts for the state's *de jure* political authority? How did it acquire it? How it is possible for an institution such as a state to *create* moral requirements in individuals, simply by issuing directives and commands? How could obedience be morally required? What are the limits to a state's *de jure* authority? Are there no conditions under which one is morally permitted to disobey the state? Must we obey the state even when it issues *unjust* commands? Does political authority leave room for various forms of popular dissent and protest, such as civil disobedience?

We cannot take up all of these questions here. But notice that many of these questions derive their intuitive bite from the background presumptions characteristic of a liberal political order. That is, authority strikes us as puzzling precisely because we are accustomed to viewing ourselves and our shared political world in the particular way that was outlined in Chapter 2. To repeat, we see ourselves as free and equal autonomous citizens, and on this basis we take it that the state exists to serve us; we therefore believe that the state *owes* us a justification for its existence, and its authority is contingent on the success of that justification. Thus we can pose the puzzle of political authority in a very general way: How could political authority be justified to free and equal autonomous citizens?

To feel the force of the puzzle, consider that where there is political authority there is someone who or something that has the moral entitlement to your obedience. Those in authority get to tell the rest of us what we must do. And, again, under normal circumstances, the political authority's commands morally preempt our own judgments about how we should act. Political authority, that is, involves a distinction between those who give orders and those who must obey, those who are in charge and those who must follow the orders.

Notice that we readily accept that there is a relation of authority among parents and children. When the parent commands her child to sit down or be quiet, she creates the moral requirement for the child to do as she has said. And we readily accept that parental authority is both extensive and exclusive (though, of course, not entirely without constraints). However, parental authority is fundamentally different from political authority in that parents and their children are not equals; the parent–child relation is intrinsically hierarchical. Yet from our liberal political perspective, citizens are equals, and the state is not a parent to its citizens. Yet political authority seems to be intrinsically hierarchical. How could authority be justified to free and equal persons?

Consider again the philosophical anarchist position that we encountered in Chapter 2. The anarchist's view is that there is no *de jure* authority; there is only *de facto* authority, and perhaps the widespread *belief* in the political authority of states. Much of the intuitive force of anarchism derives simply from the thought that, as authority is inconsistent with liberty and equality, there could be no justification of political authority among free and equal moral persons. Let us call the anti-anarchist view *statism*; it is the view that *de jure* authority is at least possible. Anarchism seems to have the upper hand precisely because statism looks so implausible. Is the anarchist correct?

4.2.1 Consent and Contract

So, how could authority be justified to free equals? One answer seems obvious: The state's authority derives from the consent of its citizens. The state commands, and we are required to obey, because we *agreed* to that arrangement. Consider the closely related phenomenon of promise-keeping. Imagine that, on Monday, I promised to take you out for dinner on Friday at a restaurant of your choice. Friday comes and as it turns out I'm not in the mood for eating out. Nonetheless, the fact that I made the promise on Monday means that I have an obligation to take you to dinner on Friday. We might say that in making the promise on Monday, I bound my future self's will; I made it the case that my future self would be required to take you out to dinner, even if by the time Friday comes I would rather stay at home. Next, imagine that Friday comes and although I'm happy to take you out to dinner, you choose an Italian restaurant whereas I'd much rather eat at a Greek restaurant. As I promised on Monday to take you to the restaurant *you choose*, I have again bound my will to yours; that you have chosen the Italian restaurant means that I am obliged to eat there with you. In both cases, my promise to you was a kind of agreement I made on Monday with my future self to eat with you, where you choose, on Friday night. In promising, I agreed to an arrangement whereby I would do as you choose; I made it the case that I must submit to your will. In promising, I in effect conferred upon you a kind of authority; in this case, I gave you authority with respect to my Friday-evening meal plans. This is to be sure a pretty low-level kind of authority. But it nonetheless is a case in which I have consented to an arrangement whereby my will would be subordinated to yours. We might even say that this is simply *what promising is*, at least in its garden-variety instances.

Of course, promising is a complex phenomenon. It is not difficult to imagine cases where an individual is morally justified in breaking a promise, and, in any case, every promise comes with implicit boundaries and limitations. My promise to take you to dinner on Friday tacitly comes with an understanding that you'll select a restaurant that's relatively local (rather than in another country, for example) and not exorbitantly expensive. There are similarly implicit conditions under which the promise becomes null. For example, my promise to take you to dinner on Friday evening does not persist in the case in which on Friday afternoon an emergency calls me to the bedside of a dying close relative. And there is a range of circumstances for which I can rightfully expect to be excused from satisfying my obligation. For example, if I wake on Friday with a severe case of food poisoning, I can justifiably expect you to "take a rain check" on our dinner together. And if I have an exceedingly stressful day at work on Friday, I might reasonably expect you to agree that we should reschedule dinner for another evening. The important thing to keep in mind, though, is that, except under circumstances of extreme emergency, it would be *wrong* for me to simply *not show up* for our dinner; even in the cases where I am justified in breaking the promise, I typically need for you explicitly to *release* me from the obligation.

There are many ways in which promising is similar to entering into a contract. Consider a simple case in which we agree that if you clean my office on Saturday I'll pay you fifty dollars. We might say that this contract is a kind of mutual promise. I promise to give you fifty dollars provided you clean my office on Saturday afternoon, and you promise to clean my office on Saturday afternoon provided that I will pay you fifty dollars for doing so. Each party agrees to provide something to the other on the condition that the other provides something as well. We often think of contractual relations as strictly legal, and some contracts are; but for the most part contracts specify *moral* (as well as legal) obligations. By agreeing to our contract, you incur a moral obligation to clean my office, just as I incur the obligation to pay you fifty dollars for cleaning it. If either of us fails, we may be subject to legal sanction, but we would also be *morally blameworthy* for failing to deliver on the deal we struck. In any case, in agreeing to our contract, you agree to devote your Saturday afternoon to serving my purposes (within limits, of course). Similarly, in agreeing to our contract, I agree to transfer some of my resources (fifty dollars) to you. If Saturday comes, and you find that you'd rather watch television than clean my office, you nonetheless are obliged to clean my office. And if Saturday comes and I find I'd rather spend my fifty dollars on new books, I still must pay you fifty dollars for cleaning my office. That is, our contract *constrains* our wills; we are each morally required to act as we agreed to act, regardless of how we might prefer to act on Saturday.

Now, as with promising, there is a much longer story to be told about the moral force of contracts. Our aims at present do not allow us to examine these complexities. We note instead that the thought that the political authority of the state derives from some contract or deal has been popular throughout the history of political philosophy. Indeed, the *social contract* theories of Thomas Hobbes, John Locke, Jean-Jacques Rousseau, and Immanuel Kant remain central to the field. And that is with good reason, too. Surely we are at home with the idea that one can place *oneself* under the authority of another while retaining one's status as a free and equal person. If this familiar authority-generating phenomenon can be extended to the state and its claim to political authority, we would have a solid answer to the philosophical anarchist and, more importantly, assurance that a *de jure* authoritative state is at least possible. Moreover, the general form of this model of agreement seems intuitive: in the social contract, citizens agree together to each give up a measure of freedom and equality to the state in exchange for the protection and stability that the state can provide.

It's an admittedly powerful thought; however, the social contract account of political authority is beset with difficulties. To begin, notice that in the simple case above of a contract whereby you would clean my office for fifty dollars, we overlooked several crucial details that must be presupposed if that agreement is in fact to be morally binding. First, we tend to think that contracts bind only when they are entered into freely. A contract agreed to by a person who is under duress, threatened, vulnerable, or profoundly ignorant regarding what he is agreeing to is not binding, nor does a contract bind if one party is relatively powerless to reject the terms offered by the other party. When the thief sticks a gun to your head and says, "Your money or your life!" he is *not* proposing a contractual agreement; nor is a ship captain who threatens to throw you overboard in the middle of the sea unless you clean his office. Similarly, children cannot be party to binding agreements, and neither can those who are severely cognitively impaired or compromised. To put these conditions positively, in order to bind, the parties to a contract must be free to decline the agreement—there must be a viable *alternative* to accepting the terms offered. In addition, they must be relatively equal in bargaining power, and they must be able to know to what they're agreeing. We might say also that, in order to be binding, a contract must include terms establishing some process by which grievances, disputes, and complaints amongst the parties could be addressed; there must be, at least, a formal *exit*, a way to *dissolve, invalidate,* or *revise* the contract.

The difficulty should now be obvious. Does any of the above hold of your relation with your state? Did you at any point agree to its terms? Were you ever even asked? Were you ever in a position to negotiate, from a position of relatively equal power, with your state over the terms of your agreement? Was there ever a viable option of *exit* from your agreement? Was there an alternative to accepting your state's authority? The answer to all of these questions is *no*. There was no point at which you negotiated a contract with your fellow citizens to form your state; no act of will on your part conferred political authority to your state, so it seems that you have incurred no obligation to obey its commands.

Perhaps not all is lost for the contract view. Some social contractarians agree that there was no point in the past that a grand contractual bargain was struck resulting in a state with political authority. Moreover, they readily concede that the actual histories of existing states tend to be blood-soaked tales of ruthless and brutal conquest. The social-contract theory, they say, is not meant to be an account of the *founding* of any particular state; it is instead an account of your existing state's political authority. The thought driving the social-contract theory, then, is that you are obliged to obey your state because you *in some sense* have consented to be ruled by, and under the authority of, your state.

Now you must ask, in what sense have you consented to be subject to your state's authority? Some say that you have consented to your state's authority simply by *living* within its territory. As John Locke put it, the state has authority over you because by living within your state's territory you indeed have given your consent to its rule; your consent is, as Locke argues, *tacit*. Surely Locke cannot be right about this. One cannot consent to an arrangement without knowing that one is doing so. That is, it seems as if consent must have some kind of *intentionality* condition such that one cannot consent unknowingly or by accident. Think again of the comparison with promising. Even if we could make sense of the idea of an *unintended* promise, we would not recognize it as binding. Tacit consent is no consent at all.

Others attracted to social contractarianism hold that the state's authority derives from the fact that *were* you to have been offered the chance to strike a deal to confer political authority on your state, it would have been rational for you to have agreed. This view, which is known as the *hypothetical consent interpretation* of the social contract, holds that if it *would have been* rational for you to agree to your state's terms had you been asked, then, from the moral point of view, things are as they would be had you in fact agreed. In other words, according to the hypothetical consent interpretation, the state has political authority if it would have been rational for you to agree to its terms had you been asked. This view looks like an improvement on the tacit-consent view in that it does not involve the claim that one can unknowingly give consent. But it still looks like a feeble argument in that it is difficult to see why a *hypothetical* agreement should have any binding force under non-hypothetical conditions. Consider an analogous case: Suppose I take fifty dollars out of your wallet. Shortly thereafter, you discover this fact and accuse me of theft. In response to the accusation, I contend that I in fact am *entitled* to the fifty dollars on the grounds that I cleaned your office, and *had you been asked* to pay me fifty dollars for the work, it would have been rational for you to agree to do so. What would you make of that kind of defense of my surreptitiously reaching into your wallet and removing fifty of your dollars? To again recall the comparison with promising, a hypothetical promise is not a special kind of promise; similarly, hypothetical consent simply is not a kind of consent. We are looking to justify political authority by appealing to our agreement to place ourselves under the rule of our state; we make no advance in that endeavor by arguing that it would have been rational to agree had we been asked.

4.2.2 Consequentialism

Perhaps the contract theory has unnecessarily complicated the matter? The thought driving social contractarianism seems to be that a moral obligation to obey the state can arise among free and equal persons only by way of their consent or agreement. This suggests a more general principle according to which positive moral obligations to others typically cannot simply befall us, but in some way must be *incurred by* us. Of course, there are certain moral obligations that simply accrue to us; these are generally known as "negative duties," such as the duty not to harm others or infringe on their rights, and so on. There might also be duties associated with emergency circumstances that can simply befall us, such as the duty to rescue a drowning child (provided we're able to swim), and the duty of bystanders to provide assistance to the victims of a car accident. There may even be related duties to give some portion of one's income to charitable or humanitarian causes and such. But it seems that the contractarian is committed to the thought that the duty to obey one's state's commands cannot simply befall us; if there is such a duty, it must derive from some act of our will.

Consequentialist accounts of political authority deny this fundamental contractarian principle. According to the consequentialist, all that is required for there to be a duty to obey is for it to be true that recognizing the general duty of citizens to obey their states produces better consequences than the anarchist alternative. In short, the consequentialist argues that the state's *de jure* authority derives from the fact that a world without politically authoritative states would be a moral disaster.

The consequentialist view has the virtue of posing the question of political authority in *comparative* terms. According to the consequentialist, when we are asking for a justification of political authority, we are in part asking for a comparative assessment of the following kind: Which is better, a social world where people recognize a duty to obey their state, or one in which they do not? Indeed, an intuitive response to philosophical anarchism often implicitly takes this form. Upon hearing the anarchist's critique of political authority, people almost instantly ask about the feasibility and desirability of the alternative. As odd as the very idea of political authority may sound to those who conceive of themselves as free and equal persons, the philosophical-anarchist alternative of a social world without politically authoritative states sounds even stranger. And that is the nub of the consequentialist argument. There is such a thing as *de jure* authority and thus citizens have a duty to obey politically authoritative states, even though such a duty marks a significant loss of freedom and equality simply because the alternative is far worse.

This argument looks promising, and it seems to have common sense on its side. But there are reasons to think that consequentialist justifications of political authority cannot succeed. First, note that the consequentialist view rests the case for political authority on an empirical claim, namely that recognizing political authority has better consequences than rejecting it. Of course, the burden is on the consequentialist to specify with precision the consequences she has in mind; *in what way* are we better off if we accept the duty to obey one's state? Are we happier? Safer? Less vulnerable? Better able to pursue our personal ideal of the good life? Yet even assuming that this question could be answered satisfactorily, there is still the empirical issue of whether the consequentialist's claim that we are better off accepting political authority is true. When making comparative assessments, it is important to think carefully about the options being compared. To be sure, there is good reason to think that a world in which everyone rejected the very idea of political authority would be very different from our own, and there would be many respects in which such a world would involve distinctive risks, threats, and harms. But now consider some of the things that states do: They go to war, they invade, they incarcerate, they spy, they intimidate, they assassinate, they confiscate, they lie, they indoctrinate, they enslave, they oppress, they execute, and they torture. And they do all of these things on a large and systematic scale. It is important to notice that in drawing up this short list of state activities, I did not restrict myself to the actions of dictatorial or "rogue" states; these activities are common among even the *morally best* existing states. To be sure, there are many things that states do that are good: They educate, they protect, they stabilize, and they create conditions under which people can live relatively happy lives. Of course it is not clear that a world without the recognition of political authority *couldn't* include institutions that provide these goods. So how can the conequentialist be so confident that anarchism would be worse?

There is a second problem with consequentialism. Arguably it misconstrues the nature of political authority from the start. Recall that we said above that political authority is the moral entitlement to obedience, and obedience involves a kind of *submission* of one's own judgment. When one obeys a police officer's command, one takes the fact that the command has been issued to be *sufficient* for requiring that one act as commanded. Anything short of this is not really obedience, but merely *compliance* with the officer's command. Given that the consequentialist argues that recognizing political authority brings about comparatively good consequences, it looks as if the consequentialist is offering a defense not of political authority and the corresponding duty to obey, but of something less weighty, such as a duty to *comply*. Indeed, we might say that the consequentialist cannot really defend the duty to *obey* at all, but only a duty to *comply* so long as compliance is the best instrument for achieving the best consequences. In the end, then, it seems as if the consequentialist cannot accommodate the state's claim to *exclusive* and *particular* authority over its citizens; on the consequentialist analysis, one's duties toward one's own state are no different from a tourist's duties toward the state she is visiting: compliance with the laws is the best policy. But that's not obedience.

4.2.3 Fair Play

The prospects for social contractarian and consequentialist justifications of political authority look dim. So let us consider a different kind of view that incorporates elements of the views we have already examined. Here the idea is not that the state's authority derives from a bargain we struck with others; the thought, rather, is that the state's authority derives from a more basic moral duty we each owe to our fellow citizens, namely the duty to do our part in sustaining a social and political order. Think of it by way of an analogy: Imagine that you find yourself among a community of persons who volunteer their time, effort, and labor to the maintenance of some collective good or resource, such as a community garden. You very much enjoy the garden, yet you resolutely decline to contribute in any way to its maintenance. Wouldn't those contributing to the garden be right to morally complain about your nonparticipation? Wouldn't they be right to regard you as a freeloader? And wouldn't there be some force to their moral argument that in using and enjoying the collective resource you incur a moral obligation to contribute something to the enterprise of maintaining it? It seems so.

The fair-play account then asks us to regard society as a kind of collective enterprise that, due to its large scale, requires there to be a politically authoritative state. As others pitch in to contribute the maintenance of society—in part by obeying the state's commands—we, too, must do our fair share. Our duty to obey follows from our duty to not freeload on others' sacrifices and efforts. In this way, we owe obedience to the state because we owe a kind of reciprocity to our fellow citizens. We have a duty to obey because disobedience would be *unfair* to our fellow citizens who, through their obedience, are each doing their part to sustain the social order.

One feature of the fair-play account that is worth mentioning is that it rests on the premise that society is a cooperative venture among individuals for mutual benefit. This presumption helps it to capture the common intuition that only a constitutional and democratic state can be politically authoritative; dictatorships and oligarchies fail to be authoritative because the social systems they support cannot plausibly be seen as a cooperative enterprise among individuals. That is, central to the fair-play account is the idea that society is something we do *together*; and it proposes a conception of political authority according to which the duty to obey follows from our responsibilities to our fellow citizens.

Accordingly, the fair-play view seems to have distinctive advantages over the others we have considered. Yet, as you may have expected, there are difficulties confronting the fair-play account. One such difficulty concerns the extent to which it makes sense to describe existing large-scale societies as cooperative enterprises for mutual benefit. Large-scale societies are quite different from community gardens. And even relatively well-ordered modern democratic states are highly stratified such that there are severe disparities between individuals' contributions to the social order and the benefits they receive. The anti-freeloading thought driving the community garden case depends upon the assumption that the benefits of the garden and the burdens of maintaining it are more or less evenly distributed; individuals pitch in roughly equal amounts of time and effort, and everyone gets roughly the same benefit. Imagine someone in the community who, for some reason or other, is unable to benefit from the garden and so does not contribute to it; wouldn't it be unreasonable to call her a freeloader? Hence it looks as if the fair-play account draws its force from an implausible analogy between small-scale collective projects and large-scale social systems.

Consider a further difficulty. Let us concede the premise that the social order is a collective enterprise much like a community garden. We can also grant that freeloading on the time and effort of others by enjoying the garden but contributing nothing to its maintenance is morally wrong; one indeed has the moral duty to contribute to the shared endeavor. In the garden case, then, freeloaders are morally blameworthy, and perhaps the contributing members of the community would be justified in restricting the freeloader's access to the garden. One might wonder, though, whether the contributors indeed have an *entitlement* to the non-contributor's time and effort. In any case, it is clear that the contributors may *not* force the non-contributors to put in their fair share. Recall, though, that in claiming political authority the state claims not only a moral entitlement to be obeyed, but the right to employ coercive force to secure compliance and punish noncompliance. Again, it seems as if the analogy that forms the core of the fair-play view does not succeed.

4.3 The Dangers of Authority

We have been looking for a justification of *de jure* authority. We have found that some of the more popular and intuitive views confront serious difficulties. But maybe this provides an occasion for a different kind of statist thought. One might think that *maybe* the anarchist is ultimately correct to say that there is no such thing as *de jure* authority, but *maybe* there's a way to defend political authority that we have not yet considered. What, really, is the anarchist alternative? Is it any more plausible than the statist view that political authority is possible? In any case, the dismantling of the view that states are politically authoritative looks extremely risky. So maybe the right conclusion to draw is that we ought to accept that at least *some* constitutional democratic states are indeed politically authoritative until we see a *decisive proof* in favor of the anarchist's position.

In philosophical circles, the kind of thought sketched above is sometimes called *burden shifting*. It's easy to see why. The idea sketched above is that the anarchist should not be permitted to win the argument by default. That we as yet lack a decisive justification for political authority does not mean that political authority is definitely unjustified. Moreover, as the anarchist alternative seems so risky and undeveloped, we should reject anarchism if at all possible. The statist thought, then, is that we ought to accept the idea that political authority is possible until decisively shown otherwise. The argumentative burden is hence shifted to the anarchist.

Burden shifting maneuvers in philosophy are notoriously slippery. This is because it is so difficult to tell how to objectively assess them. Who really has the burden of proof in the dispute between the anarchist and the statist? Where should our philosophical defaults lie? These are complicated issues in philosophical methodology. But here the statist gives the anarchist a pretty clear reply. Note that the claim in part is that there are significant risks inherent in the project of rejecting the claim that *de jure* authority is possible; that is, the statist holds that, regardless of its truth, anarchism is dangerous. The anarchist replies that the acceptance of authority is risky as well. And here the anarchist has pretty compelling evidence.

4.3.1 The Milgram Experiment

The experiments conducted in 1961 by the Yale psychologist Stanley Milgram are by now well known, so a brisk sketch should suffice. Milgram's experiment involves three participants, who we may call The Experimenter, The Teacher, and The Learner. The Experimenter wears a white lab coat and presents himself to The Teacher and The Learner as a scientific expert researching human memory. The Teacher is a voluntary participant who has responded to an advertisement calling for volunteers to take part in an experiment about human memory; he also believes that The Learner is also a voluntary participant who responded to the same advertisement. What The Teacher does not know is that The Experimenter and The Learner are confederates. The Experimenter tells The Teacher it is his job to teach The Learner a list of word associations. The Teacher sits before a large board of electric switches, and is instructed by The Experimenter to read a long list of word pairs, giving The Learner a chance to learn the associations. Then The Experimenter instructs The Teacher to serially read only the first of each word pair, and The Learner, who appears to be attached by electric wires to the switchboard, is instructed to reply with the corresponding word in the pair. The Experimenter tells The Teacher that when The Learner makes a mistake, The Teacher is to verbally correct him by stating the correct word pair, and also administer an electric shock to The Learner. Moreover, he is told that with each error The Teacher is to increase incrementally the severity of the shock to The Learner. What The Teacher does not know is that The Learner is an actor who in fact is not connected to the switchboard and does not receive any shocks. Moreover, The Teacher does not know that the experiment is not really about human memory at all; it is, rather, an investigation into The Teacher's willingness to obey a perceived authority (The Experimenter). How much pain would The Teacher be willing to cause The Learner, simply because The Teacher was instructed to do so?

Milgram's results, confirmed by multiple experiments and with several variations on the design, are startling. As the experiment progresses, the shocks that The Teacher believes himself to be administering to The Learner become increasingly severe, and quickly The Learner (who, again, unbeknownst to The Teacher, is an actor who is in fact not suffering any shocks) begins to complain about the pain. Then The Learner begins to protest more overtly by screaming (apparently) in pain, verbally expressing that he is uncomfortable with the severity of the shocks, and even verbally claiming that he no longer consents to being part of the experiment. Eventually, The Learner simply groans and weeps in response to the shocks. Whenever The Teacher expresses to The Experimenter hesitation in continuing, The Experimenter commands The Teacher to continue by saying things like, "You must continue," "The experiment demands that you continue," and "You have no choice but to go on." What Milgram found is that most people in the role of The Teacher—over 60 percent in most runs of the experiment—are willing to continue shocking a stranger, with severe levels of voltage and against the stranger's expressed will, simply because The Experimenter, a presumed authority, issued the command to continue.

The further details of the Milgram Experiment are fascinating, and anyone who is not familiar with them is urged to investigate further. But the relevant upshot of the experiment should be clear. In the experiment, those in the role of The Teacher proved to be all too willing to subordinate their own will and judgment to the presumed authority of The Experimenter, in effect relinquishing their own sense of right and wrong. Simply because a presumed authority prodded them to do so, most of those in the role of The Teacher inflicted what they believed to be permanently damaging electric shocks on an innocent stranger who had actively withheld his consent to such treatment. We may put the point slightly differently: Conceiving of ourselves as under an authority dissolves our sense of our own moral responsibility. That's surely dangerous.

4.3.2 The Stanford Prison Experiment

A 1971 experiment conducted by Stanford psychologist Philip Zimbardo is similarly disconcerting. In an effort to study the sources and nature of abuse within prisons among inmates and guards, a makeshift prison was constructed on Stanford's campus, and twenty-four male volunteers were randomly assigned roles of "prisoner" and "prison guard." The prisoners were placed in cells, outfitted in uncomfortable uniforms, and their proper names were exchanged with impersonal numbers. Guards were told that although they were not to inflict physical harm on the prisoners, they were to invoke in them a sense of dehumanization and powerlessness.

That the experiment, which was supposed to continue for two weeks, was shut down after only six days is revealing. What happened is that, as those in the role of guard became more acclimated to exercising power over the helpless prisoners, they became increasingly hostile, abusive, and even sadistic in their treatment of the prisoners. Even mild forms of resistance among the prisoners were met with excessive degrees of retaliation from the guards. And some prisoners similarly internalized their assigned role, seemingly freely adopting attitudes and adjusting their behavior in accordance with their assigned identity as a convicted criminal.

Again, for those readers who are not familiar with them already, the details of the Stanford Prison Experiment are worth exploring in greater detail. The lesson to draw at present is that, just as believing oneself to be under another's authority can morally distort our sense of responsibility, believing oneself to be in authority can have a similar effect. Again, when we take ourselves to have authority over others, we take ourselves not only to have the *power* to force others to do as we command; we take ourselves to be *morally entitled* to their obedience. Accordingly, even the slightest resistance or hesitation on the part of those over whom we take ourselves to have authority can appear to us as extreme moral offense and disrespect, a challenge to our authority that must be forcefully responded to. In short, conceiving ourselves to have authority over others looks morally dangerous.

4.4 Conclusion

Robert Nozick claims that "the fundamental question" in political philosophy is "Why not have anarchy?" We have seen in this chapter why one might agree with Nozick. We have been exploring the concept of political authority and the difficulties it occasions, especially in light of our background liberal commitments to individual freedom and equality. In the previous section in particular, we considered a statist argument that concedes to the anarchist that, at present, we lack a decisive justification for political authority, but nonetheless prescribes our continued belief in political authority on the grounds that the widespread rejection of political authority is morally and socially dangerous. We presented that argument as a kind of burden-shifting maneuver that aims to put the anarchist on the defensive; according to the argument we were considering, statism is the default and should be given up only once the anarchist has provided a decisive defense of anarchism. We then considered the anarchist's response. As dangerous as anarchism may sound, there are significant dangers that come with the statist position as well. Widespread but misplaced belief in political authority is at the core of the most morally egregious collective human behavior known to history. Given the morally sketchy track record of states, why accept statism as the philosophical default?

Here, the only response may be to return to the first two chapters of this book. For better or worse, we begin doing political philosophy from where we are, with the social world that we have inherited. As it turns out, we have inherited a world of states that claim political authority. And, as puzzling as political authority might be, we have some compelling general views concerning the kinds of states that *merely* claim political authority, but in fact only exercise force. The world's dictators certainly have no entitlement to the obedience of the people living under their rule. Tyrannies are not politically authoritative, no matter how effective their exercises of power might be. Now, surely there is a moral difference worth marking between dictatorships and liberal constitutional democracies that the anarchist cannot adequately accommodate. Remember, on the anarchist view, there is no *de jure* authority, and so the only difference between a democracy and a tyranny is a difference of *degree*. The anarchist can say that tyrannies are morally *far worse* than democracies, but nonetheless must hold that from the point of view of political authority both kinds of regime are morally on par. To the anarchist, all states are, at base, tyrannical.

To my ear at least, this sounds implausible. A social order where the state does indeed claim political authority, but also sees itself as serving its citizens rather than simply ruling over them, strikes me as different *in kind* from the social order secured by the tyrant. This seems even more clearly the case where the state also recognizes a public constitution and the rule of law that strictly constrain the state's authority and specify a range of individual rights against the state. And, again, a state that in addition is *democratic*—with regular elections, full suffrage, a free press, and broad civic participation—looks even more obviously different in moral kind from tyranny. Finally, a state that additionally embraces a commitment to *social justice*, including the protection of human rights and the fair distribution of the social and material benefits of social participation, looks far superior to any state that does not. In short, a state devoted to liberal democracy looks morally *distinctive* rather than merely a less awful form of tyranny.

The anarchist has a simple reply to these thoughts. She will respond that no matter how rosy a picture one paints of liberal democracy, an argument for its political authority is still lacking. Indeed, the anarchist could go further by saying that she of course supports liberal democracy; she may affirm that if there are going to be states at all, they should all be liberal democracies. But to this, she will add that, nevertheless, no state has *de jure* authority, no person or institution has the moral entitlement to be obeyed.

We seem to have reached an impasse between the anarchist and the liberal-democratic statist. Let me very quickly try to sketch a statist position that could accommodate some of the anarchist concerns. Thus far, we have proceeded as if *de jure* authority is the moral entitlement to obedience. To repeat, if we assume that a police officer has political authority, then when he commands you to freeze, you thereby have the moral obligation to freeze, even if you know the officer has mistaken you for a fleeing bank robber. That is, as we have said above, the commands of a political authority are *sufficient* to impose on you a moral obligation to act as directed. From this emerges the idea that political authority always involves some kind of *submission* of the will and judgment of those subject to it. And that idea is what rightly raises the hackles of the anarchist. The anarchist insists that submission must be inconsistent with equality and freedom.

Maybe the statist view can be weakened so that political authority does not involve that degree of submission. Let us consider what we might call *deflated authority*. A state has *deflated authority* when its commands are sufficient to provide only what we might call a *pro tanto moral reason* to act as directed. A reason is *pro tanto* if it is generally weighty, but can be overridden and never fully decisive all by itself. On this view, a police officer's command to freeze provides a morally weighty but nonetheless *pro tanto* reason to freeze, a reason whose force depends ultimately upon the presence of certain background conditions. That is, on this deflated view, we say that the officer's command suffices to give me a weighty moral reason to freeze, but whether I am thereby *obligated* to freeze is still a matter that depends upon other matters that I must judge for myself. To be more specific, the deflated-authority view holds that in a reasonably well-functioning liberal democracy, and under the broad range of normal circumstances, the *default* is set on obedience, but only slightly so. When circumstances deviate from normal—when democratic conditions are compromised or when the commands issued are suspicious—individual moral judgment is required. Obedience, hence, is never full-scale submission; we must obey a command only when we have judged that the requisite background conditions have been satisfied.

The moral entitlement to your obedience, then, is something that the state must continually earn. Political authority is *conditional*.

What, then, would be the conditions under which a presumptive authority's command would in fact be *de jure* authoritative? A full analysis of this question will have to wait for another occasion. But we might say that a liberal and constitutional democratic political order that stably secures a basic baseline of justice for its citizens and does not commit human-rights abuses is politically authoritative in the deflated sense—there is at least a *pro tanto* obligation to obey its commands within the range of normal circumstances. The justification for accepting that some states are politically authoritative in this deflated sense could rest upon a kind of fair-play argument: We have inherited a world of states that claim political authority. Political authority is surely a puzzling phenomenon, but it is not clear whether there is a workable alternative. So we should be *suspicious* of claims to authority, especially when these are made under unfamiliar or non-normal circumstances, or reflect a claim to further *expansion* of political authority. We should also reject the idea that the state's political authority could be *established* once and for all; it is, again, something that is *contingent* on the state proving a capable moral agent. Also, we should recognize that only a liberal and constitutional democratic order, in which there are public processes in place for popular control and oversight of the state's activities, could be politically authoritative. This, in turn, leads us to recognize that the political authority of the state depends upon our collective participation in the democratic processes of self-government. Our collective enterprise, then, consists in sustaining a politically authoritative social order.

For Further Reading

For an excellent survey of the philosophical issues, with a state-of-the-art bibliography, see Thomas Christiano's entry on authority in the online *Stanford Encyclopedia of Philosophy* (http://plato.stanford.edu/entries/authority/). Three essential and classic treatments of the issue of the authority of law are Plato's *Crito*, Henry David Thoreau's "Civil Disobedience," and Martin Luther King's "Letter from a Birmingham Jail." An excellent contemporary exploration of disobedience and protest can be found in Kimberley Brownlee's *Conscience and Conviction* (New York: Oxford University Press, 2012). In addition to the anarchist literature mentioned at the close of Chapter 1, interested readers should consult *Is There a Duty to Obey the Law?* by Christopher Heath Wellman and A. John Simmons (New York: Oxford University Press, 2005). Joseph Raz's edited collection *Authority* (New York: New York University Press, 1990) contains many important contemporary essays on the topic; see, especially, R. B. Friedman's "On the Concept of Authority in Political Philosophy," H. L. A. Hart's "Commands and Authoritative Legal Reasons," Thomas Nagel's "Moral Conflict and Political Legitimacy," and Raz's own "Authority and Justification." See also

Hannah Arendt's analysis in "What Is Authority?" (Chapter Three of her *Between Past and Future*, New York: Penguin Books, 1954). Stanley Milgram's *Obedience to Authority* (New York: Harper Torchbooks, 1974) describes the Milgram experiments and contains a sophisticated philosophical analysis of the morality of obedience. See also Philip Zimbardo's *The Lucifer Effect* (New York: Random House, 2007), which contains similarly fascinating thoughts about the dangers of obedience.

Current work on authority and the democratic state can be found in William Edmundson's *Three Anarchical Fallacies* (Cambridge: Cambridge University Press, 1998), Christopher Morris's *An Essay on the Modern State* (Cambridge: Cambridge University Press, 1998), and Thomas Christiano's "Justice and Disagreement at the Foundation of Political Authority" (in the journal *Ethics*, Volume 110, October 1999) and his "The Authority of Democracy" (in the *Journal of Political Philosophy*, Volume 12, 2004). See also George Klosko's *Political Obligation* (New York: Oxford University Press, 2002), Cynthia Stark's "Hypothetical Consent and Justification" (in the *Journal of Philosophy*, Volume 97, 2002), and Allen Buchanan's "Political Legitimacy and Democracy" (in the journal *Ethics*, Volume 112, July 2002). Michael Huemer's *The Problem of Political Authority* (London: Palgrave Macmillan, 2013) contains several concise and compelling arguments against political authority while also laying out a fascinating vision of anarchist society.

5 Justice

- Our Concept of Justice
- Conceptions of Justice
- Conclusion
- For Further Reading

5.1 Our Concept of Justice

The term "justice" pervades our political environment. We refer to our legal system as our "justice system." The US government features a "Department of Justice." We call the officers of the US Supreme Court "justices." At many colleges and universities there are departments of "criminal justice." In the Netherlands, there is an "International Court of Justice." When police officers catch a criminal, we say that the latter has been "brought to justice." These examples may suggest that justice is exclusively a legal term; however, we also speak of justice more broadly. In many Western religions, for example, justice is listed among the most important personal virtues. And in the Judeo-Christian tradition in particular, God is portrayed as striking a delicate balance between justice and mercy. Perhaps somewhat puzzlingly, we also speak of "cosmic" and "poetic" justice, where both seem to involve cases where an agent's own bad deeds facilitate his or her downfall. And it is not uncommon to hear it said of a performer, such as an actor or a soloist, that he failed to "do justice" to a difficult role or piece of music.

What seems to underlie these disparate deployments of the term "justice" is the idea of people getting their due, or getting their "just deserts," whether in the form of a deserved punishment or reward. We might say, then, that justice prevails when individuals get what they are due. Accordingly, *we* enact justice, both individually and collectively, when we give others what is their due. To be sure, there may be special cases in which we are permitted to give to another *more* of a reward than she strictly deserves; and there are special cases where we would be justified in giving her *less* of a punishment than what she deserves. Still, it would be difficult to fathom a case in which it would be permitted to give *less* of a reward or *more* of a punishment than what is deserved. Justice requires us to distribute harms or burdens, but not in excess of what is due. Still, when justice requires us to reward or benefit others, we may be strictly required only to not benefit them *less* than what is called for. There are cases in which justice may have to be balanced against other values, such as beneficence, mercy, generosity, and temperance. But one can admit this much without having to drastically amend our initial thought that justice is a matter of giving people what is their due.

It would be difficult to find anyone, philosopher or otherwise, who would strongly dispute this analysis of justice. This is a good indication that the above analysis is too simplistic. It might not be too far from the truth to say that part of what makes an idea philosophical is that there is some philosopher who stands ready to dispute it. Yet even simplistic analyses can provide a basis from which to begin forming philosophical ideas. The claim thus far is that justice prevails when people get what they are due. Hence, in order to think about justice, we must also think about what people deserve. One way to think about what people deserve is to think *expansively* about what makes a human being *worthy* of good (or bad) things. Another way to proceed is to think *constrainedly* about what people are owed. Unsurprisingly, the former approach treats justice as a very broad moral category, encompassing an entire conception of the good life for human beings. By contrast, the latter sees justice as primarily focused on how certain specific benefits and burdens are to be allotted. As it turns out, the expansive approach is common among philosophers writing outside of the liberal tradition within which we have been working, whereas the constrained view is common among liberal philosophers. But it is nonetheless important to explore the contrast between the two approaches.

5.1.1 Expansive and Constrained Approaches

The ancient Greek philosopher Plato devoted his magnum opus, *The Republic*, to the topic of justice. Central to that work is the abiding question *"How ought we to live?"* That's surely a deep and important question. But it also is broad. Notice the ambiguity in the pronoun "we." The question at once asks each individual how he or she should live, while also pressing the question to us collectively—how should *we* live (together)? Consider also the complexities surrounding the idea that we (individually and collectively) have a *life to be lived.* Our lives are of course multifaceted affairs, encompassing political, social, familial, personal, and even private aspects. The question "How ought we to live?" seemingly applies to all of these many dimensions. Accordingly, *The Republic* discusses a wide range of topics along the spectrum from the political to the personal and private—including government, law, money, war, education, religion, art, marriage, sex, and death—all in the service of examining the topic of justice.

Like many other philosophers throughout the history of the discipline, Plato adopts an expansive sense of justice. He takes justice to be the generic name for that which is good in human life. On his conception, the life of justice is the morally best life, almost by definition; the just man simply is the morally best man. *The Republic* is Plato's attempt to prove that the life of justice truly is the best kind of life; he aims in particular to defeat an opposing (and still popular) view according to which the really best life a man can live is one in which he enjoys the widespread *reputation* for being completely just, but in fact is ruthless, excessive, dishonest, and selfish.

As one should expect, Plato's views are philosophically sophisticated. He seems ultimately to have thought that justice is not simply the amalgam of all the other good things that a human life can manifest, but the *proper organization* or *harmony* of those goods within a human life. Consequently, he held that justice resides in the *structure* of the good man's soul. We need not get bogged down in the complications arising from Plato's use of the term 'soul'; suffice it to say that on Plato's view justice is the result of the *proper ordering* of a man's drives, ambitions, emotions, and rational faculties. To be slightly more precise, Plato held that a man is just when his inner life— his desires, emotions, ambitions, and beliefs—is ruled by reason. That is, the just man desires only what reason determines is desirable, he takes offense only at what reason declares offensive, and he pursues goals only when reason endorses them as worthy. The unjust man, by contrast, is one who is ruled by his non-rational elements, his desires and ambitions, regardless of their rationality. Accordingly, Plato likened injustice to internal civil war; it is the war of one's drives and desires against one's rationality. Hence Plato saw justice as the master, all-encompassing virtue. He held that, in justice, all of the other goods that a human life could manifest are unified and harmonized; a life that is just lacks nothing that could make it better. Consequently, an unjust life is necessarily morally incomplete, lacking, discordant, or defective in some fundamental respect.

It is this attention to the way in which various goods are organized that enables Plato to countenance a tight connection between our individual and collective lives. Plato argues that as justice in the individual consists in the proper ordering of his soul, the justice of a city consists in the proper ordering of its constituent parts, its social classes. More specifically, Plato argued that as the just man is one who is ruled by his rational faculties, the just city is one where the most rational citizens rule over the others. Hence *The Republic* famously endorses a highly stratified political order in which a small minority of wise philosophers rule as kings. *The Republic* is also renowned for its scathing criticisms of democracy, which Plato regards as the rule of the ignorant mob and thus fundamentally unjust.

Plato's suggestion that justice demands that philosophers rule as kings has been subjected to a great deal of criticism and ridicule over the years. So for now we will leave aside our likely reactions to Plato's positive political proposal (this will be discussed briefly later in this chapter, pp. 101–103). Instead, we should attend to one of the central philosophical underpinnings of Plato's view. Notice that Plato regards justice in the individual and justice in the city as *one and the same* thing. In fact, he seems to have thought that the just city is simply a larger manifestation of the justice in a single person. In Plato's view, the best man and the best city have the very same structure: reason rules all else. And in both cases, justice is the name for the culmination and unification of all of the other goods. We might say that, for Plato, justice provides the single and all-encompassing moral lens through which individual lives and political orders, among much else, are to be normatively evaluated.

The above provides only the slightest sketch of Plato's *Republic*, and so should not be regarded as anything beyond minimal. The main point in discussing Plato has been to give you a flavor of the expansive sense of justice that he employs. Again, this expansive approach to justice is to be contrasted with our contemporary approach, which tends to be far more constrained. To be sure, we too use the terms "just" and "unjust" to describe a variety of goods and bads. We speak of a "just man," a "just law," a "just cause," a "just war," and a "just society," among much else. And we even use the term in more extended senses than these, as is demonstrated by some of the examples with which this chapter began. But still our contemporary deployments of the concept of justice do not carry the copious scope of Plato's usage. We do not tend to speak of justice as the all-encompassing good of a human life; nor do we tend to think of justice as the master virtue or harmonizer of every other good. When we talk of a "just man," we typically ascribe to him the trait of fairness, impartiality, or evenhandedness in performing the duties of some assigned role; in calling him just, we do not mean to claim that his life is an overall or unmitigated moral success. Instead, we tend to think that justice is but one of the goods a human life can achieve. Hence we tend to think that a just man's life could nevertheless be defective in other moral respects; the just man might yet be unhappy, or stingy, or stubborn, or unkind, for example. To put the point in a different way, we tend to think that not *every* moral failing is an instance of injustice.

Moreover, unlike Plato, we tend not to think that the best person and the best society have the *very same property*. In fact, when morally assessing individuals, we employ normative concepts that are different from those we use when evaluating how things stand politically. When we morally assess an individual, we readily reach for normative concepts like kindness, honesty, courage, integrity, generosity, reliability, and the like. By contrast, we most naturally use the terms associated with justice when assessing political matters, such as laws, policies, official decrees, officials, governments, and states. That is, we primarily think of things like laws and political institutions as the items that can be just or unjust, and we tend to regard actions by governments or on behalf of states as manifesting justice and injustice. Consequently, as mentioned above, when we do call a *person* just, we are most often assessing her behavior within an assigned role, and frequently the role is one of social or political significance; she is just in virtue of her dutiful performance as a police officer, a judge, a citizen, a soldier, or a holder of political office.

A further contrast with Plato now comes into view. We tend to see a *fundamental* moral difference between individual lives and political systems. These are, in our contemporary view, two rather different subjects of moral evaluation. This is evident in the fact that there are some actions that we take to be permissible or even obligatory for individuals to enact that we nonetheless regard as morally impermissible for governments to perform. For an obvious example, consider cases of preferential treatment. When a government provides extra benefits or opportunities to some while denying them to others, we rightly criticize it as discrimination, bias, and perhaps oppression. Similarly, when a government official gives special beneficial treatment to her friends and family, we rightly criticize it as cronyism and nepotism. However, we also think that a parent who does *not* exhibit special regard for his own children and does not provide benefits distinctively for them is to be criticized for being uncaring, distant, and perhaps guilty of negligence. The same goes for spouses and friends; these are moral relations that *require* us to show partiality towards some and not others. The idea of an individual who nonetheless is fully impartial between her friends and strangers is barely intelligible; we would be inclined to say of such a person that she simply has no friends. Yet impartiality is precisely what is demanded of governments and those acting within official political roles.

Consider also that we tend to think that governments and states are permitted to act in ways that no individual person is allowed to act. For example, as we have discussed in earlier chapters, we generally believe that states can *punish* those who break its laws; furthermore, we allow that under certain conditions these punishments can be rather severe. We also hold that states can *force* citizens to do certain things, including fight in wars, pay taxes, and refrain from taking certain drugs, among much else. And we tend to think that states are permitted to hold people in jails and prisons, sometimes for life. These days, some even hold that, under special circumstances, governments are morally permitted to subject suspected terrorists to torture. We would *never* recognize in an individual the moral permission to do such things.

As a final contrast with Plato, notice that we find intuitive a distinction that Plato must find utterly alien, namely, the distinction between *what is good for a government to do* and *what a government is permitted to do*. We readily recognize that there are some *good* things that a government could do, but is not allowed to do. For example, suppose that our society would be morally far better were certain racist words never spoken. It seems obvious to us that the goodness of a society where those words are never uttered does not permit the government to criminalize the uttering of them. The question of what good things the state could bring about is distinct from that of what the state is *allowed* to do. Importantly, we tend to think that the latter is a question distinctively about *justice*. Although one might agree that a society where certain forms of racist speech were eradicated would be an overall good, one might still hold that no government is permitted to censure speech of that kind.

For someone who, like Plato, sees justice as the manifestation and harmonizing of all other goods, the very thought of there being goods that could be achieved only by injustice would sound incoherent. Yet to our modern ears, the thought sounds commonplace and obvious. Again, this is because we tend to hold a *constrained* view of justice. We are prone to think that justice is but one kind of good; more specifically, we see justice as a distinctively *political* good, and we see the evaluative terms *justice* and *injustice* to apply primarily to political matters. Fair enough. But we must ask, what kind of political good is justice?

5.1.2 Justice as the First Virtue

Plato saw justice as the master virtue governing the whole of individual and social life. Our competing, constrained, view is well captured by a slogan offered by the twentieth-century political philosopher John Rawls. Early in his magisterial book *A Theory of Justice*, Rawls claims that *justice is the first virtue of social institutions*. Slogans are often deceptively simple, so let's unpack this one.

The first thing to note about Rawls's slogan is that it further tightens the constrained view of justice. We said above that justice applies primarily to "political matters." That may be true, but it is a bit too vague. It simply prompts the question of which matters are the *political* ones. Rawls's slogan offers some assistance. It firmly identifies *social institutions* as the primary focus of justice. That is, it says that social institutions are the primary entities to which the evaluative terms "just" and "unjust" apply. Again, by contrast with Plato, the constrained view holds that the terms "justice" and "injustice" attach in the first instance to social institutions, rather than to souls and whole societies.

This institutional focus complements ideas developed in our first two chapters. Recall that we emphasized that the political world is an artifact of our own creation; even though we individually did not *found* the civic order within which we were born and presently live, we nonetheless sustain it. And within that order there are political institutions that shape and regulate our shared life. This shaping and regulating involves many kinds of action, but key among them are the establishment of rules and laws, defining institutional roles, identifying individual rights, liberties, and responsibilities, and, crucially, distributing the various benefits and burdens of social living. Again, as we have seen in previous chapters, these benefits and burdens are significant, and accordingly the regulation that is required in order for there to be a sustained and stable social order necessarily will involve *coercion*. Put otherwise, in order for there to be a social world of the kind with which we are familiar, there will have to be institutions that have the authority and power to force individuals to do things they otherwise might not do. To say that justice is primarily focused on social institutions is to say that when we are thinking about justice, we are thinking about the *proper* use of coercive force; we are thinking about what social institutions *are permitted to do* in the service of maintaining a stable social order.

Recall that in Chapter 4, on authority, we examined the problem of how relations of authority could exist among free and equal individuals. At the close of that discussion, it was proposed that a certain *deflated* conception of political authority could be justified. On this view, a liberal and constitutional democratic political order that stably secures a basic threshold of justice for its citizens and does not commit human rights abuses is politically authoritative. Let us suppose that this proposal succeeds. We can see now that even if relations of authority could be justified, there is an additional question regarding the *proper exercise* of coercive power on the part of the state. What are the proper limits of state power? For the sake of what ends may the state exercise its power? What are the things that the state is *required* to force people to do? What are the things that *no* state may (rightly) do? These are the questions that a theory of justice aims to answer.

Now let's identify what it means to say that justice is the *first virtue* of social institutions. The thought is twofold: First, the justice of a social institution is sufficient to render it morally acceptable, no matter what its other failings may be; second, injustice renders a social institution morally unacceptable no matter what other social or political goods it might realize. To say that justice is the *first* virtue of social institutions is not to say that it is the *master* virtue or the culmination of all other goods that social institutions may manifest; it is, rather, to say that justice is a necessary condition for the moral acceptability of a social institution. That is, without justice, a social institution must be regarded as morally unacceptable.

To get a better sense of the matter, imagine a society that realizes a number of important social goods—including, say, civil peace, stability, and efficiency—but nonetheless features powerful institutions that tightly control the speech and movement of its members; consequently, the society has no free press, and strictly forbids its people from traveling outside of the society. Or imagine another society that also realizes the social goods specified above, but has institutions that impose a dramatic class division according to which a small segment of the population lives in freedom and luxury while a large majority serves the few as slaves. These two societies are objectionable on a number of distinct grounds, but the one thing we are inclined to say about them both is that they are unacceptable simply due to the fact that their institutions are unjust. And we would want to go further to say that their injustice consists in the fact that the central institutions of the society fail to respect the freedom and equality of their members. This suffices to render the two societies morally unacceptable, despite the fact that peace, stability, and efficiency are undeniably good.

5.1.3 The Circumstances of Justice

We have said thus far that justice is the normative lens through which we evaluate social institutions. More specifically, we said that questions of justice are primarily questions concerning the proper exercise of the coercive power the social institutions wield. That justice concerns the exercise of coercive political power suggests that in a world without coercion there would be no questions of justice. This is quite right. On the constrained approach, questions of justice arise precisely because we find ourselves living under circumstances in which coercive institutions are necessary. Specifying some of these circumstances will be helpful as we move forward.

To begin, it seems clear that in a world where basic resources required for life and welfare—food, shelter, materials for clothing, and so on—were overly abundant and easily accessed by all, there would be no need for coercive institutions, and thus no need for justice. The same holds in a world where such resources were exceedingly scarce or inaccessible. Accordingly, what is sometimes called a "moderate" scarcity of resources is one of the circumstances of our world that makes justice necessary. Put otherwise, it is because of moderate scarcity that there needs to be a *distribution* of resources, and thus there need to be institutions that manage the distributing. Similarly, were all individuals fully altruistic and perfectly good, there would be no need for institutional coercion—we would all simply do right by each other, and no one would need to be forced to do anything. Finally, that there's room for reasoned disagreement among sincere persons of goodwill regarding the proper allocation and distribution of resources means that there needs to be a system of social institutions in place that can moderate such disagreements as well as enforce a scheme of distribution. Justice is the normative category we employ when evaluating the institutional distribution of resources.

In specifying these circumstances of justice, we are simply identifying those empirical conditions of our world that give rise to justice as a normative category. A world markedly different from our own—where there was no scarcity, perfect altruism, or complete unanimity, for instance—would recognize no such concept because there would be no need for it. This may seem an obvious point, but it assists us in noting that views about justice must adopt certain presuppositions in order to count as views *about justice*. For example, views that simply stipulate perfect altruism or full compliance with what morality demands may be pleasant to contemplate, but they are not views of justice. The same goes for views that begin by asserting an unlimited plentitude of resources or a systematic lack of neediness among persons; such views describe a world in which the concept of justice is wholly without purchase. Slightly more controversially, we could say that views that reject the very thought that resources need to be *distributed* rather than simply allotted by fortune and fate (sometimes called the "natural lottery") are not views about justice either. Of course, views like the ones we have just mentioned are often proposed as if they were views about justice; yet we can see that they reject one or more of the circumstances of justice and thus are not views about justice at all.

Now we can see more clearly that the concept of justice goes hand in hand with the idea of a social and political world with which this book began. Where there is a large-scale social world, there is need for political institutions like states. And where there are states, there will be coercive institutions charged with distributing the various benefits and burdens of shared social and political life. And where there are institutions that exercise coercive force with the aim of realizing and maintaining a certain social order, there will be a need for a conception of justice.

5.1.4 Justice and Equality

Thus far, we have said that justice prevails when the state, through its institutions, *properly* exercises its coercive power; injustice consists in the *improper* exercise of such power. So now we must ask what renders an exercise of the state's coercive power *proper*.

Again, philosophers throughout the history of the discipline have proposed a range of answers, many of which fall outside of the broadly liberal philosophical framework that we have been working within. For example, once again consider Plato. He apparently thought that society is just when it imposes a strict three-way class division between a ruling class, a warrior class, and a laboring class. An individual's placement in a class is largely determined by the class of his or her parents. Further, Plato envisioned each of these classes as having a distinct set of functions and responsibilities within the society; he also thought that these different functions give rise to correspondingly different entitlements. Thus *The Republic* outlines different social rules for each class and specifies the different systems of education appropriate for each. Plato even proposes strict social regulation of sex, marriage, family life, and child-rearing. Infanticide is proposed as a fitting method for maintaining each class's proper size. Ultimately, it could be said that Plato's just city encompasses three distinct sub-societies, each with its own distinctive way of life, its own privileges, and its own laws. Again, according to Plato, justice is the proper ordering of the society's three elements: the ruling class makes the rules, the warrior class enforces the rules and fights the wars, and the laboring class works and consumes.

Plato's vision of the just society will no doubt strike you as deeply flawed. In fact, you are likely to condemn Plato's proposal as a foolproof recipe for *injustice*. But why? What in it seems so objectionable? There are, to be sure, many defects worth discussing, not least of which is that Plato's ideal society is profoundly non-democratic. (We will discuss democracy in Chapter 6.) For now, it seems that a basic defect in Plato's vision is that it does not recognize the *equality* of its citizens. In fact, equality is denied in multiple ways. The citizens are organized from birth into distinct classes, and the classes themselves are subject to different laws. Moreover, different classes are educated and raised differently. They are thus unequal with respect to social entitlement and responsibility. Most obviously, the three-class system includes a distinct class of rulers, which means that the citizens are also unequal with respect to political standing and political power.

According to our contemporary sensibilities, these forms of inequality are blatantly inconsistent with justice. Going further, we can affirm that justice requires a kind of equality. We could even go further still and say that coercive political power is properly exercised only when that exercise is consistent with equality. To our ears, statements like these carry a kind of familiar and reassuring resonance. After all, the claim that there could be no justice where there is no equality could make for a stirring slogan. But equality is a multifaceted concept; thus, to affirm a close link between justice and equality is merely to utter a platitude until we specify what we mean by equality.

Sometimes when we speak of equality, we mean something like *equal treatment*, and by equal treatment we typically mean *sameness of treatment*. But it is obvious that there are many cases of distribution where sameness of treatment is not in line with what justice requires. Surely justice requires that criminals and their victims are treated differently; the former should be punished and the latter should be compensated. Similarly, with respect to cases involving achievement and effort, we would say that sameness of treatment is not what justice calls for. For example, the student who studies for the exam and answers every question correctly has earned an A, whereas the student who slacks off, does not study, and answers most questions incorrectly has not; they should get different grades. There are also cases in which distribution is supposed to track something like merit, and here sameness of treatment would also be unjust. The batter with the best batting average should get the award for best batter, and the student with the highest grade-point average should be named class valedictorian. To give everyone an award for best batting average or highest grade-point average would be a departure from justice (not to mention problematic on other grounds as well).

Some will point to considerations such as these as a way to oppose the thought that justice involves a kind of equality. But this conclusion is too hasty. The considerations above instead show that the kind of equality that justice calls for is *not* sameness of treatment, but equality in some other sense. What sense could this be?

Think again of Plato's conception of the just society. What we find objectionable about his proposal is not simply that people are treated differently, but rather that their differential treatment is based upon a system by which individuals at birth are assigned membership of one of three social classes that are hierarchically arranged. As was mentioned above, one's class membership determines how one will be raised and educated, which occupations one may pursue, whether one can marry and have children, whether one has any say in making laws and deciding social policy, and much else. Plato's view violates equality because it embraces a *social hierarchy* according to which some are granted special statuses, benefits, and entitlements that are denied to others, simply on the basis of birth.

We see, then, that equality can mean *anti-hierarchy*, the rejection of official *subordination*, or, positively, the demand for *sameness of status*. Equality in this sense requires the rejection of special social entitlements and privileges granted solely on the basis of such things as rank, title, lineage, caste, and station; equality opposes "second-class citizenship," natural subordination, birth privilege, and royalty. Equality in this sense is hence consistent with there being differences in treatment; it allows that some benefits should be differentially distributed according to merit, effort, achievement, and desert. Equality is opposed to the idea that there are some people who are entitled to special social benefits or privileges simply in virtue of their family lineage or their socioeconomic status, for example. Thus, equality in the relevant sense requires not equal treatment, but *treatment as an equal*, or what is sometimes called *equal concern* or *regard*.

With this more nuanced understanding of equality on the table, we can gain some traction on the question we posed at the beginning of this section. Recall that we had identified justice as the *proper* exercise of the coercive power of the state's institutions. This then prompted the question of what makes the exercise of this coercive power *proper*. We can now say that the exercise of the state's institutional coercive power is proper when it is consistent with treating each and every citizen *as an equal*. This means that exercises of coercive power based upon invidious distinctions between citizens or appeals to systems of social hierarchy and birth privilege are unjust. Similarly, this means that social systems rooted in the premise that some people are naturally subordinate to others are unjust. Expanding slightly, we could say that justice requires that all citizens are subject to the same set of rules; a minimal condition for the justice of a system of coercive social institutions is *equality under the law*.

Although this helps us to get some sense of what justice is, everything we have said thus far has been really only preliminary. The claim that justice prevails when social institutions exercise coercive power only in ways that are consistent with treating everyone as an equal is an important truth. However, it does not say very much. The next question is obvious: What does it mean for the state and its social institutions to treat all citizens as equals?

5.1.5 Moving Ahead

It should be mentioned at this point that the territory we are about to explore is arguably the most active region within contemporary political philosophy. This is largely due to the staggering impact made upon the field by John Rawls and his 1971 book *A Theory of Justice*. It is no exaggeration to say that to this day political philosophers working on justice (among other topics) must position their views in relation to Rawls's. This is understandable, as Rawls's work is, for an uncommonly broad range of reasons, pioneering. *A Theory of Justice* has stimulated dozens of research trajectories regarding justice within political philosophy and related disciplines such as political science, economics, sociology, and law. So agenda-setting is

Rawls's work that many readers who are already familiar with political philosophy are likely to find it odd that this chapter thus far has not endeavored to summarize Rawls's theory of justice. As I said in the Preface, our task is not that of summarizing the great books in the field, but rather of beginning to think our way through central philosophical questions. Hence we will not endeavor to sketch Rawls's theory of justice, nor canvass the highlights of the enormous subsequent literature it has provoked. Our task is to examine some of the more influential approaches to justice. We cannot hope to cover all of the ground here; in fact, in the remainder of the chapter we can hope only to scratch the surface.

5.2 Conceptions of Justice

Let's step back a moment to take stock. We begin from the social and political context within which we find ourselves: States and their institutions exist for the sake of establishing and maintaining a social order among free and equal persons. A common and stable social world brings with it immense benefits to its citizens, but it also creates significant burdens. Given certain facts of our world—what above were called the *circumstances of justice*—the state's task requires that coercive force be applied in *distributing* these benefits and burdens. Justice prevails when that force is exercised and applied in ways that manifest equal regard for all citizens.

It should come as no surprise that philosophers who otherwise agree about this general picture of the social and political world, and much else that we have discussed thus far, nonetheless adopt different conceptions of justice. These different conceptions reflect different views regarding what it means for the state and its institutions to show "equal regard for all citizens." In this section, we will canvass a few of the leading ways to interpret this complex idea.

We can begin, however, by noting that two deeply intuitive but fundamentally opposed thoughts about "equal regard" present themselves almost immediately. One thought holds that, in order to show equal regard for all of its citizens, a state must see to it that they have *equal shares* of some good or resource. This approach would entail that whenever one encounters an *inequality* of shares of the relevant good or resource among a population of citizens, there is good reason to suspect that there is injustice. In other words, part of showing equal regard for all citizens is guaranteeing them an equal share of some to-be-specified good or resource. According to another intuitive thought, equal regard does not require that citizens be guaranteed an equal share of any good or resource; this approach holds instead that the government shows equal regard when it distributes the specified goods and resources according to processes that count each citizen as an equal. This approach could view even drastic disparities in shares of goods and resources as consistent with justice, provided that the unequal allocation is the product of a distributive process that recognizes the equality of each citizen.

Broadly speaking, we may call the first of these two intuitive interpretations of "equal regard" *egalitarianism*; the second may be referred to as *non-egalitarianism*. But it is important to remember that *both* views are committed to the idea that justice requires a kind of equal regard; that is, egalitarian and non-egalitarian views are both committed to equality. Egalitarians and non-egalitarians differ about what equal regard requires.

5.2.1 Minimalism

Let's begin with a formidable non-egalitarian view that we will call *minimalism*. On any of the views that we will be considering in the remainder of this chapter, justice is fundamentally concerned with discerning the proper constraints on the state's coercive force. Consequently, one intuitive way to think about justice is to see the state itself as among the primary sources of injustice. States are, after all, enormously powerful and, as history shows clearly, they are capable of the most horrendous injustices. It is all too easy to think of real-world cases in which modern states have oppressed, subjugated, enslaved, deprived, marginalized, exploited, tyrannized, denigrated, tortured, tormented, and slaughtered their own citizens. We also know very well that it is extremely difficult to *stop* states from committing such horrors once they have begun to do so. And, again, recent history provides ample instances in which the most brutal tyrannizing emerges out of the state's professed concern to further the general good of its people.

Moved by such considerations, the minimalist understands justice as primarily a matter of *constraining* the state's power over the individuals that compose its citizenry. To put the idea succinctly, the minimalist holds that the state shows its citizens equal regard, and thus satisfies the demands of justice, when it recognizes their equal right to maximal liberty. Importantly, this recognition requires not only that the state not interfere with individual liberty, the state must also provide to all equal and adequate protection of that liberty. This means that, according to the minimalist, justice demands that each individual citizen is provided the greatest sphere of noninterference and free choice possible, given that all citizens are entitled to an equally broad sphere. Citizens hence are left to their own devices to form and maintain social relations, to pursue whatever it is that they individually deem worthy (within the requirement to respect the rights of others), to expend their resources as they see fit (again within the same broad requirement to respect the rights of others), and to voluntarily enter into contracts and other agreements with each other.

Thus the just society is one where the state acts only when action is necessary in order to maintain a social order in which each can exercise his or her liberty. Given that the state's role is highly circumscribed, it is relatively easy to describe. The state must protect individual rights, and this requires that it support a police force and maintain a military sufficient to fight potential invaders, both internal and external. Free citizens must also be able to hold property and to buy and sell their resources; this means that they must be able to enter into agreements and legally binding contracts. Thus, the state must establish and maintain legal and economic institutions, including markets of various kinds, which facilitate orderly trading and enforce property rights. As the exercise of liberty can occasion conflicts among individuals, the state must also provide for the impartial resolution of its citizens' disputes; consequently, it must provide for a functional system of law, conflict resolution, enforcement, retribution, and punishment.

Hardly anyone would dispute that the above are central functions of the state. The distinctive claim of the minimalist is that the state may do *no more* than these core tasks; it must instead get out of the way and allow for individuals to exercise their liberty however they see fit. The state, on this view, thus is seen as something like a combination of a night watchman and an umpire. Both images invoke the idea of an *impartial observer* who intervenes not for the sake of promoting some predetermined result, but only when rules have been broken and disputes have arisen that threaten the standing social order. Importantly, the minimalist is concerned to constrain what the state may do even to further the common good; she sees state action designed to promote goods beyond the equal protection of individual liberty as an instance of unjustified coercion. According to the minimalist, common goods that are not strictly necessary for protecting individual liberty—public parks, museums, and municipal waste disposal, and the like—are to be provided, if at all, through the voluntary contributions of those individuals who see value in such things. Hence the term *minimalism* seems apt.

The key to minimalism is the claim that equal regard—and hence justice—is essentially *backward-looking*; that is, minimalism is centrally the claim that the justice of a given distribution of social benefits and burdens across a population of citizens is primarily a matter of *how* that particular distribution came to be. For any such distribution, if it was produced by a series of voluntary exchanges among free individuals that involved no rights violations, then that distribution is consistent with justice. This is to say that when determining whether a given distribution of social benefits and burdens is just, one need not look to see *who has what*; one needs only to find out whether anyone's share was *wrongly acquired*. To put the point in a different way, the minimalist holds that there could be even dramatically *unequal* distributions of some good that are nonetheless not cases of *unequal regard*.

A simplistic example will help to bring this core aspect of minimalism into clearer focus. Imagine that Alex and Betty have divided a cake amongst themselves. For simplicity's sake, let us stipulate that prior to dividing it, neither had any greater claim to *ownership* of the cake than the other; they were, we shall presume, equally entitled to the cake. Now, after dividing it, Alex has only 10 percent of the cake, and Betty has the remaining 90 percent. Is this distribution consistent with justice? To be sure, we can say that the distribution is clearly *unequal*; Alex and Betty obviously do not have equal shares of the cake. But the minimalist will claim that the question of the justice of the 10/90 split in shares of cake is simply the question of how it came to be. The minimalist will ask, did Betty *threaten* Alex into accepting a much smaller share? Did she *steal* any cake from Alex? Did Betty *deceive* or *manipulate* Alex in order to get a much greater share for herself? More generally, the minimalist will ask whether the 10/90 distribution is the product of any *wrongdoing* on Betty's part. If the answer is *no*, the minimalist is prepared to call the distribution of cake just.

It is easy to see how such a drastically unequal allotment of a common resource could be fully consistent with justice as the minimalist conceives of it. Consider: Perhaps Alex simply does not particularly like cake, and so is happy to have only a little. Or maybe Alex agreed to allow Betty to have an extra 40 percent of the whole cake in exchange for something that he values more than cake, like forty dollars of Betty's money. Perhaps they agreed to draw straws, and Alex drew short. Or it could be that Betty finds cake especially pleasing, and Alex knows this and enjoys furthering Betty's happiness. In all such cases, the resulting 10/90 distribution of shares of cake is the product of Alex's and Betty's *voluntary* choices; the minimalist contends that *any* allotment of cake amongst Alex and Betty that is produced in this way is a just distribution of cake.

Now, we might stipulate further that Betty is a particularly unpleasant person and there is some sense in which Alex *deserves* more cake than Betty. Or we could stipulate that Alex is much *hungrier* than Betty, and so might *want*, perhaps even *need*, more than 10 percent of the cake. We could similarly imagine that Alex is a connoisseur of desserts, and so would get far more *enjoyment* out of the cake than Betty would. But, on the minimalist view, none of these stipulations suffice to render the 10/90 split *unjust*. Again, that the distribution was produced in a way that involved no infringement on individual liberty is sufficient for the justice of the result.

As I said above, this is a highly simplified example. And it is worth repeating that the version of minimalism we are discussing presently is a view of justice for social institutions, not private exchanges of cake between individuals like Alex and Betty. Yet the point of the example of Alex and Betty should be clear. Minimalism holds that equal regard, and thus justice, requires that the state coerce *only when* coercion is necessary in order to preserve and protect the social and political conditions under which individuals can exercise their equal liberty. Once these conditions are secured by the state, what individuals choose, how they elect to exercise their liberty, and what distributions of benefits and burdens result are simply not matters of justice. To be sure, the minimalist can say that certain distributions of social benefits and burdens may be bad, lamentable, sad, tragic, inefficient, irrational, unfortunate, or even morally wrong without thereby being unjust. To repeat, according to the minimalist, justice concerns *only* the question of how a distribution came to be.

There is, of course, much more to say about minimalism, and current political philosophy is alive with debates between minimalists and their critics, as well as among proponents of competing versions of minimalism. Before moving forward, we note briefly two of the central problems with minimalism.

The first problem we will consider emerges from the fact that minimalism presupposes a strictly negative conception of liberty. The minimalist holds that justice is a matter of protecting individual liberty, and liberty is fundamentally the absence of state interference with individual choice and action. Now recall the many difficulties that emerge from this simple-sounding conception of individual liberty. As was argued in Chapter 3, it is easy to imagine cases in which individuals are acting precisely as they choose, yet— perhaps due to ignorance, shortsightedness, foolishness, incompetence, or irrationality—nonetheless seem unfree. With slight modification, this point could be applied easily to the minimalist conception of justice. Think again of our cake example. Alex agrees to a 10/90 split, giving Betty a far greater share of the common resource. The minimalist holds that this allocation is fully compatible with justice, provided that it was arrived at without violating Alex's liberty. We can stipulate that in arriving at the 10/90 split, Betty did not in any way coerce Alex. Still, it could be the case that Alex entered the negotiations over the cake at a severe disadvantage relative to Betty. Perhaps Alex is ignorant of the kind of good that a cake is, or maybe he has an irrational fear of bargaining, or maybe Betty is an expert bargainer and Alex is wholly inexperienced, or perhaps Alex has been subjected for a long time to prevailing societal pressures that have convinced him that he is Betty's inferior, and thus less deserving than she. It is not difficult to imagine other ways in which Alex could be free from Betty's coercion, but nonetheless *vulnerable* to being taken advantage of by Betty. Thus the absence of coercion of Alex by Betty does not suffice to render Alex her equal; accordingly, the resulting allocation of cake might fail to manifest equal regard in any viable sense.

We can capture this point more generally by saying that, just as the negative conception of liberty seems insufficiently sensitive to the ways that *internal* obstacles can defeat an individual's liberty, the minimalist conception of justice is insufficiently sensitive to the ways in which individuals can be unequal and yet equally protected from unjustified coercion. Consequently, the minimalist's view of the just state as one that properly serves as a night watchman and an umpire looks inadequate for showing equal regard to all citizens.

Consider next a different kind of difficulty. In describing the cake example, we introduced a simplifying assumption that Alex and Betty had an equal entitlement to the cake that they were to distribute amongst themselves. Upon reflection, one might find this a strange stipulation. Cakes do not suddenly pop into existence, but must be *made* with ingredients and *baked* by someone; in any case, it is not clear precisely what one means by simply stipulating that Alex and Betty have an equal entitlement to the cake. In real-world contexts, of course, background information of the kind we have simplified away usually matters quite a great deal in determining who is entitled to what. Yet even allowing the simplifications, there still is a question of how minimalism can account for the *initial* acquisition of a good (like a cake).

Think of it this way: Minimalism offers an account of justice that seems most at home in contexts where property is to be *transferred* from one individual to another. It says, again, that the allocation resulting from the transfer of any good is consistent with justice if the process by which it was transferred involves no violations of anyone's liberty. The minimalist view hence presupposes a social world in which individuals already have entitlements to certain goods and resources, just as Betty and Alex are presumed to have *equal ownership* of the cake. But how did this ownership arise in the first place? The goods of the world did not suddenly pop into existence, already tagged with labels specifying who owns what. In fact, when you think about it, ownership as such—the very idea of property—is a surprisingly puzzling phenomenon. And it becomes all the more puzzling on the minimalist picture once we notice that our current system of ownership, including the rules by which we allocate and transfer property, is rooted in a series of actions that undeniably involved the violation of others' liberty. To be frank, many of the goods we purchase today are produced in a system of global slave labor, much of our country's infrastructure and industry were built under conditions of extreme domestic inequality and domestic slavery, and the geographical territory we occupy was initially acquired by means of genocide, violent conquest, and theft. No current allocation of any good, and no present-day transfer of property, is likely to be untainted by prior extreme violations of individual liberty. Minimalism thus might entail that the contemporary world of states is irremediably unjust. Perhaps it also entails the more striking conclusion that no one currently owns anything.

5.2.2 Utilitarianism

Utilitarianism is a moral theory that offers a unified account of the whole of morality, encompassing not only the morality of individual actions but also the morality of social and political institutions, including states; consequently, utilitarianism offers a distinctive conception of justice. To get a sense of this view of justice, one must first examine utilitarianism as a moral theory. So this is where we will begin.

Utilitarianism is a complex doctrine, and it comes in a staggering number of varieties. However, utilitarianism's core can be summarized as follows. Utilitarianism holds that whatever is to be morally evaluated—be it an action, a policy, a law, an institution, or what have you—is good just in the degree to which that thing produces pleasure and diminishes pain. For clarity's sake, let us stipulate that *happiness* is simply the presence of pleasure and the absence of pain; one is happy, then, to the degree that one experiences pleasure and is pain-free. Adding a little more detail, we can say that utilitarianism identifies happiness as the ultimate and intrinsic value, and then defines the goodness of an action (policy, law, institution) with the *quantity* of happiness it produces. The utilitarian then reasons that, as happiness is intrinsically good *no matter who is experiencing it*, the morally *best* action (policy, law, institution) is that one which *maximizes* happiness for the population of individuals it affects. Hence the fundamental utilitarian moral principle, the "Greatest Happiness Principle," says that we ought to act so as to produce the greatest happiness (defined as pleasure and the absence of pain) for the greatest number of people (all counted equally).

This is still far too coarse an account of utilitarian moral theory, but it suffices for our present purpose of examining the utilitarian conception of justice. To again put matters very roughly, utilitarianism holds that a social institution is just insofar as its actions and policies maximize overall pleasure (and minimize overall pain) in the population of its citizens. One can see from this that utilitarianism employs a distinctive interpretation of equal regard. In holding that pleasure is good (and pain is bad) no matter who happens to be experiencing it, it treats each individual's happiness—more precisely, each person's interest in experiencing pleasure and avoiding pain—as equally important, giving equal weight to each individual's interests in the calculation of the overall goodness of a law, policy, or institution. That is, the utilitarian holds that justice requires that social institutions maximize the overall quantity of happiness for society, taken as a whole; accordingly, justice forbids acts that further happiness for only a small portion of the population while creating greater quantities of displeasure overall. Equal regard, then, is construed as an *equal weighting of* interests, which in turn is construed as *equality of input* into the calculation of overall happiness.

Though utilitarianism is committed to this sense of the equality of all citizens, it must be emphasized that it is a *maximization* doctrine; again, the Greatest Happiness Principle says that happiness must be *maximized*. And this is why utilitarianism is a non-egalitarian view. According to the utilitarian, justice does not *require* that anything be made equal or distributed in equal shares; rather, it demands that something (namely, overall happiness) be *maximized*. To be sure, there may be cases in which overall happiness is maximized when some good or benefit is distributed in equal shares to all citizens; utilitarians need not deny that. But in such cases, what makes the distribution *just* is not the equality of the shares, but the fact that this alloca-tion is what maximizes overall happiness. Hence, according to the utilitarian, there may also be cases in which overall happiness is maximized when there is great *inequality* in the allocation of some good; in such cases, justice would require an unequal distribution.

Notice next an important contrast between utilitarianism and minimalism. Like the minimalist, the utilitarian cares about the processes by which any given allocation of social goods and burdens is produced; manifesting equal regard is primarily a matter of the procedure by which things are dis-tributed. In this way, both views have a backward-looking view of equal regard. However, unlike the minimalist, this is not *all* that the utilitarian must consider. After all, the Greatest Happiness Principle calls for equal input into a process that is aimed at the *production* of happiness, and thus is fundamentally forward-looking. In assessing a social institution and the way it allocates social benefits and burdens, the utilitarian must make sure that everyone's interests were considered equally, and then look to see whether the resulting allocation in fact maximizes overall happiness.

It should come as no surprise that utilitarianism has been highly influential as a conception of justice. After all, its central message looks immanently plausible: Justice prevails when social institutions maximize happiness (and minimize unhappiness) across the population they serve. In addition to this undeniably reasonable moral doctrine, utilitarianism also embodies an attractive empirical stance. It says that the justice of a social institution or policy is simply a matter of the quantity of happiness it produces in the population it affects; consequently, utilitarianism makes justice wholly an empirical matter, something that can be investigated, even *measured*, by social scientific methods. In a way, utilitarianism makes doing justice easy. One needs only to develop a way of measuring individual levels of happiness, then one can compare the happiness produced by any given policy to alternative policy options, and the one that produces the most happiness is the one justice requires. As one might have already recognized, a good deal of current work in the discipline of Economics tends to presuppose some form of utilitarianism.

This is not to say that utilitarianism is without flaws. Indeed, it should be mentioned that utilitarianism is not only greatly influential, it is also hotly debated, and the philosophical back-and-forth between advocates and opponents of utilitarianism has been ongoing and vigorous for well over a century. Consequently, the catalogue of objections to utilitarianism (and utilitarian replies) is vast and continually expanding. Here we can only canvass a tiny segment of this territory by considering two difficulties confronting utilitarian conceptions of justice.

The first difficulty concerns individual liberty and entitlements, and one could imagine it being pressed by the minimalist (though others could press it as well). The utilitarian alleges that the maximization of overall happiness is *sufficient* for the justice of an institution, law, or policy. But one could conceive of circumstances in which the violation of some particular individual's liberty might be conducive to that end. To employ a common example, imagine that Carl is a fervent proponent of an extremely unpopular political viewpoint, and his fervor leads him to express this view widely and often. Imagine that Carl's view is so unpopular, and his fellow proponents are so small in number and so deeply reviled in society, that the suppression of the expression of his view would in fact serve to increase dramatically the overall level of happiness in the society. Here is a case in which not only *may* the state suppress Carl's expression, it arguably *must* suppress it as a matter of justice. Or take another case in which you are in possession of a cake. Imagine further that your acquisition of the cake involved no wrongdoing whatsoever; you baked the cake from scratch using ingredients you produced yourself, and so on. Finally, let's say that you enjoy cake quite a lot. But now imagine that your neighbor Fred *really* enjoys cake; in fact, we can say that Fred derives an *extraordinary* amount of happiness from eating cakes. In fact, let's stipulate that Fred is unique in that he derives more happiness from eating cake than a few hundred cake-loving people derive from eating cake. We might say that, at least when it comes to cake, Fred is incredibly efficient at transferring a resource into happiness. The happiness that Fred would derive from eating your cake would far outweigh the displeasure you would experience from having your cake taken away from you. On the utilitarian conception of justice, then, it seems as if justice might require that Fred be given your cake.

The cases involving Carl and Fred may sound far-fetched. And perhaps they are. But the critical point being raised against the utilitarian conception of justice is a *conceptual* one; that the circumstances described in the cases are unlikely to actually arise does not change the fact that it seems as if the utilitarian must claim that justice requires something that intuitively seems *unjust*. In the case of Carl, it seems as if the utilitarian cannot recognize the importance of individual liberty; in the case involving Fred, it seems as if the utilitarian cannot duly acknowledge your *entitlement* to, or *ownership* of, the cake. In both cases, it looks as if utilitarianism fails to capture something essential to justice.

Consider a second kind of problem. The utilitarian regards justice strictly as a matter of the *overall* happiness that prevails in a society; to repeat, social institutions are just insofar as they effectively maximize the quantity of happiness in society. This means that the *sum* of happiness in a society is what matters for justice. This means that utilitarianism is insensitive to the *distribution* of happiness across the members of a population. So imagine again that there is a cake to be distributed among a group of people, and Fred, who is especially efficient at turning cake into happiness, is one of the members of the group. Let us next stipulate that of all the ways to allocate the cake, there are two that maximize happiness in the group; that is, there are two different ways of allocating the cake that produce the *same* and *highest* quantity of happiness. One such allocation gives Fred all of the cake, and none to the others. The second allocation is more equitable, giving everyone a roughly equal share. As we have stipulated that both allocations produce the same overall amount of happiness, the utilitarian must be indifferent between them; they are, according to the utilitarian, morally equivalent. Yet it is likely to strike you as intuitive that the more equitable distribution is *in some sense* morally better than the alternative, despite the fact that they produce identical quantities of happiness. In other words, we tend to think that the more equitable distribution has a moral value that is independent of the sum of happiness in the group. Seeing *all* value as simply a quantity of happiness, the utilitarian explicitly rejects this thought.

One way of encapsulating this second problem has been proposed by John Rawls, who claims that utilitarianism cannot take seriously the distinctness of individuals. In considering only the overall sum of happiness, the utilitarian is blind to the moral difference between making Fred extremely happy (and doing nothing for the others) and making everyone a little bit happier.

In other words, the individual drops out of the utilitarian picture, except as a site of some quantity of happiness. From this, we can see that the utilitarian retains part of what we found objectionable in Plato's view. Recall that we took issue with the very idea that justice in the city should be taken to be the *very same thing* as justice within the individual. We worried that any view that analogized individual morality and social justice risked losing sight of the special moral status of individuals. It looks as if utilitarianism is vulnerable in precisely this way.

5.2.3 Egalitarianism

We have considered two formidable non-egalitarian conceptions of justice. Let us turn now to egalitarianism. Recall that egalitarianism is the view that the state and its institutions show equal regard for all citizens when certain goods are distributed in equal shares among them. Put in a different way, egalitarianism is the view that the state treats us as equals when it ensures that each of us has an equal share of whatever it is that the state must allocate justly. We can say then that, unlike minimalism, which takes equal regard to be a backward-looking requirement, the egalitarian sees it as requiring equality as an *outcome*. Egalitarianism is in that sense like utilitarianism in being a *forward-looking* doctrine. However, an obvious contrast with utilitarianism is that egalitarianism does not require that some quantity of good be *maximized*, but instead that something must be distributed in shares that are *equal*.

Many of the complexities of egalitarianism are evident in the little that has been said. For example, as egalitarianism is committed to an equal distribution of shares of some good (or goods), there immediately arises the question of what good (or goods) is to be distributed. We can say, then, that in calling for equal shares, the egalitarian must answer the question "Equality of *what*?" That is, egalitarians must propose a view of what might be called the *currency* of justice, the item or entity that is to be equalized.

At first glance, there are two obvious candidates for the currency of egalitarian justice (though later in this chapter we will consider a third, pp. 120–123): welfare and resources. Of course, social institutions are *capable* only of distributing certain kinds of goods, including political rights and entitlements, and beneficial material instruments such as money, property, and wealth; they cannot *directly* distribute welfare. But this fact does not settle the "Equality of what?" question against welfare. Some have reasoned, intuitively, that the *value* of goods like rights and money lies in their contribution to individual well-being, or welfare. *Welfarist* egalitarians, then, hold that welfare is the currency of justice; they claim that justice requires that social institutions ensure that individuals enjoy equal shares of welfare. Inequality of welfare is thus unjust, and social institutions must distribute goods like rights and money so that each individual enjoys an equal level of welfare. Crucially, welfarism adopts from utilitarianism a hedonist conception of value; the welfarist seeks to equalize individual levels of some psychological state such as "satisfaction" or "pleasure."

The appeal of welfarism is clear. The view embraces many of the virtues of utilitarianism, while its egalitarian commitment seems to avoid some of utilitarianism's problems. But a serious difficulty is lurking. If welfarism claims that justice requires that social institutions ensure an equal level of welfare for all citizens, then those individuals who are hard to satisfy will be, *ipso facto*, entitled to greater shares of society's resources. To employ a vivid example common in the professional literature, consider Helen, an individual whose level of welfare plummets unless she is able to drink very expensive champagne at every meal. Welfarism holds that Helen is entitled to the supply of expensive champagne necessary to keep her level of welfare equal to everyone else's. Now contrast Helen with Irene, who gets adequate pleasure from the simplest things, and accordingly her overall level of welfare remains stable and high in the absence of expensive champagne. The welfarist must hold that Irene is entitled to far fewer social resources than is Helen, simply in virtue of the fact that she is easy to please. More specifically, the welfarist must conclude that Helen is entitled to a socially subsidized unending supply of expensive champagne, while Irene has no such entitlement. But that seems absurd and, moreover, not at all egalitarian.

This simple argument has led many egalitarians to abandon the idea that welfare is the currency of justice. Of these, some adopt a modified welfarist position, holding that justice requires equality, not of welfare, but of *opportunity* for welfare, or *access* to certain sources of it. But, alas, these views need to specify what the relevant sense of *opportunity* is in play, and, in the end, the opportunity-based welfarist views are hard to distinguish from welfarism's primary egalitarian competitor, *resourcism*. Resourcists hold that social institutions show equal regard for all citizens when they distribute an as yet to be specified collection of resources equally; for them, the currency of justice is resources of some kind. According to resourcism, then, welfare inequalities among individuals are not *in themselves* unjust; justice is consistent with significant disparities of welfare.

Now, it is clear that justice cannot require the equalization of shares of *every* resource. It would be implausible to say that justice calls for an equal distribution of resources like books, pick-up trucks, hot dogs, grand pianos, pencils, and apple trees. Although resourcists divide over the precise details, they all tend to hold that justice requires an equal distribution of what might be called *key social resources*; sometimes these are characterized as the central benefits that emerge from our ongoing social cooperation. The resourcist typically has in mind resources that tend to be useful to individuals as such, regardless of their particular pursuits or values. These are goods like basic political rights and liberties, the ability to participate in governance and political office, access to education, healthcare, and various public services, and economic resources like money, income, and wealth. More precisely, then, the resource egalitarian holds that justice demands that such resources be distributed equally among all citizens.

A complication instantly emerges. One could easily imagine instances where a certain degree of *inequality* in, for example, wealth, might be to the benefit of everyone. That is, we might envision circumstances in which the possibility of additional wealth would incentivize some to invest additional time and effort into the production of goods and services that improve *everybody's* share of wealth. In such a case, allowing for the inequality provides everyone with more wealth than they would have under strict equality. In order to accommodate the intuitive thought that such inequalities should be permitted, resource egalitarians often hold that equality in the distribution of key social resources is the *default* requirement for justice. This enables the resourcist to acknowledge that, in cases where it benefits *everyone*, inequality is permitted (and perhaps is required) by justice. Hence the resourcist can allow a certain level of economic inequality. However, establishing equality as the *default* is consistent with denying that inequality in basic rights and liberties is ever tolerable; the claim here is that, unlike certain economic inequalities, inequality of basic rights and liberties is *never* to the benefit of all.

Thus far, we have sketched in very broad strokes the basic commitments of egalitarianism. What has been said thus far is relatively uncontroversial among most egalitarians; to be sure, resourcists and opportunity-welfarists will disagree over some crucial details, but the general picture thus far should be satisfactory to them. Lest this give the impression that egalitarianism is a uniform philosophical program, we should next examine a major rift within the egalitarian ranks. This dispute concerns not the *currency* of egalitarian justice so much as its *point*. That is, egalitarians disagree strongly over *why* showing equal regard for all requires social institutions to distribute key social resources in equal shares (unless some non-equal allocation is better for everyone). There are many views in play; however, we will begin by considering only the two most influential. The first holds that the point of egalitarian justice is to make the distribution of key social resources track broader moral intuitions about personal responsibility; call this view *responsibilism*. The second holds that the point of egalitarianism is to secure the conditions under which citizens can participate politically as equals; call this view *democratic egalitarianism*. We will take these up in turn.

5.2.3.1 Responsibilism

The responsibilist holds that, in order to show equal regard for all citizens, social institutions must see to it that inequalities in key social resources are due to individual *choices* rather than advantageous (or disadvantageous) *circumstances*. Put otherwise, the responsibilist holds that, in order to be consistent with justice, inequalities must be the result of things for which individuals can be rightly held responsible; when an individual has less of some key social resource *due to no fault* of his or her own, that inequality is unjust.

The attraction of this view is not difficult to spot. Responsibilism hitches justice to the deep moral truth that each of us has a life to lead, and leading a life involves *taking responsibility* for one's choices. The responsibilist then says that the state treats us as equals when it, first, recognizes that our lives are equally important, and, second, acknowledges that each person is responsible for his or her own life. Taking these together, we can say that the responsibilist holds that justice requires that each person must be provided an equal chance to *make something* of his or her life, but also must be allowed to live with the consequences of his or her life choices.

More detail is required. The most influential variety of responsibilism is called *luck egalitarianism*. Luck egalitarians hold that the best way to track individual responsibility is to make a distinction between what individuals *do* and what *befalls* them, between *choice* and *luck*. The luck-egalitarian claim, then, is that inequalities in key social resources are consistent with justice only when they are the products of individual choices and not bad (or good) luck. Consider an illustrative example. Imagine a society whose central institutions distribute key social resources on the basis of eye color, such that those with blue eyes are given greater shares than the others. On any plausible conception of justice, this arrangement would be unjust, and obviously so. The luck egalitarian gives a highly plausible account of the injustice in such an arrangement; she argues that eye color is a matter of luck, not individual choice, and is therefore an inappropriate basis upon which to allocate key social resources.

Now contrast this arrangement with one that affords certain key social resources, such as income and wealth, to individuals on the basis of hard work and effort. Under this scheme, those who work harder tend to get greater shares of various economic benefits than those who do not. The luck egalitarian, again, offers an intuitive account of why such inequality is consistent with justice. She says that the inequality resulting from individual differences in effort and ambition have their source in people's *choices*, and are thus permitted by egalitarian justice. Importantly, the luck egalitarian holds that permitting inequality of this kind is *required* if social institutions are going to manifest equal regard for all citizens. As we said above, showing equal regard in part requires that individuals be held responsible for their lives. This means that those who choose to work hard should be permitted to enjoy the extra benefits of having done so, while those who choose instead to take it easy should have less. Finally, think of a person who, due to a physical disability from birth, is unable to work. Here again luck egalitarianism seems to be able to deliver a sensible result. She can say that, as the disabled person's inability is not attributable to any failing on his part, he is nonetheless entitled to a share of social resources that compensate for the disability.

As these examples suggest, responsibilism—especially in its luck egalitarian formulation—is intuitive. Yet the core of the view invites significant difficulties. As was said above, responsibilism relies upon a distinction between what individuals do (and can be held responsible for) and what befalls them (and they cannot be held responsible for); the luck-egalitarian variant formulates this as a distinction between luck and choice. The trouble lies in the fact that this distinction is ultimately very difficult to draw with the required precision.

To see this, consider the simple example above. Whereas it seems obvious that eye color belongs on the "luck" side of the luck–choice distinction, it is not clear that hard work is exclusively a matter of choice. After all, it is plausible to think that the capacity for hard work is at least in part a matter of one's psychological makeup; one must have certain dispositions such as ambition, patience, and wherewithal to work hard toward some goal. And with respect to certain goals that one might strive to achieve, one might need a certain level of cognitive ability and raw talent in order to sustain one's effort. In other words, the capacity for hard work might depend in part upon individual traits that are the result of fortunate developmental or even genetic circumstances. Consequently, the hard worker might owe much more to good luck than it seems. Finally, it is plausible to think that, in many cases, a talent is the result of some combination of raw potential (luck) and the effort to develop it (choice). What then?

But even if we suppose that the distinction between what people do and what befalls them—between choice and luck—can be drawn decisively, there is another difficulty. The problem I have in mind was initially raised against luck egalitarianism by Elizabeth Anderson in her influential essay titled "What Is the Point of Equality?," but her critique points to a flaw that is likely to be endemic to responsibilism as such. Recall that the luck–choice principle requires us to see those factors of an individual's life that affect his holdings but cannot be attributed to his choices as either good or bad luck. But consider the disabled person. It is obvious that justice requires that the state provide additional resources—for example access ramps to public buildings, accommodations in public transport vehicles, closed-captioned services, special healthcare provisions, and so on—to the disabled. But do we really want our conception of justice to officially be committed to saying that disability is a matter of bad luck?

Various disability communities have been working for decades to combat precisely this kind of condescending and pitying stigma. But even if it seems to you that disabilities *are* best treated as instances of misfortune, consider the analogous case of persons with unattractive physical features. Being ugly is a significant cause of social disadvantage; the physically unattractive tend to be paid less than their more appealing counterparts, have less-active social lives, and have a harder time finding suitable mates. Clearly, one's physical appearance isn't always a matter of choice. Does luck egalitarianism commit us to supporting—as a matter of justice—a program of publicly subsidized cosmetic surgery for those who are deemed to be physically unattractive? If so, do we really want our conception of justice to require the state and its institutions to be officially in the business of evaluating the attractiveness of its citizens? Wouldn't that be demeaning to us all?

5.2.3.2 Democratic Egalitarianism

Considerations of the kind that were just reviewed have led many egalitarians to reject responsibilism as an interpretation of the point of egalitarian justice. Some have proposed an alternative known as *democratic egalitarianism*. The democratic egalitarian holds that the reason that the state and its central institutions must distribute key social resources equally (unless an unequal distribution is better for everyone) is that justice requires the state to establish, sustain, and, if possible, enhance the social conditions under which individuals can participate as equal democratic citizens. We might say that whereas responsibilists hitch justice to our broader conception of personal moral responsibility, the democratic egalitarians tie justice to our broader conception of democracy.

But what is this broader conception of democracy? For present purposes, we can say that in a democracy the major political institutions and policy decisions are in some way the result of the citizens' collective will. This means that in a democracy there must be channels and processes by which citizens can express and register their individual wills. And this in turn requires that a kind of *social equality* prevails among all citizens. In a democracy, then, citizens must be able to participate in the activities of political self-government *as equals*, and *on an equal footing*. Accordingly, differences of race, class, gender, religious affiliation, economic status, and so on must not be permitted to transfer into differences in political power. To put the point in a slogan, we can say that in a democracy there is no second-class citizenship.

A full discussion of democracy will be the focus of Chapter 6, but this sketch suffices to allow us to see the force of the democratic-egalitarian view. Consider the following. Many of the most intuitive cases of injustice—for example slavery, racial segregation, sexism, religious discrimination—centrally involve official or state-sanctioned relations of hierarchy, subordination, and oppression; such relations contravene democracy, thus the democratic egalitarian has a parsimonious account of their injustice. Next, return to our earlier example of the arrangement where the state allocated key resources on the basis of eye color; this order also involves a failure of the state to treat citizens as political equals, and is objectionable on democratic-egalitarian grounds. Lastly, the democratic egalitarian can make good sense of the requirements of justice regarding the disabled; unlike the luck egalitarian, the democratic egalitarian need not see disability as an unlucky affliction with horrible effects for which affected individuals must be socially compensated. The democratic egalitarian, rather, can see that justice calls for providing the disabled with additional resources because the state has the responsibility of ensuring that all citizens are able to participate in democracy as equal citizens. The democratic-egalitarian aim in such cases, then, is not to socially make up for the disability, but instead to ensure that the disability does not interfere with an individual's standing as a political equal among his or her fellow democratic citizens.

Pulling these ideas together, we see that the democratic egalitarian opposes all social inequalities that obstruct or dissolve the kind of social equality that is necessary for democratic collective self-government. Put otherwise, democratic egalitarianism requires the equal distribution of key social resources—including political rights and entitlements, as well as material goods like wealth and income—unless there is an alternate distribution that *improves* or *enhances* relations of democratic equality among all citizens.

Democratic egalitarianism looks promising on several fronts. First, it has advantages over responsibilism in that it need not get bogged down in matters concerning the vexed distinctions between an individual's acts and his or her circumstances; it need not rely upon a shaky distinction between luck and choice. Second, democratic egalitarianism looks well attuned to modern-day sites of injustice. As we said above, it need not attempt to explain the injustice of, say, sexist discrimination by appeal to the fact that being a woman is a matter of (bad?) luck. Rather, it can say directly that such discrimination violates the kind of political equality required for democratic citizenship. Along the same lines, democratic egalitarianism can criticize the ways in which inequalities of money and class distort contemporary democracy. As we know all too well, money plays a role in democratic politics today that is objectionable; in a society where money can buy access to public officials and mass audiences—and consequently where those without large sums of money are routinely marginalized and shut out—it seems plausible to think that our conception of justice should be closely tied to our deeper democratic ideals.

But the democratic egalitarian's tight connection between justice and democracy also occasions significant difficulties. Here we will consider only three. The first is that the democratic egalitarian's identification of justice with the project of securing and deepening the egalitarian social relations requisite for democratic citizenship is not very informative until we know what democratic citizenship demands. Yet, as we will see in Chapter 6, democracy is a deeply contested ideal; consequently, there are several distinct conceptions of citizenship. The problem, then, is that the democratic egalitarian has analyzed one vexed conception (namely, justice) by appealing to another vexed conception (namely, democracy). Of course, the case for democratic egalitarianism seems powerful when we are considering the most noncontroversial instances of social injustice. Indeed, the democratic egalitarian appears to provide an intuitive account of the injustice of slavery, segregation, and other forms of discrimination. But the test of a conception of justice should be how well it guides our judgment in cases where it is unclear what justice requires. To say that justice requires in such cases whatever is necessary to foster proper relations of equal citizenship is simply to push the question of justice back on the question of what equal citizenship is all about. And that latter question is not easier to answer.

A related problem concerns the intuitive idea at the core of democratic egalitarianism that justice requires the elimination of social hierarchy, oppression, and subordination. Here we must ask, "What makes a social relation hierarchical and oppressive?" Surely, we would want to *explain* the badness of hierarchy and the evil of oppression by appealing to the concept of justice. It is tempting to say that hierarchy is the existence of an *unjust* difference in power, subordination is an *unjust* difference in status, and oppression is the *unjust* exertion of power by one over another. But this kind of analysis is disallowed by democratic egalitarianism, as the democratic egalitarian explains injustice by appeal to concepts like hierarchy, oppression, and subordination.

A third difficulty concerns one of democratic egalitarianism's direct implications. To put it succinctly, if justice is concerned with establishing and sustaining relations of equality among citizens, then it looks as if democratic states have no duties of justice to those who are not citizens. We will have occasion at the end of this chapter to touch briefly upon questions concerning *global* justice, questions of what relatively wealthy and resource-rich states might as a matter of justice owe to less fortunate states and their citizens. However, at present the concern is slightly different. Modern democratic states are home to many individuals who are not citizens: permanent non-citizen residents, migrant workers, refugees, asylum-seekers, foreign students, employees of foreign corporations, and ambassadors, among many other residents who neither have nor want the privileges of democratic citizenship. Democratic egalitarianism entails that whatever duties democratic states owe to such non-citizens, they are not, strictly speaking, duties of *justice*. This is counterintuitive, as it is obvious that democratic states can enact policies and institutions concerning non-citizen populations that are *unjust*.

5.2.3.3 Capabilities

The problems we have canvassed with responsibilism and democratic egalitarianism have led theorists in recent decades to revisit the "Equality of what?" question. Recall that earlier we discussed two initial candidates for the *currency* of egalitarian justice, namely, welfare and resources. We saw that difficulties with welfarism led welfarists to identify *opportunity* for welfare (or *access* to social sources of welfare) as the proper metric of equality, and, as we said above, that modification seems to make welfarism into a kind of resourcism. (What, after all, is an *opportunity* for welfare but a resource of a certain kind?) A distinctive version of egalitarianism rejects the idea that key social resources are the appropriate currency of egalitarian justice, and therefore rejects both responsibilism and democratic egalitarianism. This alternative view, which is called the *capability approach*, begins with a powerful critique of resourcism. We begin by looking at this critique.

The capability theorist's criticism of resourcism begins by accepting the welfarist thought that resources are intrinsically *instrumental* goods, and that, consequently, the value of a resource lies exclusively in how it can be used to achieve well-being. But the capability theorist does not draw from this the welfarist conclusion that welfare must be the currency of justice; instead, the capability theorist observes that individuals differ in their ability to transfer resources into well-being. To see this, consider that two individuals with an equal share of key social resources might nonetheless be socially unequal if one of them is, for example, disabled. This inequality results from the fact that a disabled person will need to devote a far greater share of her resources to meeting her basic subsistence needs than a nondisabled person. In turn, this means that the disabled person will have far fewer resources than the non-disabled person to devote to other projects necessary for well-being or flourishing. Accordingly, even if we suppose that the disabled person has a larger share of resources like income and wealth, she might nonetheless be deprived and far less well off than her nondisabled compatriots with con-siderably less wealth. To put the point in a different way, the capability approach insists that differences in individual *needs* entail crucial differences in individuals' ability to transfer resources into well-being; from this, the capability theorist concludes that achieving equality of resources is *insufficient* for showing equal regard for all citizens. Citizens with equal shares of key social resources may nonetheless be socially unequal, because they are unequally able to utilize their resource share as means to pursue and participate in activities that contribute to their overall well-being.

This sketch of the capability approach's critique of resourcism gives a sense of its positive program. The capability theorist holds that equal regard requires equality in *capability* to achieve some specified threshold level of human well-being. This might sound similar to the idea that justice requires equality of opportunity for welfare, but notice the crucial difference that, unlike the welfarist, the capability theorist does not identify well-being with preference satisfaction, or any other kind of psychological state; rather, the capability approach identifies well-being with certain central human *functions*. An individual's well-being is measured by the degree to which he functions in ways that characteristically contribute to human flourishing. Justice, according to the capabilities approach, requires that the *capability* to function in those ways be made equal among all citizens. Of course, the *capability* to function in flourishing ways is different from the actual functioning. The currency of egalitarian justice, then, is the *ability* to develop to some threshold degree certain distinctively human traits, to be able to adequately cultivate in oneself characteristically human ways of doing and being.

From what has been said, it should come as no surprise that one crucial task confronting the capability theorist is to develop a list of those capabilities that are necessary for human flourishing. To be sure, some constituents of such a list are obvious and noncontroversial. For example, it is clear that in order to live a flourishing and distinctively human life, one needs to be able to meet one's nutritional requirements, to be able to shelter and clothe oneself, to be able to live without crippling anxiety and fear of bodily assault, and to be able to develop the cognitive, affective, and emotional faculties that are dis-tinctively human. Accordingly, it seems obvious that any individual who is deprived of these basic capabilities is living an undignified life, and any individual from whom these capacities are *withheld* is being treated unjustly.

Note that this list of basic capabilities contains nothing that cannot be captured by other forms of egalitarianism. The distinctiveness of the capabilities approach becomes more evident once one realizes that, although the above list of basic capabilities may be obviously *necessary* for human flourishing, it is not *sufficient*. Arguably, in addition to capabilities for basic subsistence, one also needs to be able to live socially with others and to participate in distinctively human social activities. Perhaps, then, the list of capabilities needs to be expanded to include things like the ability to cultivate friendships and other intimate and loving relationships with others, to be able to socially interact with others in ways that are not based in domination or humiliation, to be able to play a role in the shaping of one's physical and social environment, to be able to exercise one's practical reason and devise one's own plan for one's life, to be able to explore the world of ideas, and so on. But even these additions might not be sufficient, for there are other abilities that seems necessary for a fully human life, including the ability to make art, to sing and dance, to express oneself freely, to enjoy sex, to engage in physical recreational activities, to play games and sports, to laugh, and to experience awe and wonder. Again, we tend to think that any individual who is *denied* opportunities to develop such capacities is being deprived of things that enrich and enhance human life. And for the capability theorist, such deprivation is unjust.

But there is the rub. In analyzing justice in terms not of resources but components of human well-being, the capability theorist appears to build into her conception of justice a distinctive and controversial conception of the good life. Recall from our earlier discussion in Chapter 2 that the state must be *impartial* among permissible but controversial conceptions of the good life. In order to do this, the state cannot endorse or promote any particular conception, but must instead secure and sustain the conditions under which individuals can determine for themselves (within broad constraints) how to live their lives, what kind of life is worth living, and what is truly valuable in life. As it derives its conception of justice from an ideal of human flourishing, the capabilities approach seems incompatible with state impartiality.

To be fair, the capability theorist will respond that her conception of justice requires only the provision of the *capability* to function in the specified ways; it does not require citizens to actually do anything. The capability theorist concludes from this that her view is consistent with state impartiality among permissible conceptions of the good life.

But this reply looks hollow. One may wonder what it could mean for the state to make equal the *capabilities* to make art, enjoy sex, play sports, express oneself, and explore the world of ideas without *encouraging* citizens to engage in such activities, even if only to experience what they are like. And if the state undertakes to *encourage* citizens to engage in such activities, it fails to be impartial among permissible conceptions of the good, for many such conceptions flatly *deny* that sex is something to be enjoyed, for example. Here the capability theorist might retrench and say that equalizing the capability for these components of human flourishing involves nothing as drastic as *encouraging* citizens to engage in the corresponding activities. All that is required, it may be claimed, is only that the state *makes available* occasions for acting in those ways. Yet this retrenchment looks suspiciously close to saying that the state must provide each individual the *resources* necessary for developing capacities characteristic of human flourishing. The capabilities approach might not be distinctive after all.

5.3 Conclusion

We have traveled a great distance in this chapter; still, the foregoing discussion is merely the tip of the iceberg. In fact, there are many central issues concerning justice that we have not even mentioned. To cite only one glaring example, the foregoing discussion has proceeded as if justice were exclusively *local*, strictly a matter of how states treat their citizens. However, there is good reason to suspect that justice also has a *global* or *international* scope; that is, as many contemporary philosophers have argued, states can owe duties of justice to *other states* and *citizens of other states*. Once it is recognized that, in the global order, states often act in ways that impact lives across national borders, it becomes easy to see how the views we canvassed in this chapter can be reformulated into theories of *global* justice. And, as you may expect, there is consequently an ongoing debate over whether justice is exclusively local or also global.

The debates between localists and globalists cannot be pursued here. I simply leave open the question as to whether duties of justice obtain across state borders, for even the globalists hold that states owe duties of justice to their own citizens. That is, no theorist holds that justice is *exclusively* global. And, in any case, there may be more than a little wisdom in the idea that, in order to get clear about whether justice has a global dimension, one should first try to figure out what justice demands domestically.

So where are we, then? The overarching task throughout these chapters has been to see whether the state and its coercive institutions can be justified, and, if so, how. A result reached previously is that one condition of justifiability is that the state must secure for its citizens what justice demands; we began from the intuitive idea that justice demands that the state and its institutions treat each citizen as an equal, with equal concern. The different conceptions of justice we examined offer distinct interpretations of equal regard. Is any correct?

Now, one insight at the heart of democratic egalitarianism seems undeniable. Whatever else one might say about equal concern, it must involve the elimination of political or state-sanctioned subordination, hierarchy, and domination. A society composed of distinct social classes with accordingly different political entitlements, or a society in which only men can vote and only those with pale skin can hold property, is obviously unjust. To be sure, one might identify the injustice in such arrangements with the lack of individual liberty or the overall unhappiness that would prevail under such circumstances. And these features of the social arrangements we are considering surely render the societies that instantiate them seriously *bad*. But there is a distinctive and additional way in which such arrangements are condemnable.

Social orders that permit political subordination, hierarchy, and domination not only allow those favored by the arrangement to harm those who are not; such arrangements also serve to render those who are politically sub-ordinated relatively *powerless* to object to, protest, and change the standing order. In other words, societies based in hierarchy, subordination, and domination not only establish an unequal political order, they also withhold and deny those at the bottom the tools to try to change things. This is a failure of the kind of equal regard that is central to democracy. A democratic society, then, must incorporate into its conception of justice the core of the democratic-egalitarian view.

This leads us to say that justice is centrally concerned with establishing and sustaining the social and material conditions required for democratic citizenship. Now, as I mentioned above, there are significant disputes over what democratic citizenship is really all about. However, there is nevertheless an intuitive core that is common to the competing conceptions of citizenship: equal basic political liberties, including not only the typical menu of individual basic rights, but also equal protection under the law, rights of due process, and equal access to political office and decision-making processes. Any proposed conception of democratic citizenship that did not recognize such provisions as essential would have no claim to being a *democratic* conception. Given this, it would be difficult to deny the further implication that, as severe disparities in material advantage causally produce inequalities in basic liberties, democratic citizenship requires some degree of material well-being, and this calls for provisions for things like public education, economic assistance of various kinds, and healthcare. Of course, all of this requires governmental infrastructure and, naturally, official systems of taxation.

This broadly democratic-egalitarian view is, of course, severely under-specified. We might call it a *minimal* democratic-egalitarian view (keeping in mind that it is quite distinct from the view we above called *minimalism*). It is difficult to see any proposed conception of citizenship that *denied* any of the above as a properly democratic conception. Thus it looks as if a minimal democratic-egalitarian conception is, at the very least, the right place to *begin* in thinking about justice for a liberal and constitutional democracy.

Note that minimal democratic egalitarianism looks decidedly resourcist in its conception of justice's currency. This is troubling, as surely there is *something* to the criticism of resourcism advanced by the capabilities approach. In order to achieve the kind of political equality sought by the democratic egalitarian, it is likely that we will have to look not only to each citizen's share of key social resources, but also to their ability to employ them. Can this central insight of the capability theorist be accommodated by the minimal demo-cratic egalitarian without thereby inviting the difficulties that the capabilities approach invites?

Maybe so. Recall that the main problem we found with the capabilities approach has to do with the tendency of that view to continually expand its list of core human capabilities. This tendency is the result of the fact that the capabilities approach treats capabilities as tied to human flourishing. Perhaps the minimal democratic egalitarian can adopt a view of core *democratic capabilities* or the basic political functioning of democratic citizens. Instead of talking about capabilities for things like play, dancing, feeling awe, and physical exercise, the minimal democratic egalitarian can limit herself to capabilities for political informedness, historical understanding, political participation, and public action; these would require the development of capacities for critically thinking, engaging in public discourse, weighing different considerations relevant to pressing political and social issues, imagining and understanding opposing viewpoints, and so on. In addition, the minimal democratic egalitarian could also adopt the capability theorist's concern with making public and political environments accessible to the disabled and accommodating for the elderly. In short, some such conception of the core *democratic capabilities* is available to the minimal democratic egalitarian.

But the crucial thought underlying the minimal democratic-egalitarian view I have just sketched is that it is able to recognize that, at some point, the specifics of justice—the precise design of the tax structure, the content and extent of public education, the forms of public assistance, and so on—must be topics of ongoing debate, criticism, and reevaluation. That is, one can establish in one's theory of justice a fairly elaborate minimal threshold that must be met in order for democracy to persist, and then leave the further specifics to ongoing democratic processes. It is fitting, then, that we turn next to the topic of democracy.

For Further Reading

As always, the great texts in the historical tradition of political philosophy must be grappled with; these include, minimally, Plato's *Republic*; Book V of Aristotle's *Nicomachean Ethics* and his *Politics*; and the masterworks mentioned previously of Hobbes, Locke, Rousseau, Kant, Bentham, and Mill. All of the contemporary work on justice proceeds against the long shadow cast by John Rawls's landmark *A Theory of Justice* (Cambridge, MA: Harvard University Press, 1971). The secondary literature on Rawls is far too voluminous to catalogue here. For a comprehensive and synoptic treatment of the whole of Rawls's political philosophy, consult Samuel Freeman's *Rawls* (New York: Routledge, 2007). One of the best ways to enter into the contemporary debates over justice is to begin by looking at some of the more influential criticisms of Rawls; see the papers collected in Norman Daniels's *Reading Rawls* (Stanford: Stanford University Press, 1989) for early critical reactions, and the most current assessments can be found in Jon Mandle and David Reidy's edited volume *A Companion to Rawls* (Oxford: Wiley-Blackwell, 2014). Criticisms of Rawls that claim to stand outside of the liberal framework can be found in Michael Sandel's *Liberalism and the Limits of Justice* (Cambridge: Cambridge University Press, 1982); Iris Marion Young's *Justice and the Politics of Difference* (Princeton: Princeton

University Press, 1990); Michael Walzer's *Spheres of Justice* (New York: Basic Books, 1983); and G. A. Cohen's *Rescuing Justice and Equality* (Cambridge, MA: Harvard University Press, 2008). See Robert Nozick's *Anarchy, State, and Utopia* (New York: Basic Books, 1974) for a defense of minimalism; and for a utilitarian view, see Robert Goodin's *Utilitarianism as a Public Philosophy* (Cambridge: Cambridge University Press, 1995).

The literature on egalitarianism is vast. One place to begin is Ronald Dworkin's two seminal papers "What Is Equality, Part I" (*Philosophy & Public Affairs*, Volume 10, 1981) and "What Is Equality, Part II" (*Philosophy & Public Affairs*, Volume 10, 1981). From there, one should read Amartya Sen's Tanner Lecture, "Equality of What?," which is reprinted in Sterling MacMurrin's edited collection of *Tanner Lectures on Human Values* (Salt Lake City: University of Utah Press, 1980), Richard Arneson's "Equality and Equal Opportunity for Welfare" (*Philosophical Studies*, Volume 56, 1989), and G. A. Cohen's "On the Currency of Egalitarian Justice" (*Ethics*, Volume 99, 1989). Two influential critiques of luck egalitarianism are Susan Hurley's "Luck and Equality" (*Aristotelian Society Supplemental Volume* 75, 2011) and Samuel Scheffler's "What Is Egalitarianism?" (*Philosophy & Public Affairs*, Volume 31, 2003). As was mentioned above, Elizabeth Anderson's "What Is the Point of Equality?" (*Ethics*, Volume 109, 1999) remains the most trenchant critique of luck egalitarianism, and it is also a compelling defense of democratic egalitarianism; see also her *The Imperative of Integration* (Princeton: Princeton University Press, 2010). A version of luck egalitarianism is defended by Kok-Chor Tan in two excellent articles, "Justice and Personal Pursuits" (*Journal of Philosophy*, Volume 101, 2004) and "A Defense of Luck Egalitarianism" (*Journal of Philosophy*, Volume 105, 2008). The most forceful articulation and defense of the capabilities approach can be found in the work of Martha Nussbaum. See, especially, her "Human Functioning and Social Justice: In Defense of Aristotelian Essentialism" (*Political Theory*, Volume 20, 1992), and her books *Women and Human Development* (Cambridge: Cambridge University Press, 2000) and *Frontiers of Justice* (Cambridge, MA: Harvard University Press, 2006). For a series of recent papers examining the differences between resourcism and the capabilities approach, see Harry Brighouse and Ingrid Robeyns's edited collection *Measuring Justice: Primary Goods and Capabilities* (Cambridge: Cambridge University Press, 2010). Carl Knight and Zofia Stemplowska's collection on *Responsibility and Distributive Justice* (New York: Oxford University Press, 2011) provides a good guide to the state of the art in responsibilist views of justice.

6 Democracy

- The Familiarity of Democracy
- The Fundamental Ideal
- Classical Conceptions of Democracy
- Two Contemporary Trends
- Conclusion
- For Further Reading

6.1 The Familiarity of Democracy

It might strike some readers as odd that the discussion of democracy occurs so late in this book. We began with the methodological commitment to beginning with the social world as we encounter it, and, after all, unlike some of the ideas that have been discussed, democracy is familiar, perhaps obvious. We all know what democracy is, so why didn't the book begin there?

There is indeed a sense in which we are all already well acquainted with democracy. Chances are that if you are reading this book, you live in a democracy, and this means that democracy's major institutions and processes—elections, campaigns, debates, courts, systems of political representation, and so on—are close at hand. That you live in a democracy also means that the language of democracy pervades your life. From the time you were very young, you learned what it means to settle disputes "democratically," and even as a child many of your appeals to ideals of fairness and equality had a democratic flavor. This, of course, is to say nothing of the constant appeals to democracy in your everyday political talk. Judging from the facility with which you employ the concept, democracy seems rather simple.

Being familiar with a concept is different from understanding its content. In fact, familiarity can sometimes serve as a block to philosophical understanding. We do not often take the time to think about things that seem to us obvious; we tend to glide over what's familiar. However, despite appearances, democracy is a surprisingly complicated, even puzzling, idea. Moreover, our everyday attitudes toward democracy are complicated, perhaps even conflicted. Nothing is obvious about democracy.

6.1.1 Popular Attitudes toward Democracy

As I write this sentence, large segments of the world's population are engaged in long-term struggles for democracy. In pressing their call for democracy, many individuals are openly defying standing dictators, and in many parts of the world publicly demanding political reform in the direction of democracy is a serious crime. Consequently, those who openly support democratic reform do so at considerable risk to their own well-being, if not their lives.

Not unrelatedly, many of the military and diplomatic actions taken recently by the United States and other democratic nations—including the costly invasions of Iraq and Afghanistan, as well as additional interventions in other parts of the Middle East—have had democratization as among their official goals. In fact, in contemporary democratic societies, the need to support, enrich, protect, and spread democracy both domestically and around the world is commonly cited as a justification for government action of various kinds. What's more, this justification is, perhaps unsurprisingly, frequently successful. Long before President Wilson articulated his famous case for declaring war on Germany, thereby entering the United States in World War I, democratic citizens had thought that one of the central purposes of the democratic state is to make the world safe for democracy. We still generally hold to this view.

Yet, as events currently unfolding across the globe demonstrate, the process of democratization is not easy. Alas, making a democracy where there was once tyranny requires a lot more than replacing a dictator with elected officials. It is no exaggeration to say that the road to democracy is perilous, beset with a good deal of uncertainty, civil unrest, and social instability. This is why pro-democracy social movements are so hard to sustain. The ousting of the dictator is often the easiest part of democratization. Far more difficult is the subsequent task of effecting the social and cultural transformations that are required if democracy is to take root. That democratization is often so difficult partly explains why those of us who are already citizens of stable democracies tend to see those struggling for democracy as courageous and heroic, and worthy of considerable political—and financial—support.

6.1.2 Familiar Criticisms of Democracy

In light of the ongoing struggles for democracy across the globe, it might seem churlish to confess that, even at its best, democracy is hard to love. Those who live in established and stable democracies know that democracy is often exasperating, and sometimes infuriating. Consider only a few lines of complaint, many of which are likely to be familiar to you, or anyone else living in a modern democracy. It is well established that democratic citizens are woefully uninformed even about the most basic facts of their constitution and the workings of the political system it establishes; they likewise are reliably ignorant when it comes to the major political issues of the day. These high levels of ignorance contribute to the ease with which democratic voters are manipulated by charming politicians and their professional handlers. It is hard to deny that contemporary democratic elections are far less about political ideas than commercial polish and slick marketing; what wins modern elections is firm handshakes, reassuring smiles, fashionable clothing, confident rhetoric, comforting promises, and catchy slogans rather than clear thinking, cogent ideas, and civic purpose. Moreover, there can be little doubt that contemporary democracies are plagued by ongoing difficulties concerning the ways in which money and other forms of social power can be transformed into disproportionate political influence, effectively undermining democracy's ideal of political equality. Add to all of this the fact that in the United States and elsewhere voter turnout for major elections is commonly below 50 percent. But perhaps that is of no importance, as decades of work by political scientists, economists, and mathematicians has concluded that it is impossible to design a system of democratic voting that guarantees that its results will in fact reflect the majority will. Winston Churchill may have been too generous when he described democracy as "the worst form of government, except for all those other forms that have been tried." It might, in the end, really be no better than certain nondemocratic alternatives. Perhaps it's worse.

These familiar complaints about democracy have a distinguished history in political thought, beginning with Plato. In his *Republic*, Plato likened democracy to a ship lost at sea, a vessel under the control of popular sweet-talkers rather than those with knowledge of navigation. Subsequent philosophers have tended to side with Plato; for most of the history of political philosophy, democracy has been either wholly renounced as the rule of the incompetent mob, or accepted with considerable trepidation. Yet one need not plumb philosophy's distant past to find serious reservations about democracy. In studying the documents surrounding the founding of the United States, one will almost immediately encounter instances in which the term democracy is used with overt scorn. Many of the founders of the United States saw themselves as establishing not a democracy, but a republic. To them, democracy was just as Plato had described it—the direct rule of the ignorant masses—and for that reason obviously objectionable. Yet the founders were, of course, opposed to monarchy and thus recognized the need for some form of popular rule. Their alternative, then, was an *indirect* system of popular rule. Under republican government, the people rule by means of their chosen representatives, and their will is constrained by rules and procedures established in a constitution. Although the establishment of the United States was marked by heated debates between advocates of democracy and those who favored a republican form of government, today we embrace the republican form of government established in the US Constitution, but we call it democracy. That is, when we talk about democracy today, we almost always mean a system of indirect popular government by means of political representatives, all bound by a public constitution that establishes rules, procedures, and entitlements that, among other things, protect individuals from the will of the majority. Since the time of the founding of the United States, the concept of democracy has undergone a fundamental shift.

The history of this shift in the concept of democracy is fascinating, as is the tradition of antidemocratic political philosophy, but these topics lie beyond our purposes here. Even if we identify democracy with representative and constitutional popular rule, many of the standard criticisms of democracy still have force. To see this, conduct the following simple experiment: Take a moment now to visit the website of an organization that promotes political policies and ideas that you oppose especially strongly. Spend some time reviewing the reader-comments section of the site. Follow the threads, paying special attention to the ways in which your political opponents describe your political allies and your views. Note your reactions. Then try to feel good about the fact that those commenters are your fellow citizens, each with the same voting power as you. Good luck!

6.1.3 Resolving a Tension

We thus have hit upon an odd tension in our popular attitude toward democracy. When thinking as democratic citizens about the rough and tumble of politics, we are prone to complain a great deal about the workings of our democracy. We readily deride our fellow citizens, as well as our elected representatives and officials, for being too foolish, fickle, or dishonest to fulfill their democratic duties. And, as a quick survey of your local bookstore's section on Politics or Current Affairs will demonstrate, the disparaging of our democracy is big business. Best-seller lists are saturated with accounts of the corruption, incompetence, and dysfunction of democratic government; apparently we *like* to be shown how bad our democracy is. Democracy is not only hard to love, but our reading habits suggest that we love to hate democracy.

Yet this is most certainly not the whole story. No matter how hard democracy is to love, we do love it. Although popular political talk is often highly critical of our democracy, no one seriously rejects democracy as a form of government; no one goes so far as to advocate a nondemocratic alternative. In fact, despite all of the complaining, democracy is almost always hailed as an unmitigated political good. We could go further: Democracy is often presented as a necessary precondition for all other social and political goods, from freedom, fairness, equality, and justice to security, peace, and prosperity. Consequently, to characterize a government action, policy, or institution as necessary for democracy is almost always to praise or recommend it. In popular political talk, the term serves a legitimating function; we are generally inclined to presume that anything that is democratic must be good or right, and we rarely apply the term to arrangements or institutions that we aim to criticize.

It seems, then, that we have a love–hate relationship with democracy. The question is whether these two widespread but seemingly incompatible attitudes can be reconciled.

Here's one suggestion for rendering them consistent: Our popular attitudes toggle between two different perspectives from which to evaluate democracy, which we might call the *ideal* and the *real*. When thinking of democracy as a political ideal—as a philosophical conception of government—we tend toward the view that democracy is the only acceptable mode of government; we think that any political order that does not aspire to the democratic ideal is a moral and political failure. By contrast, when we talk of democracy "on the ground," so to speak—as the functioning system of processes and institutions by which we are governed—we find a great deal about which to complain. Again, citizens are foolish, politicians are dishonest, the elections are bought, the system is inefficient, and so on. What we praise as an unmitigated social and political good is the democratic *ideal*, or perhaps the *aspiration* identified in the ideal of democracy. What we complain about is the condition of our attempts to realize that ideal in our real political order. We love democracy, but find that our actual political order falls far short of that ideal.

Now we can see that the familiar complaints about real democracy derive their force from democracy as an ideal. That is, when we criticize democracy on the grounds that its citizens are uninformed, we are implicitly appealing to the ideal that a democratic citizenry should be politically informed; similarly, the criticism that politicians are deceitful hucksters draws its force from the ideal that, in a democracy, politicians should be driven by civic duty. When we criticize democratic politics as it is practiced, we are generally lamenting the ways in which our existing democracy is failing to achieve the democratic ideal. The complaints are often calls for improved effort in living up to that ideal.

If the above is roughly correct, then our love–hate relationship is not so puzzling after all. We are critical of our democracy *for the sake of* diagnosing its shortcomings relative to the democratic ideal, perhaps with the hope of *improving* our democracy. Some may wish to go further to say that the two attitudes with which we began are not incompatible at all; they will claim that the critique of democracy "on the ground" is itself a central *part of* the ideal of democracy. In other words, one could argue that criticism of democracy is what good democratic citizens do.

We will consider that intriguing claim in the concluding section of this chapter. For now, we must fix our attention elsewhere. I suggested above that the familiar complaints about the real world of democratic politics derive their force from the fact that we wholeheartedly accept the democratic ideal. Accordingly, we turn to an examination of that ideal.

6.2 The Fundamental Ideal

Before proceeding directly to our task, it might be helpful to emphasize that our query has mainly to do with the nature of democracy as a philosophical conception of proper governance. We are not at present concerned with important questions about the design of democratic political institutions, the interpretation of any of the existing democratic constitutions, the nature of democratic political campaigns, the strategizing of political parties, or the voting behavior of citizens and elected politicians. These are matters studied by political scientists, legal theorists, and sociologists, among others. Our aim is distinctly philosophical. We seek to identify, clarify, examine, and evaluate the democratic ideal. It is this ideal that the familiar institutions, offices, and processes of existing democratic states are meant to instantiate. Questions about how that ideal may be realized or approximated in the concrete are largely empirical matters that lie beyond our purposes in this book.

6.2.1 Democracy as a Moral Ideal

So we turn to the task at hand. The fundamental thought that drives the democratic ideal can be expressed in different ways. To appeal to the Greek origin of the word, in a democracy the people (*demos*) have the ruling power (*kratos*). That's correct as far as it goes, but etymology can elucidate only so much. A more informative formulation owing to Abraham Lincoln says that democracy is government of the people, by the people, and for the people. That statement nicely captures the idea that in a democracy the people rule themselves, that democracy is collective *self-government*. It also calls attention to the fact that democracy is to be distinguished from hierarchical regimes, where one segment of the population rules over the rest. Again, Lincoln's description is correct, but there's more to the democratic ideal than this. Consider the following alternative formulation: Democracy is the proposition that those who are bound by political laws, policies, and rules should have an equal say in political decision-making. This formulation differs importantly from its predecessors in that it identifies democracy as a *normative claim*, a claim about what *should be*. More specifically, it identifies democracy as the claim that the people *should* rule themselves. But it goes further. It places at the heart of democracy a conception of *political equality*, and affirms that citizens should have an *equal say* in authoring the rules by which they live together. In doing so, this formulation enables us to see that the familiar processes of democracy—voting, elections, campaigns, multiple and opposed political parties, debates, press conferences, and such—have their bases in the underlying moral claim that, as citizens, we are equals. Democracy hence involves the moral claim that our fundamental political equality *requires* collective self-rule and *disallows* the rule of some or one over the others. Democracy says that *because* we are political equals we must have an equal say in making the rules by which we live together as a society; our political equality *entails* that we are equal sharers in the task of governance. In this way, democracy is fundamentally a *moral ideal*.

The moral dimension of democracy is worth special emphasis because we are prone to think of democracy in a non-moral way. We tend to identify democracy with a procedure for decision-making in which each person who will be bound by the decision gets exactly one vote, and the majority rules.

To be sure, on almost any view, democracy indeed *involves* collective decision-making by votes, with majority rule. But as was just suggested, that model of collective decision-making is so closely associated with democracy only because it is a common interpretation of the underlying moral ideal of democracy: self-government among political equals.

This occasions a point I have made previously in this book. Important moral ideals are complex, and, due to their complexity, such moral ideals do not interpret themselves; they must be interpreted. Philosophical theories offer *conceptions* of such ideals. Thus, we must ask, what does the democratic moral ideal mean? What *is* self-government among political equals? It should come as no surprise that the moral ideal that lies at the heart of democracy is subject to a range of interpretations. This is why there are several distinct philosophical conceptions of democracy. Each conception offers a view of what it takes for a system of government to qualify as a system of self-government among equals.

As was mentioned a moment ago, we are all familiar with the conception of democracy according to which democracy is realized when, with respect to any collective decision, each individual who will be bound by the decision gets exactly one vote, and the majority rules. Call this familiar view *equal-vote majoritarianism*. Now, of course, large-scale democracies are far more complex in their collective decision-making processes than this suggests. For example, we previously noted that modern democracy is *representative* democracy, and this means that most laws and policies are not decided by a popular vote, but by parliamentary processes involving bodies of elected representatives, and some of these processes are not majoritarian. It should be mentioned also that in the United States the President is elected by the Electoral College rather than by popular vote. Moreover, certain key public offices—including the justices on the Supreme Court—are not elected at all, but rather are *appointed*.

Let's place these complications aside by assuming that any such deviation in practice from the simple system of equal-vote majoritarianism will be either *itself* a product of an equal vote, or else necessary in preserving the democratic order and protecting democratic citizens. We cannot linger on the details, but it is not difficult to see how certain departures from equal-vote majoritarianism might be so justified. One could argue that certain judicial offices are appointed rather than elected precisely so that judges can do their job fairly and impartially, without having to be concerned with winning reelection. It could similarly be argued that modern democracies are representative precisely because individual citizens prefer to leave the burden of large-scale political decision-making to individuals who can give their full attention to such matters. To be sure, it is not difficult to anticipate arguments to the effect that representative democracy or a society that allows unelected judges to interpret its laws is no democracy at all. But, again, we will leave these matters aside. The first question we need to address is whether equal-vote majoritarianism is indeed sufficient as a conception of the democratic ideal.

6.2.2 The Schoolyard View

We'll begin by considering a highly simplified image of equal-vote major-itarianism. Seeing the questions and problems that are occasioned by this simplified view will help us when we turn to the more nuanced conceptions.

Suppose that three friends—Ann, Betty, and Cara—wish to go to the movies together tonight. Their local cinema is showing two films; one is a bittersweet romantic comedy, and the other is an action-packed thriller. They must choose one to see. How should they decide?

Imagine that that Ann, Betty, and Cara are all indifferent. They want to see a film *together*, and none of them cares which one they see. So they simply flip a coin, and head to the theater. This case is obviously too simplistic to reveal anything about democracy. A small group of individuals want to do something together, and, as they are all indifferent about which film to see, there is no conflict or disparity among them; they want to see a film toge-ther, and their only task is to settle the matter of which theater to walk into. We might say that theirs is a problem not of governance, but merely of setting a plan.

So we need to complicate the example slightly. Now imagine that Ann, Betty, and Cara are not indifferent with respect to the matter of which film to see. That is, imagine that for each member of the group, there is one movie among the two on offer that she most wants to see tonight. Of course, it could be that Ann, Betty, and Cara all want to see the *same* movie, that they are unanimous in their movie preference. That would be a happy coincidence; but, again, in order to get a handle on democracy, we need to begin by supposing that the group is not of one mind about which film to see. How should they decide? There's something undeniably attractive about the thought that they should each state their preferred movie, and the group should go to whichever film the majority wants to see.

This is the simple view of democracy that we all learned as children. Call it the *schoolyard view*. It looks like a simple kind of democracy mainly because it, first, is addressed to a context where a collective decision must be made among individuals who may disagree or may have differing preferences, and, second, embodies two central norms that are most frequently associated with democracy in its full-blown variety, namely equality and majority rule. In our example, the decision process instantiates equality in that Ann, Betty, and Cara each get exactly one vote regarding which movie to see; it manifests majority rule in that the group goes to the movie that attracts the most votes. Hence the schoolyard view proposes equal-vote majoritarianism as a way to make collective decisions that treat each individual as an equal. Isn't that democracy?

The schoolyard view is in many ways too simplistic. When even slight complexities are introduced, it seems to lose much of its intuitive force. For example, suppose Ann *really* wants to see the romantic comedy and really *dislikes* thrillers, whereas Betty and Cara have only a slight preference in favor of the thriller, but are not opposed to the romantic comedy. Or consider the possibility that Ann's preference for the romantic comedy is the result of her having read several reviews by reliable critics, whereas Betty's and Cara's preference for the thriller is not informed by reviews, or anything at all for that matter. Further, imagine that Ann's preference for the romantic comedy is based on reliable reviews, and expresses her educated judgment concerning which film Betty and Cara are most likely to enjoy, whereas Betty and Cara have a long track record of picking movies that they wind up not enjoying. Next, imagine a case in which Ann strongly prefers the romantic comedy, and Betty strongly prefers the thriller, but Cara, who is generally indifferent, votes for the thriller because she knows that Betty, unlike Ann, will get angry if she votes against the thriller. Or consider the case in which Ann realizes that both Betty and Cara are in some significant way *misinformed* about the thriller; they mistakenly believe that it stars their favorite actor and has an uplifting and patriotic message, while Ann knows that it stars an unknown actor and ends with a bleak embrace of existential dread. Finally, imagine that Ann wants to see the romantic comedy, and Betty wants to see the thriller, but Betty, knowing that Cara will vote only for a film that stars her favorite actor, tricks Cara into voting for the thriller by lying to her about who its star is. In any of these scenarios, does the schoolyard view prescribe a good way to make the decision?

Things grow more difficult when we consider even slightly larger groups with greater numbers of options. For example, what if the group discovers that the local cinema is showing *four* films this evening: a romantic comedy, a thriller, a mystery, and a documentary? What if two additional friends, Debbie and Emma, unexpectedly join the group? Suppose that Debbie and Emma both most want to see the documentary, whereas Ann votes for the romantic comedy, Betty votes for the thriller, and Cara votes for the mystery. According to the schoolyard view, the group should go to the documentary. But notice that the majority voted for some other option. What steps should be taken in order to avoid this kind of result? Perhaps some scheme should be devised by which each member of the group gets to vote for a particular *ordering* of films (e.g. mystery first, thriller second, and so on). But once such a system is introduced, we confront the notoriously difficult question of how the votes should be counted. Perhaps, alternatively, the group should nominate someone (or some subset) among them to be the decider with regard to films? But how should *that* decision be made? And upon what should the decider's decisions be based: her own preferences, her own judgments about which films are good, her judgments about which films the group would choose, or her own judgments about which films that group would like best? Finally, consider that Emma very intensely wants to see the documentary, and Ann equally intensely wants to see the romantic comedy, but, unlike Ann, Emma has enough money to offer to buy popcorn for whoever votes for the documentary; arguably, Emma thereby effectively buys the votes of others in the group. Should this be allowed? Additional difficulties of this kind could be added easily.

The point is that, in any of these cases, it is not obvious that the schoolyard view prescribes an appropriate way to make a collective decision. It is important to note that the schoolyard view looks dubious not merely because it looks unlikely to produce a *good* decision; the more important point is that it also is not clear that it manifests an adequate conception of equality. The schoolyard view has it that individuals are treated as equals when they are afforded the same number of votes. Yet one might argue that "one person, one vote" does not sufficiently treat individuals as equals. We already considered possibilities where individuals are manipulated through ignorance, intimidation, dishonesty, and money. One might argue that because the schoolyard view does not take into account the intensity, ordering, and rationality of each individual's preferences concerning the film options, it cannot really respect their equality. In other words, one could contend that the schoolyard view's conception of equality—namely, equal voting—is not sufficient. More specifically, the schoolyard view understands equality simply as *equality of input*, and this kind of equality is arguably consistent with various forms of political *inequality*. Democracy, it seems, must require more than equal-vote majoritarianism.

6.2.3 Democracy, Equality, and Authority

Let's not be too hasty in dismissing equal-vote majoritarianism as a conception of the democratic ideal. Our schoolyard examples above have been simplistic, and this gives us reason to temper whatever conclusions we can draw from them about large-scale democracy. After all, democracy as a self-governing political community of equals is in several crucial respects different from a small social group of friendly filmgoers. For example, note that in the case of the filmgoers the individuals know each other and can share information; they can talk face to face, and there is a lot of room for cooperation and compromise. They could, for example, decide to see more than one movie that evening, or decide to see the romantic comedy on the given evening and the documentary later in the week. Moreover, the filmgoers' decision is low-stakes. Should they decide to see a bad movie, there's really no serious cost to anyone; at worst, they've wasted their time and a relatively small amount of their money. And in any case, if it turns out that the film they select proves to be exceedingly horrible, they can simply walk out of the theater; their mistakes are nonpermanent and, in a way, reversible. In the case of democratic politics, by contrast, decisions involve the input of individuals who do not know each other and cannot talk face to face; accordingly, the opportunities for compromise among democratic citizens are few. Moreover, democratic decisions can be high-stakes, and errors can be both costly and difficult to repair.

These differences are philosophically significant. Once we reformulate the filmgoer example to model more closely these realities of democratic politics, we may find that equal-vote majoritarianism might begin to look more plausible. Yet there is a further difference between the filmgoers and a community of democratic citizens that must not be overlooked. In the filmgoer case, no one claims *authority* over anyone else and, moreover, the group claims no entitlement to exercise coercive force over its members. Let's not forget that a democracy is a kind of state, and states claim authority over their members as well as the entitlement to use force if it is necessary to secure compliance. In the filmgoer case, if Betty does not like the result of the group's vote, she can simply decline to go to the movie; she can go home, or to another movie all by herself. She can disassociate from the group. At the extreme, Betty can suspend her friendship with the others, resolving to never socialize with them again. Of course, in taking any of these disassociating measures, Betty may be revealing herself to be a bad sport or a sore loser, and she may be criticized for being uncooperative or unfriendly. But, crucially, the other filmgoers cannot *force* Betty to join them, nor do they claim to have that kind of standing. Moreover, in refusing to comply with the outcome of the group's vote, Betty does not render herself vulnerable to the group's punishment.

Things are much different in a democratic community. When a democracy votes, an outcome is reached, and *all* are required to comply with the resulting decision; one cannot simply disassociate from the democracy and live according to one's own rules. Moreover, in a democracy, the state claims the entitlement to use *force* to secure citizens' compliance; it even claims the right to impose punishment—including severe punishment, like long-term imprisonment—on those who refuse.

Although we readily accept the idea that democracy is self-government among political equals, it must not be overlooked that democracy always involves the imposition of the majority's preference, or will, upon a minority. To put the point more dramatically, whenever a democracy makes a decision, someone (often a very large number of individuals) *loses*, and the losers are required to accept, adopt, and comply with the majority will, or else confront the coercive force of the state. Think of it this way. When your democratic state decides to adopt a law that you personally oppose, you are nonetheless *required* to obey that law. Now, of course, there are special circumstances where citizens have a moral right to civilly disobey, and there are other circumstances where some citizens might be entitled to an exemption from the law. But, on any plausible view of such matters, the vast majority of laws that are adopted in a democracy will require the obedience even of those who oppose them. What could explain this? How is such an arrangement consistent with the equality of all citizens? In a nutshell, the answer democracy offers is this: The fact that the law in question was produced in a democratic way means that you must obey it, even if you voted against it and continue to personally oppose it.

There are certainly many more details that would need to be provided before democracy can begin to look plausible as an account of authority among political equals. But we now see that the crucial issue for democracy lies with the concept of authority, which was the focus of Chapter 4. Drawing from that discussion, we can say that democracy is supposed to resolve the conflict between the political *authority* claimed by the state and the political *equality* of all citizens. Again, the fundamental idea of democracy is deeply appealing: State authority and individual equality are reconciled when the state is, in *some* sense, nothing but the collective will of the individuals governed by it. To formulate the thought in a different way, democracy involves the contention that we retain our equality as individuals in the face of the authority of the state when the state is—again, in *some* sense—us. Once we see this, it may appear that, given the demands and complexities of large-scale government, equal-vote majoritarianism is just right for democracy.

6.3 Classical Conceptions of Democracy

We are now well positioned to consider some of the leading philosophical conceptions of democracy. We begin by looking at a few "classical" conceptions. These are conceptions that have been in currency and influential throughout the founding of the modern-day democracies. As we'll see, the somewhat disappointing trajectory of the succession of classical conceptions provides the critical basis for the more recent views that we will discuss in the next section.

6.3.1 Aggregation

We begin by looking at an intuitive and influential style of democratic theory that may be generally characterized as *aggregative*. The aggregative view explicitly adopts equal-vote majoritarianism: Each political actor gets exactly one vote, each vote is given equal weight, and the majority rules. The thought guiding the aggregative view is that in large-scale social contexts when interests collide but a collective decision must be made we cannot bother with the considerations that were raised in the filmgoer example; we should not seek to model the intensity, ordering, or even the rationality of the individuals' preferences; nor should we focus on questions regarding the independent *merits* of the collective decisions produced by the democratic process. The aggregative view holds instead that the most important thing is that a collective decision be reached that has *some* plausible claim to representing the will of the people, the "popular will." The aggregative view holds that insofar as a decision procedure affords to each actor equal input, and aggregates the inputs into a majority decision, it realizes the democratic ideal of self-government among political equals.

This sounds simple and highly plausible. However, the central problem confronting the view has to do with the mathematical task of counting up the votes. Recall the simple problem we mentioned above where we considered five filmgoers with the following profiles: Debbie and Emma both vote to see the documentary, Ann votes for the romantic comedy, Betty votes for the thriller, and Cara votes for the mystery. On a simple adding up of the votes, the group has decided to go to the documentary. However, it is difficult to see how this result could plausibly be seen as a reflection of the "popular will" of the group; after all, the majority would prefer to see something other than the documentary. This is certainly an oversimplified example, but it suffices to show that the question facing aggregative views is how to design a voting procedure that will preclude this kind of irrationality. The details cannot be canvassed here, but famous social-choice results associated with the economist Kenneth Arrow demonstrate that there is no way to transform expressions of individual preference into a rational collective decision that could plausibly claim to represent the popular will. The aggregative view is thus imperiled.

6.3.2 Minimalism

One way to react to the seemingly insurmountable mathematical difficulties confronting the aggregative view is to conclude that the very idea of a popular will is incoherent, and thus disposable. Hence there is a family of views that retains the aggregative view's commitment to equal-vote majoritarianism while jettisoning the idea that collective decisions must be plausibly seen as representing the popular will; these views are known as *minimalist*. (Recall that in section 5.2.1 we encountered a conception of justice called *minimalism*; minimalism in democratic theory is different from minimalism concerning justice, though the views are in some obvious ways complementary.) According to the minimalist, there is no such thing as a popular will, thus the ideal of self-government among equals cannot require that collective decisions reflect it. The question is how to make sense of self-government among equals without invoking such a concept. We'll consider two minimalist attempts to do so.

There is a central minimalist thought that might have already occurred to you. One might say that the ideal of self-government among equals is fundamentally the ideal of *anti-tyranny*, rather than anything having to do with collective decisions that reflect the popular will. And one can easily anticipate how this anti-tyranny minimalism would proceed. On this view, the central aim of democracy is efficiently to deliver collective decisions within a framework that reliably produces political stability by discouraging autocracy on the part of public officials and rebellion on the part of the citizens. To fill in more details, the anti-tyranny minimalist sees democracy as a system of collective decision that offers to the citizens regular and relatively peaceful electoral events whereby they may replace officeholders who are seen to be performing poorly, and the electoral process in turn incentivizes elected officials to exercise their power with restraint and to avoid actions that are likely to prove unpopular. Those officeholders who overreach or engage in unpopular actions risk being voted out of office, and so behave moderately. Government is hence produced, and collective decisions efficiently rendered, without need of a permanent hierarchy or ruler. According to minimalism, the ideal of self-government among equals is realized where politically ambitious individuals compete in elections for a chance to rule temporarily.

Anti-tyranny minimalism hence sees democracy as a market-like arrangement under which aspiring officials compete for votes and other forms of popular support. Consequently, the view is consistent with there being within society a single and relatively small ruling *class* composed of individuals who cycle in and out of power, each ruling principally to the benefit of his or her class. In fact, the anti-tyranny view is consistent with circumstances in which every citizen but for a small and wealthy few is effectively blocked from holding political office. Remember that on the anti-tyranny minimalist view all that democracy requires is that no single *person* hold unrestrained power for too long. But, as it is consistent with a society in which members of one class rule over the rest, it appears to be consistent with a kind of social hierarchy that one would think democracy should oppose. Consequently anti-tyranny minimalism might be *too* minimal to capture the ideal of self-government among equals.

Let us turn to an alternate kind of minimalist view that is frequently called *pluralism*. Pluralism holds with the anti-tyranny view that democracy is a competition for votes among aspiring politicians. It thus accepts equal-vote majoritarianism. But the pluralist view introduces a more nuanced view of power than the one offered by the anti-tyranny minimalist. Whereas the anti-tyranny minimalist sees political power as fundamentally residing in the offices of government, the pluralist, by contrast, sees power as distributed throughout society, especially in the various kinds of groups and associations formed by individuals who share political interests. On the pluralist view, then, democracy is a constant negotiation among multiple interest groups, with competing groups exerting pressure on elected officials well beyond Election Day. The pluralist, that is, rejects the view that democracy is temporary and restrained rule by elected officials, holding instead that democracy is rule by elected officials in response to the push and pull of competing and dynamic minorities. The pluralist hence seems to avoid the problem raised above with the anti-tyranny view; democracy, according to the pluralist, requires institutions and forums where distinct popular interest groups can form, organize, operate, and ultimately exert influence. Hence the pluralist claims that democracy calls for more than elections; it also needs lobbies.

The difference between these two minimalisms is important, but perhaps not as important as what the views have in common. Both views hold that democracy is a political mechanism that produces collective decisions efficiently for a conflicted population in a way that secures social stability by incentivizing restraint on the part of politicians (lest they get voted out of office) and discouraging revolt among the citizens. But more importantly, both views deny that the democratic ideal is in any deep sense *moral*; the equality required by democracy is strictly the mathematical matter of whether each citizen gets the same voting power, and the value of democracy lies simply in the fact that it indeed protects against tyranny and instability. Consequently, minimalist views do not speak to the normative question we raised above about the basis of democracy's authority, the bindingness of democratic decisions even on those in the minority. Minimalist views tend to be motivated by the idea that these normative matters ultimately make no sense. Recall that minimalism arises from the thought that talk of the "public will" is nonsense.

However, there is reason to suspect that minimalism cannot avoid appealing to the idea of a public will after all. This is perhaps clearest in the case of the anti-tyranny version, so we'll focus there. The anti-tyranny minimalist holds that democracy produces stability partly because it offers citizens the opportunity to vote out of office those officials who seem to be doing a poor job; this threat of losing reelection is then regarded as sufficient to provide officeholders with due incentive to avoid taking extreme and unpopular actions. But if the Arrowvian social-choice results mentioned earlier suffice to show that the very idea of a "popular will" is nonsense, then so, too, should they show that democratic voting cannot be interpreted as an expression of dissatisfaction on the part of the citizens with any given official. In other words, if, as the social-choice results are said to show, democratic voting cannot be an expression of the popular will (because there is no such thing), then it is not clear how the fact of regular elections could provide any specific incentive to standing officeholders. Once the idea of a popular will is discarded as nonsense, then so, too, must we reject the idea of a democratic citizenry threatening bad officeholders by declining to reelect them. If, on the other hand, the minimalist wants to retain the view that votes are means by which the democratic citizenry expresses approval or disapproval of politicians, then the idea of a popular will is again in play, and we are led back to the aggregative view. Minimalism hence looks internally conflicted. It wants to dismiss the idea of a popular will as nonsense, yet also wants to talk about democratic elections as providing incentives for politicians to retain their popularity with the citizenry; the minimalist cannot have it both ways.

6.3.3 Stepping Back

Before moving on to examine a few contemporary conceptions of democracy, let us step back for a moment to consider a broader concern with the classical conceptions. Recall what was emphasized in section 6.2.3. Whatever else one may want to say about democracy, it must not be forgotten that a democracy is also a kind of state. As it is a kind of state, a democracy claims for itself the moral entitlement to coerce its citizens—to use force in order to get them to act in ways they otherwise would not—even though it also is committed to regarding all citizens as equals. In the chapter about authority (Chapter 4), we explored the problems that arise from the very idea of authority relations among equals. But democracy aspires to be the solution to at least one of those problems. The democrat argues that political rules, laws, and policies have their authority over the citizenry because of the way in which democracy makes its decisions. In brief, the democrat claims that, with certain special exceptions, you must obey democratic laws because such laws are, in some sense, the product of *your own* will—even in the case of a law that you voted against and continue to oppose.

That is a deeply puzzling thought. The task of most democratic theory is to try to make sense of it, and ultimately to vindicate it. One way to understand the task is to imagine a fellow citizen named Frances. She just lost an important vote and is wondering why she should comply with the democratic outcome. What could one say to her? One could obviously offer to Frances the merely *prudential* reason that unless she complies she will be subject to sanction or punishment from the state. But that kind of answer offers her no explanation of the *authority* of democracy; it only reminds her of the fact that the democratic state, like all states, wields great power. Yet this is something she is likely well aware of. All theories of democracy are committed to the idea that there's something *special* about the way democracies make their political decisions, and this special feature accounts for the authority of democratic results. Now, the classical conceptions we canvassed all offer some version of the following kind of response to Frances. They say that the reason Frances has to comply with the result she opposes is that the process by which it was produced gave every citizen an equal say in determining the outcome. And, as we have seen, the classical conceptions all see the system of *equal-vote majoritarianism* as sufficient for ensuring that each citizen has an *equal say* in determining democratic outcomes. Accordingly, one might respond to Frances by claiming that she had exactly one vote—no more and no less than anyone else—and more people disagreed with her view on the matter than agreed. So, even though she must now comply with a decision that she opposes, she is nonetheless being treated as an equal. Moreover, an advocate of any classical conception can say, further, that Frances will have the opportunity to vote again in the next election, and will thus have another chance to get her way.

The reply we have been sketching on behalf of the classical view should have a familiar ring. But one may nonetheless wonder whether it is really all that compelling. After all, in a wide range of other cases we do not take equal voting to be a good decision procedure. For example, we think it would be irrational to decide by an equal vote among the general population what medicine to take when we're feeling ill. Here the democrat could reply that the decision of what medicine to take is crucially different from the kind of *collective* decision-making that democracy must engage in. The democrat's thought continues that in a democracy we have to decide the rules by which *we will live together*, and the only way this could be consistent with our political equality is if such decisions give each of us an equal say in deciding what the rules will be.

So far, so good. But now the question confronting the democrat is whether equal-vote majoritarianism is sufficient for ensuring that each citizen has an equal say in decision-making. Here there is considerable room for debate.

Think again of Frances; her side just lost a vote and she's wondering why she should be required to comply with the democratic result. We already have told her that she must comply because the decision is the product of a process that treats everyone as an equal. But the claim that equal-vote majoritarianism suffices for giving each an equal say begins to ring hollow once we take into account the fact that, in a democracy, political *influence* and social *standing* are not equally distributed among the citizenry. To be more specific, one need not look too far back in the history of existing democratic states to find instances in which majorities have exercised various forms of social power to marginalize, silence, demote, and invalidate the interests, ideas, concerns, and even the *voices* of minority groups. In fact, we know that even today many democratic citizens overtly profess various kinds of racism, sexism, classism, and other discriminatory tendencies that typically lead individuals to ignore the voices of members of the disfavored groups. And it may astound you to know that a formidable mass of empirical evidence shows that, even in this day and age, your fellow citizens—both men and women—unconsciously tend to regard women's testimony, legal and otherwise, as intrinsically less reliable than men's!

Bigotry and unjust discriminatory attitudes and practices are not the only problems, however. We all know that, with respect to any major political office, running an effective political campaign requires unbelievable amounts of money; those without money, or access to money, have very little chance of winning public office. Similarly, we know that access to the forums and institutions that enable citizens to speak to their fellow citizens about political topics is not equally distributed across the population; again, those with large sums of money at their disposal can easily purchase advertising space in newspapers and on television, and this allows them to broadcast their political ideas to the entire citizenry; lacking the requisite financial resources, most citizens cannot match the degree of political influence that is available to the very wealthy.

The trouble, then, is this: Equal-vote majoritarianism is consistent with a background culture in which vast inequalities—of political power, standing, and influence—are prevalent. Under such cultural conditions, it seems plausible to think that equal voting is not sufficient for having an equal say in the democratic process. One might argue instead that having an equal say requires that the equal voting occur under broader cultural conditions in which everyone has something like an *equal voice*, the social standing to be recognized by one's fellow citizens as an equal, as someone with ideas, concerns, and proposals that deserve an *equal hearing*. This is the thought driving the two leading contemporary trends in democratic theory that we'll examine next.

6.4 Two Contemporary Trends

The claim underlying the classical conceptions of democracy is that equality of input in a majoritarian decision-making procedure suffices as an explanation of the authority of democratic outcomes. We just considered an argument to the effect that equal voting is *not* sufficient for ensuring that every citizen has an equal say in democratic decision-making. What else is required? The two views that we are about to encounter share a common core; they both hold that classical democratic theory conceives of the processes of democratic decision-making too narrowly. To be more specific, these current conceptions contend that the classical views employ a conception of equality that is too fixed on what happens in the voting booth, or in the public activities of political officials. The thought driving much of contemporary democratic theory is that although the democratic decision-making process may *culminate* with voting, it begins long before Election Day, in the cultural and civic activities of politically engaged democratic citizens. Now we ask, what are these activities? The two views we are about to consider—participationism and deliberativism—give different responses. As the second of these two views is by all accounts the predominant approach to democratic theory today, we will consider it in some detail.

6.4.1 Participationism

According to *participationism*, the ideal of self-government among equals involves a robust conception of citizenship that is tacitly denied by the classical views. That is, the participationist holds that classical conceptions presuppose an anemic conception of democratic citizenship; roughly, the classical theorists begin from a view of the citizen as a largely private and self-interested agent seeking a political order that suits his or her individual preferences. The participationist, by contrast, holds that democratic citizenship is a distinctive kind of public office. On this view, a citizen is not simply a private individual acting in public on behalf of his or her private interests. Rather, the democratic citizen is charged with the distinctively *civic* and *public-minded* task of contributing to the collective project of self-government.

In this way, participationists see democracy as a political and social order in which individuals must sometimes put aside their private interests and, with others, adopt the perspective of the political community, acting for the sake of the common good rather than their individual preferences. Democracy hence is envisioned as a large-scale collection of interlocking civic associations, where individuals come together to pursue aims and goods that serve the distinctive good of the whole. Thus the emphasis is transferred away from the classical focus on the need to produce collective decisions amidst conflicting preferences and toward civic processes aimed at forging solidarity, consensus, community, and a sense of belonging among equal citizens.

It may be instructive to contrast participationism with the pluralist variant of minimalism described above. Recall that pluralism holds that democracy is a system of ongoing power conflicts among social groups organized around citizen interests; these groups vie for influence with seated officials, and the officials attempt to satisfy as many, and alienate as few, groups as possible (lest they undercut their chances of reelection). Participatory democracy also adopts the broad idea that democracy is an ongoing social process, but insists that democratic participation requires citizens to adopt a fundamentally *civic* perspective. Whereas pluralism sees democratic action in terms of particular interest groups struggling to pressure officials to mold public policy around their specific preferences, the participationist sees democratic action in terms of civic groups of various kinds organizing and interacting, primarily for the purpose of establishing consensus, coalition, and mutual understanding among the citizenry. To formulate the contrast a little more starkly, the pluralist sees democracy as what we today call *lobbying*, while the participationist associates democracy with the broad range of civic activities that we sometimes call *organizing*. And whereas the pluralist sees the characteristic activity of the interest group to be that of *pressuring* politicians into supporting policies in line with the specific group's interest, the participationist, again, recognizes a broad variety of political activities—from canvassing and campaigning to letter-writing, editorializing, consciousness-raising, and community-building—in the service of building a social movement around a common interest.

Now, think again of Frances, the disappointed citizen we discussed earlier. She's just lost a vote, and is wondering why she should be required to comply with the standing result, which she opposes. The participationist can say to her that even though her favored outcome lost in the election, she must comply because the process treated her as an equal in the following way. Not only did she have the same voting power as every other citizen, but she was also afforded the opportunity to work with like-minded citizens in forming organizations and engaging in public activities designed to convince the broader population of her view. Moreover, the participationist can go further to tell Frances that although her side lost the vote, she may still engage in social and political activities designed to convince her fellow citizens to reverse their decision; moving forward, she and others may continue to organize, criticize, challenge, and, in some cases, even resist and protest the decision she opposes.

We can say, then, that participationism holds that the democratic ideal of self-government among equal citizens is realized when the process of equal-vote majoritarianism is supplemented by broad social support for democratic civic activity in which citizens can publicly interact, communicate, and try to influence each other's political views. Thus the view improves upon the classical views in that it supplies an additional kind of justification to the minority voter; she may not have gotten her way, but she was able to make her views known to her fellow citizens, and was given the opportunity to try to change their minds.

Yet the participatory model still may not be able to address the problems we raised above with the classical conceptions. The opportunity to organize and to build coalitions is surely a central element of the democratic process; moreover, the kind of civic-mindedness prescribed by participationism is without a doubt necessary for a healthy democracy. But there remain difficulties in cases where the broader culture tends to ignore or disregard the ideas, concerns, and voices of some citizens. When certain segments of the citizenry are subjected to systematic marginalization and denigration, the fact that they are afforded opportunities to publicly organize amounts to only a small improvement over the classical models. Where social standing is unequal due to the prevalence of implicit bigotry, discrimination, and unjust bias in the background culture, the participatory conception offers very little remedy. In fact, one might go further and argue that, under such conditions, the participationist places the onerous task of democratic progress squarely on those segments of the population that are likely to be the least powerful, and, not incidentally, also the most vulnerable. To put the point in another way, the participationist conception encourages citizens—both as individuals and as groups—to speak up, but it does not do much to ensure that anyone actually gets a hearing. It is difficult to see how such a conception realizes the ideal of self-government among equals.

6.4.2 Deliberativism

If the arguments just sketched hold, then the democratic ideal requires more than equal-vote majoritarianism against the backdrop of a participationist civil society; other conditions must be added if a society is plausibly to count as an instance of self-government among political equals. *Deliberativist* conceptions of democracy propose that the ideal of self-government among equals is realized when democratic outcomes are in some sense the product of processes of *public deliberation*. Hence deliberativists share with participationist views the idea that democracy is more than voting and elections; like participationism, deliberativism holds that the social and civic processes *leading up to* an election are as crucial to democracy as the act of voting. It should be added that deliberativists also tend to endorse the participationist vision of a vibrant and dynamic civil society, active with social and political organizations and associations of all kinds. But to this, the deliberativist adds a distinctive concern with the ways citizens come to form their political views and the reasons that inform citizens' votes. The thought is that, in a democracy, collective decisions derive their authority from the fact that, prior to voting, each citizen was able to engage in activities whereby he or she could *rationally persuade* others to adopt his or her favored view by defending it with reasons, and offering reasons opposing competing views. According to the deliberativist, the democratic ideal has at its core an idea of *collective reasoning*. In order for citizens to rule themselves as equals, they must reason together as equals.

That sounds rather lofty. To see more clearly what is being proposed, consider once again Frances. The deliberativist claims that Frances must comply with the democratic outcome she opposes because, prior to voting, citizens (including Frances) had the opportunity to exchange not merely their opinions and preferences, but their *reasons* in support of their views, and, as it turns out, Frances and her like-minded fellows did not manage to persuade enough people. The deliberative democratic process, then, is held to respect Frances's equality in virtue of the fact that it gives her reasons—both in favor of her own view and against other views—a hearing. But perhaps more important than this, it also enables Frances to hear the reasons of her fellow citizens, the considerations that lead them to reject her view and favor another. Accordingly, even though she must now comply with a result she opposes, Frances can see, perhaps even appreciate, the reasons that support that result, and she can see how her fellow citizens were led to adopt their views. Consequently, she can also see how she should move forward in criticizing the result and pressing for its reform. In a nutshell, the deliberativist holds that self-government among equals is realized when collective decision-making is responsive to citizens' reasons.

Deliberativism hence is attuned to the difficulties raised earlier concerning inequalities in social standing. It holds, in effect, that the democratic ideal is not realized unless all citizens' reasons are given a *fair hearing* in a social process of public deliberation, where individuals are not only willing to question the views of others, but also open to having their own political views challenged (and their minds changed). This goes some distance in showing that democracy requires institutions and policies designed to constrain the ways in which money and other forms of social privilege can be transformed into political power. Furthermore, by requiring that democratic deliberation be public, the deliberativist addresses somewhat the concern that the prevalence of bigoted and unjust discriminatory attitudes in the background culture of a democracy will undermine equality. For one thing, public deliberation must be *inclusive* of the public. Thus, informal blocks to citizens' access to processes of democratic reasoning must be eliminated. Moreover, the need for deliberation to be public also helps to root out and neutralize political views that derive from racism, sexism, and other forms of unjust discrimination. When addressing and evaluating each other's *reasons*, certain kinds of considerations are rendered irrelevant, or even inadmissible; one cannot refute a reason by simply expressing a bigoted attitude.

Deliberativism has distinctive virtues. This is why it is the predominant approach in contemporary democratic theory. However, it also raises obvious difficulties. To get a sense of these difficulties, we will need first to examine in some detail one of deliberativism's central components.

6.4.2.1 Public Reasoning

According to the deliberativist, democratic politics is conducted centrally with reasons, rather than simply with votes. Prior to voting, citizens and officeholders are supposed to share, exchange, evaluate, and criticize each other's reasons, all within a public process of collective deliberation. One natural question emerges instantly. What is a reason?

Deliberativists offer a diverse array of responses to this question; however, they seem to agree on the following. When engaging in public deliberation, citizens attempt to address their reasons *to their fellow citizens*. This means, in part, that when publicly deliberating, citizens are supposed to offer only reasons that their fellow citizens *could adopt* as their own. As was mentioned a moment ago, this means that certain kinds of considerations will be rendered inadmissible in public deliberation. For example, if you favor a drastic tax cut, and offer to me as a reason, "I like money," or "I want it," you have failed to contribute to the process of public deliberation. To be sure, that you like money and want the tax cut indeed might be *your* reasons for supporting the tax cut. However, that *you* like money and want a tax cut cannot, all by themselves, serve as reasons for *me* to adopt your view of the proposed tax cut. By declaring, "I like money," or "I want it," you have not offered me a reason to support the tax cut in question; you have only revealed information about yourself. In order to deliberate together, citizens must trade in reasons of a particular kind, namely reasons that they could potentially share.

Following the nomenclature prevalent in the current literature, let us call those reasons that are shareable in the requisite way *public reasons*. The deliberativist holds, then, that the ideal of self-government among equals is realized when collective decision-making is responsive to citizens' *public reasons*. So our question now is what makes a reason shareable, and therefore public.

It is intuitive to say that "I want it" fails as a public reason. For the reasons indicated a moment ago, "I want it" is obviously not shareable in the relevant sense. But what would a shareable reason look like? Consider the following reason for supporting the tax cut: "This tax cut will stimulate the local economy and help to lower unemployment significantly." This reason looks public in the relevant respect in that it could be shared among citizens; *that* the tax cut will have the stated effects could be my reason to support it, and it could be yours as well. But it looks public in an additional way in that it cites the *public* goods of stimulating the economy and decreasing joblessness as the determinative considerations for supporting the policy. We might say that this latter feature of the proposed reason accounts for its shareability; the reason is shareable *because* it references a social good and goal that citizens could reasonably be expected to acknowledge as worthy.

Now, it should be emphasized that to call a reason *public* is certainly not to endorse it; nor is it even to say that the reason is particularly weighty. Public reasons may yet be rejectable, and moreover they can be weak. One could acknowledge the publicity of the reason while also challenging it. For example, one could argue on empirical grounds that the proposed tax cut in fact would *not* stimulate the economy. Or one could argue that although the cut would have the indicated effects, there are more weighty public reasons against the cut. One could imagine circumstances in which the tax cut would indeed stimulate the economy and help to lower unemployment, but would also drive large numbers of citizens out of the middle class, and would drastically reduce home ownership among the poorest citizens. Under such circumstances, there would be countervailing public reasons—considerations to be entered into public deliberation and evaluated among the others.

Of course, the tax-cut example we have been looking at is highly simplified. The point at present is that on the deliberativist view public reasons are the *terms in which* democratic deliberation is conducted. With regard to any policy question, there should be a wide array of public reasons supporting a similarly broad menu of policy options, and these reasons will be of varied strength, weight, and plausibility. The task of democratic deliberation is to give due consideration to the public reasons, and to give the policy options a hearing by examining the public reasons that support each option. In this way, the requirement that citizens exchange and evaluate *public reasons* is intended to *leave open* the policy questions that democratic citizens must confront; identifying the public reasons regarding a policy proposal is supposed to *open* public deliberation of the matter, not close it.

6.4.2.2 *Complexities of Public Reason*

Although the term *public reason* is closely associated with those deliberativist views that originate with the philosophy of John Rawls, the fact is that all deliberativist conceptions of democracy must rely upon some explicit distinction between the reasons that count in democratic deliberation and those that do not. Thus far, I have used the term in this general sense, simply to mark those reasons that indeed count in public deliberation. But the devil is in the details, so to speak, and the examples offered above of how the distinction between public and nonpublic reasons should be drawn have been overly simplistic. It's time to look at a few of the complications that this distinction occasions once one attempts to draw it with the requisite detail.

We have said that what makes a reason public is its shareability. And we have also said that the shareability of a reason has to do, at least in part, with its *content*. More specifically, in the example about the tax cut, it was claimed that considerations regarding economic stimulation, the unemployment rate, the financial health of the middle class, and access to home ownership are all *public* in that they reference a goal or value that can be reasonably be expected to be widely shared among the population of democratic citizens to whom they are addressed. This suggests that the distinction between public and nonpublic reasons is largely a *sociological* matter, the claim that those reasons are public that can be recognized by some given democratic population as shareable. However, if the publicity of a reason is construed in this way, the deliberativist will quickly confront a version of the kind of the difficulty we raised earlier with the participationist and classical conceptions. To be specific, if publicity is understood as a sociological matter, then reasons for public policy that draw upon, for example, racist, sexist, classist, or homophobic considerations will count as public reasons, provided that such attitudes prevail in the society in question. In other words, the sociological construal of the publicity of reasons seems actually to *empower* bigotry in those communities where it is especially pronounced. This is a most unwelcome result. So it seems that deliberativists require some non-sociological criterion for drawing the distinction between public and nonpublic reasons.

There may be something puzzling about the very idea of a non-sociological conception of public reason. After all, the distinction between public and nonpublic reasons is supposed to help democratic citizens conduct public deliberation, and make political decisions, in a way that respects the equality of all citizens by ensuring that all citizens' views get a fair hearing. One wonders, then, about the status of a proposed conception of the shareability of reasons that is not itself based in the sociological facts regarding what reasons a given population of citizens actually share. To press the point in a slightly different way, one may ask, *"What is the appropriate kind of reason to appeal to when proposing a demarcation between public and nonpublic reasons?"* The very project seems oddly doomed.

But let's not be too hurried. One way to move forward would be to look again to the democratic ideal of self-government among political equals. The strategy would be to define the publicity of reasons by appealing to the fundamental presupposition that in various ways has been underlying this entire book, namely, that each citizen is a free and equal individual, and the corresponding need for the state to respect each citizen as a fundamentally free and equal individual. Such an appeal yields something like the following result. A reason is public insofar as its force is consistent with regarding all citizens as free and equal partners in the collective project of democratic self-government. A reason's publicity, then, would not simply be a matter of its shareability, but instead of its shareability *among free and equal democratic citizens*.

That formulation has a favorable ring to it, as it seems to neatly disqualify from publicity those reasons that draw upon the kinds of unjust discriminatory attitudes we mentioned above. It also seems to capture well why the reasons we mentioned earlier in our discussion of the tax cut should count as properly public reasons. Now we see that in the tax-cut case it is not merely that considerations regarding economic stimulation and home ownership are likely to be shared among democratic citizens; it is that such considerations *ought to be shared* among a community of individuals who regard each other as free and equal democratic citizens. Consequently, even within a community of self-centered and greedy elitists, considerations regarding the impact of a tax policy on the poorest citizens will count as a public reason, whether the elitists are inclined to regard it as such or not. Finally, this way of understanding the publicity of reasons helps us to keep in mind the tight connection that the deliberativist sees between the processes of public deliberation and the bindingness of democratic collective decisions; recall that on the deliberativist picture the bindingness and authority of democratic collective decisions owes to the fact that the democratic process recognizes citizens' reasons. With the non-sociological formulation of the distinction between public and nonpublic reasons in hand, we can add to this that, on the deliberativist view, the authority of democratic decisions derives from the fact that the decision-making process is responsive to the reasons citizens could offer *when they are showing due regard for each other as fellow citizens*.

However, serious difficulties remain. The non-sociological rendering of the distinction between public and nonpublic reasons relies upon the moral ideal of the freedom and equality of each citizen. Again, it says that a reason in support of a policy is public when it is consistent with the freedom and equality of all citizens. Yet the matter of what, precisely, it is to evince a due regard for the freedom and equality of each citizen is often *precisely* what divides citizens when they think about political policy. To cite one familiar instance, some argue that a progressive taxation structure within a broad system of public assistance for the society's poorest citizens is a way for the government to ensure that those most vulnerable to marginalization and disenfranchisement are able to act as democratic citizens. They thus argue that in order to show due regard for the freedom and equality of all citizens, society must support progressive taxation and public assistance. Others, however, hold that such arrangements actually demean the poorest individuals by encouraging them to remain dependent on the very programs and benefits that are supposed to be helping them. As we saw in Chapter 5, some hold that only a minimal or umpire state could be consistent with the freedom and equality of each citizen; they thus regard their opponents' argument for progressive taxation and public assistance to be profoundly insensitive to individuals' freedom and equality. The point is that the content of the ideals of freedom and equality are among the things about which democratic citizens are divided, and these divisions often drive citizens' public policy disagreements; our conception of the publicity of a reason needs to do the work of separating those reasons that count in public deliberation from those that do not. The strategy of drawing upon the ideals of freedom and equality in devising our conception of public reason hence looks unpromising, to say the least.

6.4.2.3 Problems with Deliberativism

Let's suppose that this particular conceptual difficulty could be surmounted. Perhaps there is a sufficiently robust and noncontroversial normative core to the ideals of freedom and equality that can be drawn upon in devising a non-sociological conception of the publicity of a reason. The deliberativist program nonetheless raises several problems. We will consider only a few here.

One set of questions has probably already occurred to you. How could a deliberative democracy be *instituted*? What would its institutions look like? Would such a democracy need to build special forums for public deliberation? How would it work? Would each citizen be given equal time to address *every other citizen*, or only some other citizens? Once one begins thinking about the logistics of deliberativism, one wonders whether democracy has the *time* to make political decisions deliberatively. This is to say nothing about the demands deliberativism seems to place on citizens. What about those citizens who have a pronounced distaste for political argument and would rather spend their free time gardening, cooking, or teaching children to read? Are they to be regarded as failing at democratic citizenship? One is reminded here of a jibe attributed to Oscar Wilde about socialism—he said it required too many meetings.

Perhaps the deliberativist could respond to these concerns. She might say that the core deliberativist ideal calls only for *the opportunity* for citizens to deliberate together, not the requirement that they do so. And, furthermore, perhaps the deliberative ideal could be realized in a system of deliberative *representatives*, thus freeing the average citizen from the seemingly unyielding burden of deliberative democracy. Yet even if these concerns could be addressed, there remains another series of fairly obvious worries. Is the entire model helplessly optimistic? Doesn't it depend upon an almost inexcusably naïve vision of politics?

Just think for a moment about the *cognitive* demands the deliberativist places upon democratic citizens. First of all, citizens must be willing to deliberate publicly with their fellow citizens. This means that they must be able and willing to think through their own political commitments, articulate to themselves their own reasons, and consider whether their reasons are sufficient. Perhaps that's not too much to ask. But citizens must also be willing to share their reasons with others, and *defend* their political views against criticism. Furthermore, they are expected to listen to the reasons offered by their political opponents. What's more, they must seriously consider the merits of those reasons. Perhaps, again, these requirements are not too strenuous, although some citizens will surely find them onerous. But deliberativism requires more. It requires that citizens must be ready to admit the possibility that their own views are mistaken, incomplete, irrational, or foolish. And they must be open to having their political convictions corrected or otherwise changed in light of their deliberative exchanges. They are expected to keep their political convictions at a certain critical distance, and stand ready to abandon what might be longstanding or even cherished commitments, should public deliberation prove them flawed. Inevitably, in the course of public deliberation, some citizens will lose face, and some will no doubt feel humiliated and exposed in the process.

Now, these cognitive requirements and expectations are perfectly appropriate for a Philosophy seminar. There, the explicit collective aim is to challenge ideas, exchange criticisms, press objections, and follow the arguments wherever they might lead, all in the hope of moving closer to truth. But a democracy is not a Philosophy classroom, nor should it be. Individuals' commitments to their political views are complicated at best, and most commonly they are far from fully rational. Most commonly, political convictions are the product of tangles of disparate forces: reasons, values, upbringing, blind spots, cultural biases, and much else. Consequently, citizens often do not have a good sense of their reasons, and are prone to various kinds of non-rational cognitive defense mechanisms; they confabulate, rationalize, overestimate the weight of the evidence that favors their own views and underestimate the weight of countervailing evidence, and so on. In fact, as it turns out, we're not especially good reasoners. And we seem to get worse when we're considering ideas and commitments in which we are *invested*. Our political ideas are often tied closely to the values, projects, and plans around which we have built our lives. Consequently, we often find it difficult to treat those views with the kind of rational detachment that the deliberativist appears to require. In brief, the deliberativist expectation that citizens put their views up for the rational scrutiny of fellow citizens seems overly demanding.

A deliberativist might concede this point, but maintain that democratic citizens nonetheless *ought to* seek to have political views that reflect their best reasons, and so they ought to stand ready to subject their convictions to the rational scrutiny of others. Perhaps they should. But now consider a new difficulty. Deliberativism obviously makes heavy use of concepts like *reason*, *rationality*, and *deliberation*. One might be concerned that these terms, and the resulting deliberativist ideal, presuppose a range of communicative norms that may themselves be unjustly exclusionary. To explain, the deliberativist's call for reason exchange and rational dialogue puts a political premium on speech that is articulate, polite, refined, and calm. Arguably, this advantages citizens who are educated, well-spoken, native speakers of the local language, and likely to be already privileged in various ways; citizens who speak with a thick accent, or are not especially articulate, or are not skilled in public speaking, are likely to be dismissed as unreasonable, and their reasons are hence likely to be disregarded. One suspects, again, that the deliberativists' conception of public deliberation is too much rooted in the practices and norms of an academic seminar.

A related concern now comes to the foreground. If, indeed, the deliberativist view advantages those who are most easily able to speak with the requisite eloquence and dispassion, it would seem that the view also advantages the political views most likely to be favored by such speakers. In privileging the speech of the educated, polished, articulate, and refined citizens, the deliberative model in turn privileges the political views associated with the advantaged social classes: the white, wealthy, male, white-collar graduates of elite universities. The concern, then, is that deliberativism's appeal to public deliberation and collective reasoning is *itself* an unwitting defense of the political *status quo*. Those who advocate radical economic and social changes to our democracy are required to adopt communicative norms that privilege the voices, and hence the views, of their opponents. Yet, as we know simply from watching the nightly news, longstanding systems of discrimination and injustice often cannot be changed simply with reasons and arguments; changing well-entrenched institutions and practices sometimes requires political action that seemingly has little to do with the exchange of reasons.

Given the aims of their view, deliberativists will need to show how their conception of public deliberation and collective reasoning can accommodate and give a fair hearing to the voices of the underprivileged. They will also have to show that the deliberativist ideal could be rendered consistent with the kind of political activism that democratic social change often requires. To be sure, contemporary deliberativists are eager to develop accounts that respond to these concerns. Unless they succeed, it may be that, even if deliberativism were logistically practicable and cognitively feasible, it might nonetheless be politically undesirable.

6.5 Conclusion

This chapter has covered a lot of ground, and it has seemed to terminate in the bleak conclusion that democracy, perhaps our most cherished political idea, might be philosophically nonviable. What are we to make of this result?

Throughout this book, we have been looking for ways to render our political order coherent. The central challenge has been to show how the authority of the state could be reconciled with the freedom and equality of the individual. In other words, we have been seeking a *justification* of the state. As was mentioned earlier in this chapter, democracy is supposed to provide a mode of governance where the state has authority because *in some sense* the state *is* its citizens; its will—expressed in its laws and commands—is the will of its people. If that idea could be made plausible, a central element of our task would be achieved. Yet, as this chapter has shown, the fundamental ideal of democracy—the ideal of self-government among political equals—is especially thorny. And it should be added that the discussion in this chapter employed many simplifying premises. The task of making sense of democracy is even more difficult than this chapter has indicated.

Early in this chapter, a famous quip of Winston Churchill's was mentioned. He once claimed, "Democracy is the worst form of government, except for all those other forms that have been tried." The remark is frequently cited with a chuckle, and its lesson is often taken simply to be that, whatever the faults of democracy, the alternatives are *so much worse* that we ought to just put up with it. Perhaps Churchill's defense of democracy as the least awful of all the awful options for government suffices as a philosophical justification of the democratic state; maybe philosophers are making a mistake in looking for more than this. But, on the other hand, there may be more to say about Churchill's comment. It might be worth asking exactly what it is about democracy that makes it the least awful option.

One answer quickly comes to mind. Democracy is unique in being a system of government that is consistent with its own reform. A democracy is perpetually reevaluating, reexamining, and often revising its policies. It, moreover, is able to reform even its more fundamental institutional and procedural structures while keeping its identity as a democracy intact. Of course, in a democracy, sweeping social change is slow and difficult, and in some cases even relatively modest reforms require unbelievable degrees of sustained effort. But the consolation for this lies in the fact that those who seek social change in the directions that you oppose also have to shoulder those same burdens. In a democracy, that is, anything can be changed, but *no one* gets to make big changes quickly or easily.

This point can be expanded. If all the options are, as Churchill alleges, bad, then surely there's something to be said for the option that can recognize this very fact, and subject itself to criticism. The result is a system of government that is both aware of its fallibility and on guard against its tendency to act too hastily when trying to correct itself. So, yes, democracy often feels like an exceedingly inefficient, even plodding and hapless, motley congeries of institutions, procedures, laws, and offices. But that's its virtue.

This dimension of democracy fits nicely with a further observation. Throughout this chapter we have spoken of the democratic *ideal*, but we did not pause to say much about what it might mean to identify democracy with an ideal. Perhaps the point of talking about democracy as an ideal is obvious, but perhaps not. In any case, in identifying the *ideal* of democracy, one acknowledges that democracy is largely an *aspiration*. To be more specific, a democratic society is one that aspires to instantiate self-government among political equals, and has met some basic institutional and procedural conditions necessary for the pursuit of that goal. These basic conditions include all of the apparatus we commonly recognize as distinctively democratic, including regular open elections, equal-vote majoritarianism, accountable public officials, a workable division of power within government, as well as a free press, freedom of expression, freedom of association, and various forms of protection for political dissent and critique. No society that does not support institutions of this kind can plausibly be regarded as aspiring to the ideal of self-government among equals.

Yet, importantly, satisfying these basic conditions is not sufficient for democracy. The aspirational element of democracy is no less crucial than the institutional and procedural components. Against the backdrop of the basic institutional apparatus, democracy requires there to be a vibrant civil society of citizen engagement and political action, including the public-deliberation activities advocated by the deliberativists. Such action helps the democracy identify new possibilities for expanding and enriching the degree of self-government among the citizens; it also helps the democracy to correct itself, to reform those aspects of the social order that are falling short of the democratic ideal. We might say, then, that a democratic society is a combination of the familiar institutions and procedures with a civic order that allows citizens to challenge, critique, test, and attempt to expand the democratic character of their social order.

This thought allows us to return to an idea that was mentioned in passing at the close of section 6.1.3. You may recall that it was suggested there that the critique of existing democratic institutions and practices is itself a central *part of* the ideal of democracy, and that good democratic citizenship partly involves adopting a critical, adversarial stance towards one's society. We now see why one might believe this. Democracy, one might think, is not merely a kind of government, nor is it simply a kind of social order; it is, rather, an ongoing social process of building a political order that more closely realizes the moral idea of self-government among equals. However, the aspiration for ongoing democratization must itself be pursued through channels that are themselves democratic. One cannot enrich democracy by authoritarian means; change in the direction of further democracy must come from within existing democracy. Accordingly, the central tool for the democratic aspiration is the *internal* criticism, opposition, and dissent of democratic citizens. It may sound paradoxical, but in order for a society to be democratic, it must protect and enable—and perhaps encourage—its own critique.

Hence a modified version of the deliberativist conception of democracy becomes visible. The ideal of self-government among equals is never fully realized, but it is approximated to a degree sufficient to render democratic decisions authoritative when equal-vote majoritarianism is supplemented by the requirement that the laws, policies, and actions of the state must be justifiable by public reasons to its citizens. This form of deliberativism demands that the democratic state be *vulnerable* to the criticisms, objections, and contestations of its citizens, that the state be *accountable* to its citizens. This articulation of deliberativism may seem to be only a slight variation on the views discussed above. However, there is a crucial, even if slight, difference. On the view I am now suggesting, the burdens of public reason-giving and public justification fall squarely on the state and its officials. Democratic citizens are not required to reason or publicly deliberate together (though they, of course, may do so); the task of making decisions and policies by following what the best public reasons recommend falls to the citizens' public representatives, who are then *answerable* to their constituents. The citizens' role then would be to act as social critics, pressing for political movement in the direction of further and enriched democracy.

Of course, this is only a very rough sketch of what might be called *contestatory* deliberativism. I think this view can be developed in promising ways to address some of the difficulties raised earlier in this chapter with other versions of deliberativism. Of course, I cannot here begin to develop these thoughts; I leave it to the reader to consider the ways that contestatory deliberativism might be further developed. But, more importantly, I invite the reader to consider the ways in which such a view, once more completely articulated, could be criticized. And what could be more fitting than that?

For Further Reading

The philosophical literature on democracy is overwhelmingly vast and varied. The following books give a good sense of the general territory of democratic thought. First, three canonical books by Robert Dahl should be consulted: *A Preface to Democratic Theory* (Chicago: University of Chicago Press, 1956); *Democracy and its Critics* (New Haven: Yale University Press, 1989); and *On Democracy* (New Haven: Yale University Press, 1998). Then five additional book-length works are worth a close look: C. B. Macpherson's

The Real World of Democracy (Oxford: Oxford University Press, 1965); David Held's *Models of Democracy,* Third Edition (Stanford: Stanford University Press, 2006); Thomas Christiano's *The Rule of the Many* (Boulder: Westview Press, 1996); Frank Cunningham's *Theories of Democracy* (London: Routledge, 2002); and Ian Shapiro's *The State of Democratic Theory* (Princeton: Princeton University Press, 2003). Influential essays on a range of key philosophical issues concerning democracy are collected in *Philosophy and Democracy,* edited by Thomas Christiano (New York: Oxford University Press, 2003).

Important background regarding the classical conceptions is found in Anthony Downs's *An Economic Theory of Democracy* (New York: Harper Books, 1957) and the more recent and highly influential book by William Riker, *Liberalism against Populism* (New York: W. H. Freeman and Co., 1982). Both of these books address results first presented in Kenneth Arrow's groundbreaking essay "A Difficulty in Social Welfare" (*Journal of Political Economy,* Volume 68, 1951). Some concerns about the ways in which Arrow's results have been employed are discussed in great detail in Gerry Mackie's challenging *Democracy Defended* (Cambridge: Cambridge University Press, 2003). For a discussion of the impact of Arrow's findings on democratic theory, one should consult David Miller's "Deliberative Democracy and Social Choice" (*Political Studies,* Volume 40, 1992), Jules Coleman and John Ferejohn's "Democracy and Social Choice" (*Ethics,* Volume 97, 1986), and Joshua Cohen's "An Epistemic Theory of Democracy" (*Ethics,* Volume 97, 1986).

A classic version of minimalism is presented in Joseph Schumpeter's *Capitalism, Socialism, and Democracy* (New York: Harper Books, 1962); Richard Posner attempts to revive Schumpeter in his *Law, Pragmatism, and Democracy* (Cambridge, MA: Harvard University Press, 2003). See also another landmark work by Robert Dahl, *Who Governs?* (New Haven: Yale University Press, 1961). The minimalist and aggregative conceptions are well critiqued in some of the influential participationist works, including Carole Pateman's *Participation in Democratic Theory* (Cambridge: Cambridge University Press, 1970); Jane Mansbridge's *Beyond Adversary Democracy* (New York: Basic Books, 1980); Benjamin Barber's *Strong Democracy* (Berkeley: University of California Press, 1984); and Carol Gould's *Rethinking Democracy* (Cambridge: Cambridge University Press, 1988). Robert Putnam's influential work on "social capital" in democracy should also be considered; see his "Bowling Alone" (*Journal of Democracy,* Volume 6, 1995) and the subsequent book of the same name (New York: Simon and Schuster, 2000).

Much of the contemporary literature on democracy focuses on issues and problems arising in the wake of deliberativism. Early summary articulations of the deliberativist program can be found in Bruce Ackerman's "Why Dialogue?" (*Journal of Philosophy,* Volume 86, 1989); Jürgen Habermas's "Three Normative Models of Democracy" (reprinted in *Democracy and Difference,* Seyla Benhabib, ed. Princeton: Princeton University Press, 1996); Amy Gutmann and Dennis Thompson's "Moral Conflict and Political Consensus" (*Ethics,*

Volume 100, 1990), John Rawls's "The Idea of Public Reason Revisited" (first published in the *University of Chicago Law Review*, Volume 64, 1997, but widely reprinted, and included in the expanded edition of Rawls's *Political Liberalism*, New York: Columbia University Press, 2005); and Seyla Benhabib's "Toward a Deliberative Model of Democratic Legitimacy" (reprinted in *Democracy and Difference*, Seyla Benhabib, ed. Princeton: Princeton University Press, 1996).

To get a sense of the landscape of deliberativism, see James Bohman's "The Coming of Age of Deliberative Democracy" (*Journal of Political Philosophy*, Volume 4, 1998); Samuel Freeman's "Deliberative Democracy: A Sympathetic Comment" (*Philosophy and Public Affairs*, Volume 29, 2000); and the articles collected in *Deliberative Democracy*, edited by James Bohman and William Rehg (Cambridge: MIT Press, 1997), and *Deliberative Democracy*, edited by Jon Elster (Cambridge: Cambridge University Press, 1998).

A few skeptical, though in some cases still sympathetic, treatments of deliberativism can be found in John Dryzek's "Legitimacy and Economy in Deliberative Democracy" (*Political Theory*, Volume 29, 2001); Lynn Sanders's "Against Deliberation" (*Political Theory*, Volume 25, 1997); Iris Marion Young's "Communication and the Other: Beyond Deliberative Democracy" (reprinted in *Democracy and Difference*, Seyla Benhabib, ed. Princeton: Princeton University Press, 1996, as well as her "Activist Challenges to Deliberative Democracy" (*Political Theory*, Volume 29, 2001); Cass Sunstein's "The Law of Group Polarization" (*Journal of Political Philosophy*, Volume 10, 2002); Robert Goodin's "Democratic Deliberation Within" (*Philosophy and Public Affairs*, Volume 29, 2000); Elizabeth Anderson's "The Epistemology of Democracy," (*Episteme*, Volume 3, 2006); and Diana Mutz's *Hearing the Other Side* (Cambridge: Cambridge University Press, 2006).

Finally, a few recent book-length discussions of fundamental philosophical issues regarding democracy should be examined. See, especially, David Estlund's groundbreaking *Democratic Authority* (Princeton: Princeton University Press, 2008); Fabienne Peter's *Democratic Legitimacy* (London: Routledge, 2011); Jamie Kelly's *Framing Democracy* (Princeton: Princeton University Press, 2012); Joshua Cohen's collection of essays *Philosophy, Politics, Democracy* (Cambridge, MA: Harvard University Press, 2009); and Helene Landermore's *Democratic Reason* (Princeton: Princeton University Press, 2012).

7   Conclusion

Politics without Certainty

We have been trying throughout this book to make philosophical sense of the political world that citizens of modern liberal democracies inhabit. To be a bit more specific, we have been trying to make sense of the idea that there could be a political authority among free and equal individuals; in this way, we have sought a philosophical justification for the modern state. Toward this end, we took up a few of the concepts central to our shared political world: liberty, authority, justice, and democracy. We explored the problems, puzzles, and difficulties each raises, but tried at the close of every chapter to articulate a tentative suggestion for how each concept might be best understood. It's time to review and take stock.

The opening two chapters laid out the task. To begin doing philosophy with the political world as we find it, we must start with the idea of a liberal democracy, that is, a democracy constrained by the rule of law and a constitutionally codified public menu of individual entitlements and protections. The liberalism that underlies democracy sets the central question of political philosophy. To explain, liberalism is the commitment to the political understanding of individuals as free and equal, each with his or her own life to live and author. States are large-scale institutions that not only wield enormous coercive power, but also claim authority, the *entitlement* to such power. Hence the central question: "Given what individuals are, can states be justified?" Why not anarchism?

Liberty was addressed first. Although it may seem obvious that states stand in need of justification precisely because they limit and reduce individual freedom, it is no easy task to devise a plausible view of what this freedom consists in. After finding significant fault with three distinct conceptions of freedom, it was suggested that we entertain a hybrid view according to which liberty is the absence of interference among autonomous social equals. A society is free, then, to the degree that each enjoys the broadest sphere of non-obstructed activity that is consistent with everyone having the civic standing and the relevant capacities for pursuing a life of his or her own. Freedom, we might say, is the absence of something (namely, others' interference) in the presence of other things (namely, autonomy and equal civic standing). Neither the absence of interference nor the presence of autonomy or civic standing suffices for freedom.

That's a mouthful. What's worse, it really doesn't say all that much. But it does indicate something important which this book has implicitly confirmed at nearly every turn: The fundamental concepts composing the philosophical underpinnings of our political order are not discrete and isolated, but rather interrelated and interdependent. To get a grip on liberty, we need to figure out social equality as well as the moral powers requisite for authoring one's own life. This means that the truth about freedom is partly composed of truths about autonomy and equality.

Suppose that's true. It might nonetheless be the case that individual liberty cannot be reconciled with political authority. Authority, after all, seems to involve a departure from social equality, and likely requires the surrender of individual autonomy. That we must stand in a certain kind of social relation to others in order to be individually free does not entail that there should be states.

We next turned directly to the topic of authority. We found, again, that it is no easy task to formulate an attractive conception of authority, especially if one is committed to regarding citizens as free, equal, and autonomous moral persons. Accounts of political authority seem to always devolve into the simple matter of some people claiming the right to push others around; thus authority is hard to reconcile with the freedom and equality of all. I proposed a *deflated* view of authority, according to which the state's commands provide *pro tanto* moral reasons to act as directed, their force being contingent upon the state satisfying certain basic (though as yet unspecified) conditions for justice and democracy. On the deflated view, unjust and undemocratic states have no entitlement to the obedience of their citizens; they have no authority, but only wield power. Democratic states that are profoundly failing at justice similarly are not authoritative; and states that enact most of what justice demands but are not democratic also fail to have authority. In cases where the state is democratic, not wildly unjust, and thus respectful of human rights, citizens must obey, but only in light of the assessment that the state has cleared basic thresholds for justice and democracy. In such a state, commands are sufficient to obligate citizens, but that obligation is contingent upon the state's being sufficiently democratic and just. Once again, we see that in order to clearly grasp one fundamental concept, we need to elucidate others. More precisely, in order to get a grasp on authority, we need to think through matters regarding justice and democracy. The next chapters were devoted to these key concepts.

Justice is a matter of the state showing each citizen equal regard or concern. After exploring several different conceptions of equal regard, it was suggested that no state can plausibly be seen as showing equal regard if it permits official systems of political subordination and domination among its citizens. Once again, we were led to the thought that the authority of the state depends upon its ability to manifest a due recognition for individual equality, even though it employs coercive power. We saw that one reason why political subordination is unjust is that subordination often renders those who are subordinated unable to object to or resist their oppression; political subordination typically consists in rendering those subordinated politically powerless to effect change. In the most egregious cases, oppression renders its victims unable even to *conceive* of change. If this kind of powerlessness is paradigmatic of injustice, then it looks as if some version of democratic egalitarianism must be correct. Justice prevails when material and social resources requisite for effective democratic participation are distributed equally, unless some unequal distribution enhances everyone's share.

Thinking about justice hence brings us to the topic of democracy. And, as we saw, although democracy is perhaps the political-philosophical idea that is most familiar to us, its precise nature is no less difficult to articulate. Democracy is often presented as the sole hope for political authority, the only system of governance that could possibly reconcile the state's coercive power with the freedom and equality of individuals. To repeat, in a democracy the will of the state is supposed to be in some sense the collective will of the citizens; thus freedom and equality are reconciled with the state's authority. Of course, everything hangs on the idea of the citizens' collective will, and so the political philosopher needs to try to make sense of it. As we saw, that's a tall order, and it is not clear whether a conception of democracy can fill it without becoming impracticable. I proposed a *contestatory* version of deliberative democracy, a model where the legislators and other government officials are required to deliberate together, and the citizenry is called upon to function as social critics, pressing the government to account for itself and its decisions, with public reasons.

Such is a rough account of the ground covered in the preceding chapters, and it should be emphasized that even these rather tentative conclusions remain controversial among political philosophers. Keeping in mind that there is still much more to say, allow me now to attempt to tie it all together. The central result of the foregoing discussion seems to be this: In order to be *de jure* authoritative, a state must be accountable to its citizens. In order to be accountable to its citizens, the state must be *vulnerable* to the criticism, questioning, challenges, and protests of its citizens; it must be able to justify itself and its actions with public reasons; and, perhaps most importantly, it must secure for all individuals the social and material resources necessary for effective democratic citizenship. The claim, again, is that when a state is sufficiently democratic and reasonably just, it enacts policies on the basis of only public reasons; thus its decisions are *justifiable* to citizens, and so citizens are obligated to obey.

To bring this thought into sharper focus, consider again the circumstance of the democratic citizen who finds herself on the losing side of an important vote. Why must she comply with the outcome she opposes? If it can be shown to her that (1) the decision procedure was sufficiently democratic; (2) the background conditions were sufficiently just; (3) the process leading up to the decision was responsive to public reasons; (4) the resulting decision is justifiable with public reasons; and (5) the state remains receptive to ongoing critique and challenge, then the justificatory burden will have been met. Of course, to show her that a democratic outcome is *justifiable* in this way is not to *convince* her that it is best, or even good. Rather, to justify an outcome in the relevant sense is simply to show that the outcome is defensible within the bounds of public reason, reasons that are accessible to her in her role as citizen. The claim is that to justify a democratic outcome in this way is to show that the duty to obey is consistent with her status as a free and equal citizen.

But what if the citizen we have been considering still objects? What if she insists that *despite* the fact that these five conditions have been satisfied, she still has no reason to comply? One might first remind her of the broad range of responses that are available to her. When confronted with a democratic decision that she opposes, she may petition, demonstrate, organize, and campaign against it. She may also satirize, criticize, challenge, and mock those officials and fellow citizens who support it. Within certain constraints, she may additionally engage in protest, agitation, refusal, and resistance; and, under special circumstances, she may even civilly disobey. That is, the kind of authority we have described allows each citizen broad latitude for political action following a democratic decision; citizens who find themselves on the losing side may nonetheless oppose the outcome and continue to press for political change in their favored direction.

But what if the citizen we have envisioned still denies that she has a duty to comply? One might note that her view is beginning to look like the flatfooted insistence the she must always get her way politically, and that others must comply with her will. Such insistence is obviously inconsistent with the freedom and equality of *all* citizens. So perhaps the best response would be to introduce a burden-shifting argument, pressing the citizen to identify the conditions and processes for political decision that on her view would be sufficient to produce authoritative outcomes. One suspects that the kind of citizen we have been envisioning holds views that indeed may be inconsistent with the very idea of a social and political order among free and equal citizens.

Still, there is plenty of room for doubt as to whether any existing democracy can be plausibly regarded as satisfying the five conditions laid out above. Moreover, one might doubt further that it is even *possible* for such a democracy to exist. But note that those who raise concerns about the empirical possibility of the kind of political order we have described seem to accept that there could be, even if only in theory, political authority among free and equal citizens. This concession is philosophically significant. For it means that, as a philosophical matter, political authority is reconcilable with citizens' freedom and equality. A justified state is *conceptually possible*, we might say. Perhaps this is only a scanty victory over the philosophical anarchist; but it's something.

It nevertheless should be acknowledged that, according to the account that has been developed, *de jure* political authority is likely to be rare. On any plausible view of the five conditions laid out above, it will be difficult for a modern state to meet the threshold for authority. In this respect, the anarchist may seem to have prevailed. Perhaps. Everything hangs on the precise details concerning the five conditions. But this is as it should be. After all, the task of vindicating political authority among free and morally equal citizens should be a difficult one. And the question of whether our state is indeed authoritative is one to which we should return again and again.

Next, imagine a more sweeping indictment. A critic could argue that our results are unsurprising, given that the entire project of this book has been based on a handful of objectionable assumptions. The critic might point out that, from the very start, it has been presumed that there *must be* a social and political order of some kind among humans. She might then continue that the starting place for the entire discussion has been a particular description of one very specific kind of social-political arrangement, an arrangement that simply takes for granted an intricate system of states, laws, offices, and individuals. It's no wonder, she may continue, that we have arrived at the conclusion that a sufficiently democratic and just state is thereby authoritative. *That* conclusion was quietly presupposed from the very beginning, our critic may allege. She may then charge that the foregoing discussions amount to nothing more than apologetics for the modern liberal-democratic state. Yet apologetics are not really arguments; consequently, what were presented a moment ago as *results* are, in truth, nothing of the sort.

This kind of criticism is worth taking seriously. In fact, I think there is a lot in it that must be conceded. It is true that the entire discussion in this book has been deliberately confined to the analysis of a small collection of concepts that will be familiar to citizens of contemporary liberal democracies; consequently, we have indeed presupposed that the liberal-democratic political order is an appropriate starting point for political philosophy. It is true that some philosophers contend that liberal democracy is intrinsically irrational, immoral, and incoherent; according to those who take this view, liberal democracy is therefore an inappropriate place to begin. But recall that our explicit aim in this book has been to see whether it is possible to make this loose and seemingly discordant assemblage of familiar ideas—liberty, authority, justice, and democracy—hang together philosophically. Had it turned out that these fundamental concepts are indeed irreconcilable, we would have hit upon a powerful argument for pursuing some philosophical alternative to liberal democracy. To be sure, that there is a way to fit the components of liberal democracy together into a cohesive philosophical package is not a demonstration that liberal democracy is the best, or even a good, mode of political and social organization. That liberal democracy is philosophically coherent only makes it a *candidate* for being a good political order.

In other words, the sweeping criticism just sketched can be met with the response that the foregoing discussions have been intended to be only the beginning of political philosophy. We began with liberal democracy because that is where we find ourselves. Accordingly, in identifying "results," I did not mean to imply that our inquiry is complete. The only thing that's coming to an end at present is this particular book. The task of political philosophy remains. And, as I have said several times in these pages, we have only scratched the surface. Nothing has been settled.

Given this, it might be best to state a more general upshot of the preceding chapters: It is as yet not clear what we should think about our political world. Although we have arrived at conceptions of freedom, authority, justice, and democracy that seem to hang together in a way that is philosophically cohesive, we have not produced anything that is even close to being a properly detailed philosophical account of liberal democracy or any of its components. Again, the most we have shown is that the fundamental elements of the liberal-democratic political order are internally coherent, and thus liberal democracy is not conceptually doomed. But we have avoided nearly all of the most important trench-work. For example, we have said that justice requires that each citizen be provided the material and social resources required for effective democratic citizenship, yet we have said nothing about what these resources are, and how great a share is necessary. In fact, we have not even asked how we should go about finding answers to such questions. Similarly, we have proposed a vision of democracy where citizens are called upon to serve as social critics, but we have not specified precisely what this role demands of individuals. That is to say, not only have we merely scratched the surface, we also have left many of the most crucial issues hanging as loose ends requiring a lot of further analysis. It is certainly possible that once we fill in the required details, it will be revealed that liberal democracy is indeed philosophically doomed. Let me emphasize that this remains a real possibility. The ultimate philosophical fate of our political world has not yet been settled. Supposing that there will be future generations of humans, our descendants in the next century may well look back on us and declare our social and political order nothing short of barbaric, inhuman, indecent, uncivilized, or worse.

When you think about it, matters regarding liberal democracy may be even more uncertain than this. In fact, things might be philosophically bleak. Anyone who keeps up with the news will be able to produce a long list of problems and issues confronting contemporary liberal-democratic states that have not been discussed at all in this book. Take a moment to flip through this morning's newspaper. Here are a few issues that are being discussed: immigration, environmental degradation, war, privacy and surveillance, refugees, torture, nuclear proliferation, terrorism, drug decriminalization, human rights, poverty, human trafficking, incarceration, and healthcare. In order to philosophically vindicate liberal democracy, one will have to develop, within that framework, plausible views concerning these issues.

It seems a daunting task. We might be able to pull some of these disparate topics together by noting that although our entire discussion has assumed that political philosophy is focused on the relation between the state and its citizens, it is undeniable that modern states exercise coercive power over large numbers of individuals who are *not* their citizens. Perhaps the most obvious example of this is war, which always involves seriously harming the citizens of other states (often unarmed and nonthreatening individuals, including children). Judging from the way in which government money is spent, war is perhaps the most central function of the modern state, but we have said nothing about it here. Similar cases are easy to identify. For example, modern states claim the authority to define and regulate citizenship in various ways. States set policies concerning who is, and who is not, a citizen; they determine who can, and who cannot, become a citizen; and they establish the processes by which one becomes a citizen. Such policies clearly exert coercive power over non-citizens. To cite another example, each state establishes laws and regulations concerning the environment; states fix standards regarding pollution, waste disposal, emissions, the use of environmentally harmful materials in industry, and so on. But, of course, the environment is not confined to any state's borders, and the lax environmental policies of one state indisputably negatively impact people all around the world. Similar thoughts apply to each state's policy on nuclear power and weapons; and these points can be easily transferred to considerations regarding each state's global economic and trade policies. Surely a state's policies and practices that impact those beyond its borders (and those non-citizens within them) must be subjected to moral evaluation; and it seems likely that a state which radically fails to show a proper regard for non-citizens—for example, by committing human rights abuses abroad—will lose whatever claim it might have to authority over its own citizens.

However, as it has focused on the relations between the state and its citizens, this book has not dealt at all with this cluster of issues. Unsurprisingly, these are extremely complicated problems, and their complexity undoubtedly owes in part to the fact that the liberal democratic framework that we have presupposed seems ill equipped to address questions of the state's obligations to non-citizens and to other states. Hence contemporary liberal-democratic political philosophy is largely focused on trying to extend the account so that it can deal with such issues. Yet this expansion thus far has yielded mixed results, and it is not clear that at the end of the day the liberal-democratic political order holds together. More philosophical work is required.

We find ourselves is a somewhat awkward position. As was said at the beginning, our lives are shaped by the social and political world in which we find ourselves. Long before we are mature enough to begin to think philosophically about the social and political conditions under which we live, we are already fully acclimated to the norms, rules, requirements, and expectations that those conditions impose. Once we begin to think philosophically about this fact, we come to realize that features of our political order that had once seemed obvious, simple, natural, and commonsensical, are in fact thorny, murky, debatable, and perhaps deeply suspicious. In response, we devise a rough-and-ready proto-philosophical understanding of how our central political commitments might hang together; but, with only a little philosophical reflection, we come to realize just how tenuous their cohesion is. Yet, despite all of this well-motivated uncertainty, our political lives go on. We continue to *live* our politics, and we are unable to start from scratch. Should we discover that our existing political system is falling drastically short of justice and thus requires improvement, we must attempt to rebuild it from within. And, given the vast power of existing states and the inertia of long-standing political traditions, one might wonder whether reform is possible. But one thing remains clear: Politics goes on, and it cannot wait for the political philosophers to reach agreement on liberty, authority, justice, and democracy. No matter how uncertain we may be about the ultimate philosophical content and cogency of these concepts, our lives are structured by *some* philosophical interpretation of them.

Here, then, is our predicament. Philosophical reflections lead us to only tentative and uncertain conclusions about the nature and worth of our political order; yet in politics, as in theater, the show must go on. What are we to do?

I think this very quandary suggests a distinctive kind of argument in favor of liberal democracy. Recall the discussion in section 4.2.3 about the *fair-play* justification of political authority. Those who promote this defense of authority liken society to a collective enterprise whose success depends upon the willingness of each individual to do his part in sustaining the political order. It is then claimed that obedience to the state is a necessary part of doing one's required share. Several objections to the fair-play view were considered in Chapter 4, though it was noted that the deflated view of authority seems to rely on some considerations of fair play. I think we are now able to press this kind of fair-play consideration a little further. To be more specific, I think our predicament points the way toward a different kind of collective endeavor to which we are individually called to contribute.

Consider the following: In order to know what kind of political order is best, and thus to discern what changes to our existing political arrangements should be made, we need to work out many difficult philosophical issues of the kind that were discussed in this book. In order to work out these difficult philosophical issues, we will need to consider a wide array of arguments, ideas, proposals, and objections from across a broad spectrum of interlocutors. But we will also need some way to assure ourselves that our philosophical reflections are informed by reliable empirical data, accurate renderings of the objections of our critics, faithful articulations of new and unfamiliar proposals and arguments, a fair representation of the field of available evidence, and so on. That is, in order to think philosophically about politics, our thinking must take place within a social and political order that permits—or, better yet, encourages—the free and open exchange of ideas, arguments, criticisms, data, and other kinds of information.

However, we need not only to be able to debate, argue, disagree, and reason together about the nature of our political arrangements; we need also to have some reason to think that these activities are not systematically distorted, misinformed, deluded, or rooted in mere deception. Thus the open and free exchange of ideas is necessary, but not sufficient, for doing political philosophy; there also need to be protections for dissenters, protesters, and critics, as well as positive encouragements for those who have historically been marginalized and shut out of political engagement to speak up. And this in turn means that there must be public venues and forums—including independent media outlets as well as actual physical spaces, such as public parks, and virtual spaces, such as blogs and social media sites—for open political discussion and disagreement. Perhaps most important of all, in addition to these institutional prerequisites for political philosophical engagement, there needs to be a commitment on the part of citizens to actually listen to one another's arguments, and to exchange arguments rather than insults, flattery, bribes, and threats.

We can summarize the foregoing argument as follows. Reflection on our existing social and political order leads us to the activity of political philosophy. But in order to do political philosophy today, we need *others* to philosophize along with us. More specifically, in order to think well about our political circumstances, we need to be able to *rely* on the cognitive resources of others; we need *them* to be competent discussants. Hence we need a social and political environment that is conducive to—or at least not destructive of—responsible philosophical deliberation and debate. We need the institutions and norms that enable us to share reasons, arguments, and evidence; we need to be able to test our ideas against those favored by others; we need to be able to criticize our government and its policies. And these norms and capacities are most firmly secured under liberal-democratic conditions. So, in a nutshell: We must politically philosophize, and in order to do so responsibly, we need an *open society*; the norms and institutions constitutive of an open society are best realized under a liberal-democratic political order. Therefore, the need to engage in political philosophy responsibly leads us to endorse liberal democracy.

That may look like a simplistic argument. It is most certainly *incomplete*. But I confess to finding it compelling. Ask yourself: What would contemporary political philosophy—including the kind of political philosophy that is wary of the very idea of political authority, or the kind that rejects liberal democracy as such—be without the protections and entitlements provided by the central institutions of liberal-democratic societies? For that matter, what could philosophy or inquiry *of any kind* be in the absence of the social and political guarantee that no conclusion, no argument, no thought, and no idea is, strictly speaking, forbidden? Could the philosophical questions we have explored in the foregoing chapters be asked, let alone pursued, under social and political conditions where certain kinds of ideas are criminal? Could we have any confidence in the value of our beliefs if we took ourselves to be operating under political institutions that officially control and constrain the exchange of ideas?

The general thrust of this argument can be captured in a different way. We conceive of ourselves as individuals with warranted beliefs, beliefs rooted in reliable information, accurate evidence, and compelling reasons. This self-conception tacitly presupposes a favorable assessment of the social and political conditions under which our beliefs are formed and maintained. In order to embrace our own beliefs about pretty much anything at all, we must assess those beliefs as *not* the products of systematic distortion, manipulation, propaganda, lies, and deception. That is, in order to sustain our conception of ourselves, we must be able to stand back from our beliefs and critically evaluate the social and political conditions under which they have been formed. This kind of critical distance is made possible by social and political institutions that enable and facilitate the sharing of information and the exchanging of reasons and arguments. In other words, in order to sustain our self-conception and embrace our own beliefs, we need to be able to engage with the ideas, reasons, and criticisms of others. And in order to do *that* we need social and political institutions of the kind most centrally associated with liberal democracy.

This gives no assurance that, in the end, liberal democracy is philosophically sound, much less morally best among all of the options. Again, in the course of philosophical examination, we may come to see that our existing social and political arrangements are unacceptable, that liberal democracy itself is inconsistent with justice and hence must be dismantled. We will then have to devise strategies for making political progress. What is not clear as yet is what a post-liberal-democratic political order would look like; unsurprisingly, it is also not clear how one might transform existing liberal democracy into a more acceptable alternative. We are, once again, stuck in the curious position of needing to critically assess our current environment while being nonetheless embedded within it. It is no wonder, then, that uncertainties abound.

But there is significant value in recognizing this fact. Philosophy is the ongoing struggle to see ourselves. And this struggle is too often preempted and co-opted by pleasant but dishonest self-depictions that portray comforting scenes of certitude, mastery, normalcy, and finality. We like to think of ourselves as inhabiting a world where it is *obvious* that everything is just as it should be. Our popular political culture preys on this; despite the substantive differences in their positions, the pundits and talk-show commentators all peddle the very same message: The truths about our political world—from the nature of individual freedom to the wisdom of some newly proposed policy initiative—are obvious to anyone who is not wicked, benighted, or foolish. The overriding assumption driving our popular politics is that all political disagreement has its source in the ignorance or stupidity of one's opposition, that for every political question there is but one obvious and simple truth, and thus that there is no political debate worth having. But if the foregoing pages have shown anything, it is that this popular view is pure fantasy. The fundamental components underlying our social and political order are open to philosophical dispute among rational, well-informed, and sincere citizens. In fact, one may go so far as to say that the driving assumption of liberal democracy is that it is possible for such citizens to disagree about fundamental political issues. If the view that prevails among the popular commentators were correct, there would be no need for politics—or philosophy—at all. We would submit our wills to the wisdom of those who know the relevant truths, and we would all live happily ever after. Our world is not that simple.

Still, we long for conditions where philosophy would be unnecessary. The comforting image of a political environment in which everything is obvious and easy is one manifestation of this longing. It is important to recognize that the activity of philosophy is itself another expression of that same aspiration. We philosophize in order to put philosophy to rest, to eventually resolve the puzzles and problems that philosophy enables us to see. Of course, philosophical problems are notoriously difficult, which is why we find ourselves asking the same questions that stimulated the likes of Plato, Aristotle, and a long line of philosophical luminaries leading up to this day. Although the completion of philosophy seems elusive, it does seem that gradual philosophical progress is within our reach. However, in order to make philosophical progress of any magnitude, we must first see ourselves clearly; we must expose to ourselves the ways we conceal our uncertainty from ourselves. Given our tendencies to self-deceive and to see simplicity where there is none, in order to see ourselves we need others to be able to look at us and tell us what they see. And, in turn, we need to be able to scrutinize them, too. That is, in order to see ourselves individually, *we* need to look at ourselves *collectively*. And part of that looking must involve the critical examination of the social and political forces that shape our lives and color our vision.

Index